Relational Databases

Barry Eaglestone BSc, PhD, MBCS, CEng

Stanley Thornes (Publishers) Ltd

First published in 1991 by:
Stanley Thornes (Publishers) Ltd
Old Station Drive
Leckhampton
Cheltenham GL53 0DN
England

British Library Cataloguing in Publication Data

Eaglestone, Barry M.
    Relational databases.
    I. Title
    005.74

ISBN 0-7487-1176-7

Typeset by Tech-Set, Gateshead, Tyne & Wear
Printed and bound in Great Britain by Courier International Ltd, East Kilbride, Scotland

Contents

3   Database languages   74

4   Relational database design   165

5   On keeping a database clean, tidy and safe   241

6   Distributed relational databases   259

7 And what next?   276

Outline solutions to selected exercises   286

Index   307

List of figures

List of tables

Editor's note

The Stanley Thornes Computer Studies Series is a series of text books with a modular structure aimed at students of computer studies and designed for use on courses at most levels of academic and professional qualification. Existing books in the series include:

Computer Appreciation and Basic Programming
Computing in a Small Business
Fundamentals of Computing
✳ Computer Systems: Software and Architecture
Microcomputer Interfacing for Control
Structured Program Design
Scientific Programming
✳ Data Processing Methods
Basic Systems Analysis
Basic Systems Design
Management of Systems Development
✳ Case Studies in Business Computing

As the series has developed and computing has grown as a subject, the need has been recognised for a number of texts which are more specialist and advanced than the earlier ones, though still focused on intermediate level courses in computing. *Basic Principles of Human–Computer Interface Design* addresses the technological aspects of interaction between humans and computers with sound advice for the system designer on the types of interface available and their appropriateness for particular applications. *Relational Databases* builds on the earlier books which cover database concepts and technology, and provides a deeper practical introduction to the most popular types of database software.
✳ *An Introduction to Fourth Generation Languages* does a similar job in relation to the powerful software tools which have come on to the marketplace to aid end-users to develop their own systems and professional staff to build prototypes very quickly.

Barry Lee
Series Editor

Preface

Relational database technology makes it easy for people to represent information as data stored in computers and to use that data to assist with the running of their businesses. It is the state-of-the-art database technology, is now relatively cheap, and can be used on all types of computers, including cheap personal computers.

This book provides the reader with an understanding of:

the ideas which lie behind relational database technology,
programs and techniques which are used to apply the technology,
the next generation of database technology which will either replace or complement relational technology.

It is assumed that the reader has some basic computer literacy but does not have any prior knowledge of database technology. The book is targeted primarily at students at undergraduate level; studying, for example, for BTEC or BSc. qualifications. Accordingly we have taken the trouble to explain ideas in plain English and to provide many illustrative examples. The book should also be of interest to the individual who is contemplating buying and using a database system. It may help the reader to appraise and make effective use of 'relation database' products.

The book is structured to provide answers to a series of questions, i.e:

1) what is a database system and what are the advantages of using one? (Chapter 1),
2) what is a relational database system? (Chapter 2),
3) how is a relational database used? (Chapter 3),
4) how is a relational database designed? (Chapter 4),
5) how is a relational database kept clean, tidy and safe? (Chapter 5),
6) how can a relational database system be distributed between a number of linked computers? (Chapter 6),
7) what comes next after relational database technology? (Chapter 7).

Barry M. Eaglestone
1991

1 The database approach

1.1 Introduction

A database management system (DBMS) is a particular type of computer program which is used to manage data stored on a computer and which enables other computer programs and computer users to make use of that data. A DBMS and a set of programs which use it to access a particular collection of data are collectively called a database system. DBMSs and database systems are now commonplace on all types of computer, ranging from large mainframe computers costing hundreds of thousands of pounds, to small personal computers costing only a few hundred pounds. Most up-to-date DBMSs are of a type called a relational DBMS (RDBMS).

RDBMSs are often easy to operate, but in order to use them to greatest effect it is necessary to have an understanding of the set of ideas and thinking that is called the database approach.

This introductory chapter explains the database approach, and contrasts it with the file-oriented approach to designing computer systems. It then goes on to give a brief introduction to relational DBMSs (RDBMSs).

1.2 The organisation

A database system exists to provide an organisation with the information necessary for it to carry out its activities. An organisation is a very general term which refers to 'any organised body or system or society' (Concise Oxford Dictionary), and the database approach is applicable to organisations in general. Database systems are used in all walks of life, e.g. manufacturing industry, businesses, service industries, education, government and scientific research. This chapter uses a small manufacturing organisation to illustrate database technology but it should be remembered that the technology is almost universally applicable.

1.2.1 The case study organisation: Fair-Childs

The case study organisation with which database concepts are illustrated is called Fair-Childs. Fair-Childs is a children's clothing manufacturer and is managed by two people, Derek and Sue Fairchild. This is a small organisation and prior to the 1980s the database approach would not have been relevant. The computer equipment, computer programs and expertise necessary to use a DBMS would have been too expensive. However, cheap personal computers with powerful and easy-to-operate database software now make database systems feasible even on this small scale.

Fair-Childs operates in yearly cycles, as illustrated in Figure 1.1. At the start of the year new garments are designed and samples are made. The garments are priced and then orders are solicited from shops. Materials for making the garments are ordered on the basis of sales forecasts, a production schedule is drawn up, and production is monitored for quality and punctuality. Completed garments are dispatched to the customers and the remittances are banked.

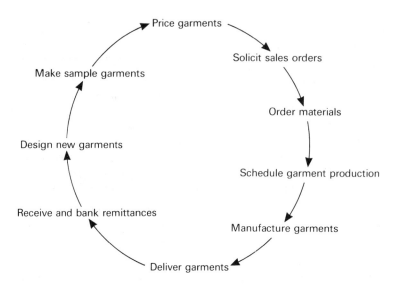

Figure 1.1   *Fair-Childs' yearly cycle of activities*

1.2.2 An organisation's information system

Jobs are done in an organisation in order for the organisation to function properly. An organisation can therefore be viewed as a system of activities. These activities may be performed by people, singly or in groups, manually or using machines, or may be automated using computers or robots. The result of these activities taking place should be that the organisation achieves its objectives.

Example 1.1

Fair-Childs may be viewed as a system of activities which take place in order to achieve certain objectives. The prime objective is *to create and sell children's clothing at a profit*.

To meet this objective Fair-Childs' employees perform the following activities:

> buying materials
> cutting and seaming garments
> selling garments
> receiving and banking remittances.

The activities in the above example are to do with turning the materials that the organisation acquires into the required products, i.e. turning money into material, material into garments, and then garments back into money (see Figure 1.2). These are examples of *materials activities*.

The materials activities of an organisation do not operate at random or in isolation. They are co-ordinated by a flow of information between activities within the organisation, and between these and relevant activities in the outside world.

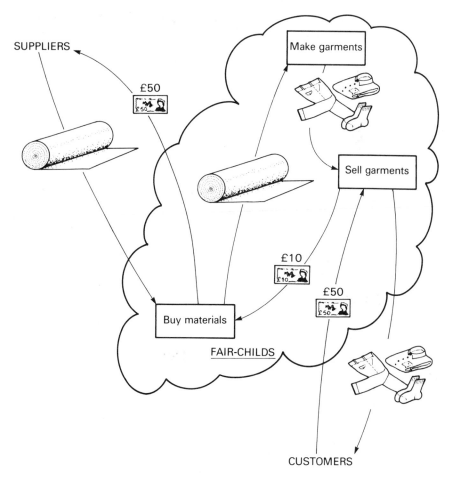

Figure 1.2   *Materials activities in Fair-Childs*

Example 1.2

In Fair-Childs, garments are made only when it is believed that they are required. The manager in charge of garment production must therefore receive information. This information will be to do with the need for sample garments, sales forecasts, and sales orders placed by customers. Other information which affects the production of garments is to do with the garment design, the availability of materials, and delivery dates. This information is generated by other activities within Fair-Childs, and also by activities outside the organisation. For example, information will be received from customers, suppliers, the bank, and the taxation office.

There is therefore an underlying system of *information activities*, i.e. jobs to do with capturing, storing, and transmitting the information required by the materials activities. These information activities are necessary in order to plan, monitor and control the materials activities. They are required for managing and directing the organisation. This underlying system of information activities is called the organisation's *information systems*. Information activities of a typical manufacturing business include activities to do with:

> financial control
> management planning
> inventory management
> production management
> research and design of products
> sales order processing.

The information system of an organisation may be represented by an information flow diagram in which information activities are depicted by boxes, and arrows connecting the boxes depict the flow of information between these activities.

Example 1.3

Figure 1.3 is part of an information flow diagram for Fair-Childs which depicts a fragment of an analysis of Fair-Childs as an information system.

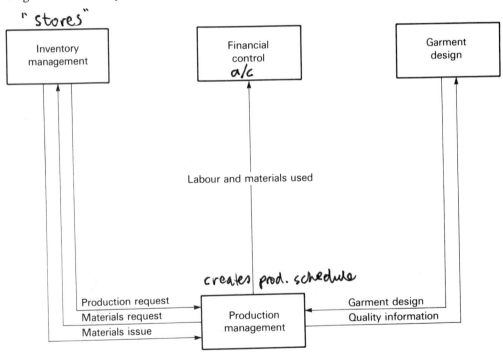

Figure 1.3   *A part of an information flow diagram depicting the Fair-Childs' information system*

'Production management' is the information activity for planning, monitoring and controlling the production of garments. This activity requires information from other information activities. 'Inventory management' is concerned with managing the stores of materials and garments, and production management creates a production schedule in response to a production request issued by inventory management. Material to be turned into garments is requested from, and issued by inventory management. 'Garment design' is concerned with designing new garments, and production management also monitors the quality of the garments produced so that quality information may be used by garment design to improve designs. Details of material and labour used in production are sent to 'Financial control' which is concerned with accounting for these production costs.

1.2.3 Informal and formal information flow

Information flow may be formal or informal. When information flow is formal, this means that the information is recorded in a specified way and is communicated using specified procedures.

Example 1.4

Sales order information will flow formally. It will be recorded on special order forms (see Figure 1.4) and copies of these will be used to communicate information about sales orders to other activities, such as sales order processing and inventory control.

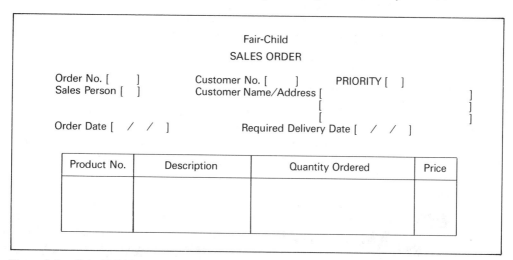

Figure 1.4   *Fair-Childs' sales order form*

Informally communicated information is not recorded in a prescribed manner. It may be recorded as rough notes in a notebook or diary, it may simply be remembered, or known intuitively. This information may be received as a result of observing other activities taking place, or by word of mouth.

Example 1.5

When pricing garments, one factor is what the market will stand. This information is known both intuitively and by observing the behaviour of the market, but is not explicitly recorded. This is an example of informally communicated information.

1.2.4 Information and data

Information is an abstract commodity (you cannot actually touch information, but you can gain information by touching something), and may be represented and communicated in many and varied ways. In computerised systems, information is represented as data. Data consists of symbols written on a recording medium to represent facts, concepts or instructions in a formalised manner so that they may be interpreted or processed by human or machine. Information, on the other hand, is in the eye of the beholder. It is the meaning that the human observer assigns to data by means of the known conventions used in their representation.

Example 1.6

To illustrate the distinction between data and information, consider the (simplified) sales order form used by Fair-Childs, shown in Figure 1.4. It includes a box which is annotated, 'PRIORITY'. Within this box either the letter 'U' or 'N' or 'L' may be recorded. These recorded symbols constitute *data* and convey information to the person who reads the form. This person will receive information that the order is urgent, normal or low priority, but the reader of the form will glean this information only if he or she knows the conventions used. If not, the reader may draw an incorrect conclusion, such as, the order is 'Unpaid for', or 'for a Northern customer', or 'for a London customer', or 'there is a mistake; this letter should be a number'.

1.2.5 The database

The formal information flow within an organisation may be viewed as messages passed between activities. The information contents of the messages must be recorded as data and must be retained within the organisation for as long as the information represented is of potential use to the organisation.

Example 1.7

A sales order (see Figure 1.4) from a new customer is a message containing information about the customer, i.e. name, address, and so on. It will also contain information about the current sales order, i.e. the articles and quantities ordered, and the order date. The customer information is relevant for as long as that customer continues to place orders with the organisation, and so it will be recorded and stored as data, possibly in a file of customer details. Information about the current order is of interest at least until the ordered goods have been dispatched and payment has been received. The order information will therefore be recorded for that period as data, perhaps in a file of current sales orders.

The total collection of data within an organisation at any time is the organisation's database. This database may be distributed throughout the organisation and may be recorded on various media, e.g. on paper records, floppy disks, microfiche or magnetic tape. However, the term database is usually used more specifically. Database usually refers to the information recorded as data and stored on computers.

1.3 The database system

Computer programs are often used to perform or assist with many of the information activities (see Section 1.2.2) of an organisation.

Example 1.8

Given the small size of Fair-Childs, the case study organisation, they would probably automate some of their information tasks using one or more personal computers.

Amongst the information activities that have to be performed by the managers of Fair-Childs is the processing of sales orders. There are a number of ways in which a computer can be used to assist with this task. For example, a computer can be used:

a) to check that the sales order forms are correctly filled in,
b) to check that the ordered clothing is in stock and if so, to produce the appropriate documents, i.e. delivery note and invoice, and also to adjust the recorded stock levels for the products which are to be dispatched,
c) to produce an appropriate request for production when the ordered products are not in stock.

Programs which perform or assist with information activities may be implemented either using a conventional file-oriented approach or using the database approach. In this section the advantages of using the database approach are highlighted by first considering the file-oriented alternative.

1.3.1 Conventional file-oriented data processing systems

In conventional file-oriented data processing sytstems, computer programs are designed to support specific information activities, and data files are designed to provide these programs with the data they need in a convenient form. Data files are organised such that the programs which use them may execute efficiently. In this type of system the database does not exist as a single integrated structure, but is distributed across a number of files.

Example 1.9

The sales order processing application in Example 1.8 could be implemented by one or more programs. If a file system is used, files must be designed to store the data required by those programs and to store the data generated by them. Files must be designed to store:

a) outstanding sales orders (these must be retained at least until the order is delivered and paid for),
b) customer details such as name and address (to be printed on invoices, etc.),
c) stock details, i.e. which and how many items are currently held in store,
d) product descriptions (including pricing information).

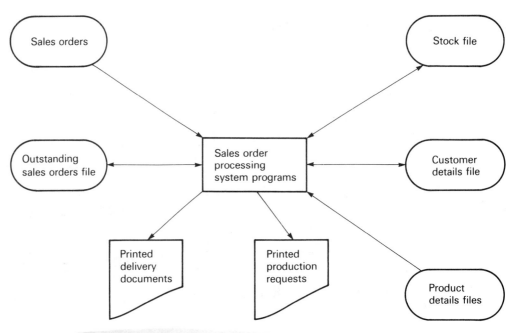

Figure 1.5   *A file-oriented sales order processing system*

One possible design for the sales order processing computer system could be to process the files of data depicted in Figure 1.5.

The above example system has characteristics that are common to both database and file-oriented systems. These are as follows.

a) Data represents information about objects of various types. The objects described in the example system are sales orders, items in stock, customers, and products.

b) Relationships between the objects about which the data represents information are represented by storing the same values in more than one record. For example, sales orders and items of stock are related, and this relationship is represented by storing product numbers in both stock file records and sales order file records.

c) Applications may share data. Though files are often designed for specific programs, they may contain data which is also required by other programs. For example, the stock file will also be required for inventory control, the outstanding sales orders file will be required for sales analysis, and the customer file data may also be required for mailing shots and for payments processing.

The above example does however illustrate some of the disadvantages of the file-oriented approach. These disadvantages stem from the following two additional characteristics.

d) The programs are central and data files are organised to be in a form convenient to specific programs.

e) Programs must have built into them knowledge about how files are organised, how records may be accessed, and the meaning of the data. In the example system, for instance, the program must know how the stock and sales order files are organised in order to access information about related items of stock and sales orders.

Three undesirable consequences of characteristics d) and e) above are as follows:

a) The system may be expensive to develop and maintain. Data is collected and organised in a form suitable for specific applications, and this collection may be a costly task. However, extra cost may be incurred at a later date when some future application needs to use the same data. The data may then have to be duplicated and reorganised into a new form, or some compromise reorganisation of existing files may be necessary. In the latter case, it will be necessary to modify existing programs so that they may process the altered file structures. Therefore neither the investment in writing programs nor the investment in collecting and organising data is preserved.

b) Data management is difficult. Data is distributed across a number of files and is used by a number of different applications programs. In cases where different applications require the same data, the data may be duplicated, possibly in different forms. When this happens it becomes difficult and expensive to make sure that data is secure, correct and consistent.

c) The system is unstable. The system is based on the ways in which jobs are done, but activities are not a stable feature of an organisation. Ways of doing things change. The introduction of a new computer system will in itself alter the activity structure of the organisation and give rise to new requirements of the system.

The next section introduces the database approach, which is data- rather than activity-centred, and consequently does not share the above three problems.

1.3.2 The database approach

The database approach to computerising information activities treats the organisation's data, i.e. its database (see Section 1.2.5), as a central resource which must be designed and managed in its own right. Design and management of the database becomes the responsibility of an individual or group of people called the database administrator (DBA).

One objective is to structure the data in the database in such a way that it has the same structure as the things about which it represents information. Applications programs are then designed around the database. This contrasts with the file-oriented approach (see Section 1.3.1) where the programs are central and data files are designed around them (see Figure 1.6).

A general objective of the database approach is therefore that the database should be a natural representation of the data with few imposed restrictions, capable of use by all relevant applications, including future ones, without duplication.

An organisation may in fact have a number of databases, and for operational convenience and reasons of clarity and self-consistency within each database it may be desirable to have some controlled duplication of data. However, the above general objective does give the thrust of the approach, i.e. data must be stored in a natural and sharable form.

To achieve this natural representation of the information as data, the database must include both data, which represents the real world objects which are of interest, and also a representation of the relationships between those objects.

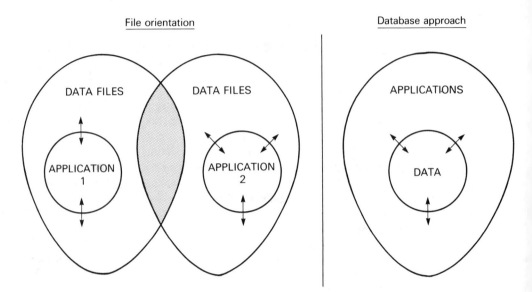

Figure 1.6   *File-oriented computer systems and database systems*

Example 1.10

A database which supports sales order processing (see Example 1.9) will include data which represents customers, products and sales orders, and will also include a representation of the relationships between them. These relationships are between customers and the sales orders that they placed, and between sales orders and the ordered products. The objects and relationships that must be represented are depicted in the following diagram.

The boxes represent different types of real world objects and the connecting lines represent the types of relationship that may exist between them. 'Crow's-feet' are used to indicate when many objects are involved in a relationship.

By representing both the objects and the relationships between them, the database models a part of the world. When users of a database view the data stored within it, they should see data objects which correspond to the things in the world that are currently of interest.

1.3.3 The database management system

The database approach is implemented using a special program called a database management system (DBMS). A DBMS makes it possible for data to be stored in a natural form and to be accessed by users, such that each user sees only the data that is of interest, though the DBMS does also allow different users to access the same data.

To appreciate how a DBMS works, it is necessary to distinguish between logical and physical data. The logical structure of data is that which is apparent to the user; it is the way that the data appears to be made up of interrelated parts. The physical data structure, on the other hand, is the way the data is actually represented on the computer storage devices. It is to do with the file structures and record access methods used, and at the lowest level, how data values are represented by 1's and 0's stored on devices such as magnetic disks.

A DBMS makes possible a natural representation of data by shielding from the user the physical data structures. It allows data to be logically structured in a way that corresponds to the actual structure of the information. In this way, the DBMS allows the user of the database to see the data in a way that reflects its meaning (see Figure 1.7). This feature, by which users take a logical view of the database which is independent of the way that the data is actually stored, is called **data independence**.

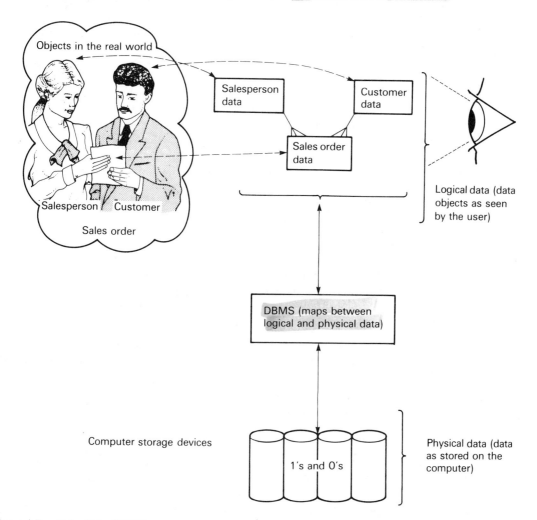

Figure 1.7   *Role of the DBMS*

Typically, a DBMS will allow a user to see a database as a collection of records, each of which represents information about a real world object. These records will be logically linked in some way to represent the relationships between the objects. A person may use the DBMS to access data about specific objects and relationships by providing the DBMS with values of some of their properties.

1.3.4 Advantages and costs of the database approach

There are five main advantages that accrue from applying the database approach.

a) The database may be tuned without it affecting the users. By tuning we mean adjusting the ways in which data are actually stored so as to make the database system run better. Changes to data storage structures which do not affect the logical structure of the database will not affect the database users, apart perhaps from changing the speed of the database system.

b) The database may evolve without upsetting existing applications. When the database is changed to represent new information, existing users should be unaffected. That is provided the information that they use is still represented in the database.

c) Data may be shared by applications, including future ones. Since the user of the data is concerned only with logical properties of data, there is no need to reorganise data for a new application.

d) Greater security and integrity control are possible. The design, maintenance and evolution of the database are the responsibility of the database administrator (DBA). The DBA must also ensure the correctness, consistency and security of the data in the database but this job is made easier because the data is collected together into a single integrated structure.

e) Greater productivity is possible. In general it is easier and faster to create applications programs in a database environment than it is in a conventional file-oriented environment. Programs are simpler because there is no need to include details of how the data are physically stored; it is easy to access data already in the database; and a database system typically includes tools that automatically generate applications programs from descriptions of what they must do, rather than how they must do it, i.e. fourth generation environments (see Chapter 3).

The result of a) and b) above is that investment in developing applications is preserved. It will not be necessary to change applications programs when the database is changed to be more efficient, or to accommodate new applications.

The result of c) above is that investment in storing data is preserved. Data will not have to be re-stored in some other form for new applications.

The costs of applying the database approach are as follows.

a) The database approach requires more hardware resources than does the conventional file-oriented approach. Applications programs in a database environment see the database through a 'user view' mechanism which masks off all but the relevant portion of the database. A program can access only the portion of the database that is needed for its application, but despite this it is still usually necessary for the complete database to be stored on-line on some direct-access storage device such as a disk. This contrasts with file processing programs as these require only the files they process to be accessible. Therefore, the database approach requires more on-line direct-access store than does the conventional file-oriented approach. This overhead may be contained to some extent by splitting the organisation's database into a number of smaller 'operational' databases.

There will also be a minimum requirement for main store and processing power in order to run the DBMS. However, even personal computers are now powerful enough to support sophisticated DBMSs.

b) Additional software is required to support the database approach. This will include the DBMS itself, software to extend programming languages so that they may access the database, special database languages and tools for building database applications, and various special programs for database administration.

c) Organisational changes will be necessary. A DBA must be established to manage the database. Programmers, analysts and users will have to be trained.

The above expenses may be prohibitive for certain applications which are relatively independent of other applications and which process small amounts of data. In particular, the expenses may be prohibitive for smaller organisations, where such applications are more typical; a smaller organisation will have fewer individuals employed on information activities, a smaller volume of work, and consequently less formal information flow.

1.4 Relational DBMSs

DBMSs are classified according to the logical data structures and languages they support, and relational DBMSs (RDBMSs) form one of these classes. RDBMSs are important because they are currently state-of-the-art and are becoming ever more widely used on all sizes of computer, ranging from small personal computers to large mainframes.

A general strength of RDBMSs is that the logical structures and languages that they support are based on a sound theoretical foundation. Relational DBMSs are based on the relational model (described in Chapter 2) which has been defined and developed with theoretical rigour. The advantage of this is that it has made much recent research possible, and users of RDBMSs have benefited from the results. For example, users have benefited from improved database design methods and database languages.

An RDBMS supports just one logical data structure; all data are logically represented within tables. The tables each have a name and are made up of named columns of data. Each row contains one value per column. This tabular representation is illustrated in the next example.

Example 1.11

The following is an example set of data to be stored in the sales order database discussed in Example 1.10.

```
Products are:   P1 Pantaloons (blue)
                P2 Pantaloons (khaki)
                P3 Socks (white)
                P4 Socks (harebell)
                P5 Pinafore (aqua)

Customers are:  C1 Nippers Ltd, 25 High St, Leeds
                C2 Tots-Gear, 5 Low St, Oxford
                C3 Super-Brat, 30 New St, Barnet

   The following sales orders have been placed:
       01 1/9/89 Nippers have ordered:
          100 × Pantaloons (blue)
           50 × Pantaloons (khaki)
       02 2/5/90 Super-Brat have ordered:
          100 × Pantaloons (khaki)
          200 × Pinafore (aqua)
```

Note that in this and later examples, only small amounts of data are used for illustrative purposes. However, readers should bear in mind that real organisations typically deal with large amounts of data; a manufacturer may, for example, produce hundreds of product lines, sell to thousands of customers, and process tens of thousands of sales orders each year.

The above data may be stored in a relational database as the set of tables in Figure 1.8.

PRODUCT

PRODUCT_NO	NAME	COLOUR
P1	Pantaloons	blue
P2	Pantaloons	khaki
P3	Socks	white
P4	Socks	harebell
P5	Pinafore	aqua

SALES_ORDER

ORDER_NO	DATE	CUSTOMER_NO
01	1/9/89	C1
02	2/5/90	C3

ORDER_LINE

ORDER_NO	PRODUCT_NO	QUANTITY
01	P1	100
01	P2	50
02	P2	100
02	P5	200

CUSTOMER

CUSTOMER_NO	NAME	ADDRESS
C1	Nippers Ltd	25 High St, Leeds
C2	Tots-Gear	5 Low St, Oxford
C3	Super-Brat	30 New St, Luton

Figure 1.8   *A relational database for the example data in Example 1.11*

Relational tables look very similar to conventional files but this likeness is deceptive. Relational tables are logical structures, whereas conventional files are physical structures. A table may be physically represented by a conventional file but there are other alternative physical representations. What is important however is not how tables are physically implemented, but how they can be used to represent data in a natural form and the operations that may be performed upon them in order to exploit the natural properties of the data.

The way relational tables capture some of the natural structure of data is illustrated in the following example.

Example 1.12

The correspondence between the real world objects and relationships identified in Example 1.10 and the relational database in Figure 1.8 is as follows.

a) A table represents objects or relationships of a particular type. For example, the PRODUCT table is used to store details of all products and the ORDER_LINE table represents relationships between sales orders and products.
b) Columns of a table represent the properties of the objects or relationships described by that table. Properties of a customer are customer number, name and address, and so the CUSTOMER table includes a column for each of these.
c) A row of a table represents an occurrence of an object or relationship of the type associated with the table. The values in that row represent the properties of the object or relationship. For example, the first row of the CUSTOMER table represents Nippers Ltd.
d) Each row includes a set of one or more values which uniquely identifies that row within the table. This is called the key value and identifies or names the object or relationships represented by that row. For example, the rows in the PRODUCT table are uniquely identifiable by the values in the PRODUCT_NO column. ORDER_LINE rows are identifiable by the combination of the values in the ORDER_NO and PRODUCT_NO columns.
e) All relationships between objects are represented by duplicating data values. For example, there is a many-to-one relationship between a customer's sales orders and that customer. This is because each customer may place many sales orders, but a sales order will have been placed by just one customer. To represent this the SALES_ORDER table includes a column of CUSTOMER_NO values which are used to cross-reference related rows in the CUSTOMER table.

An RDBMS will support one or more relational database languages for creating database tables, and for utilising the data stored in them. These languages allow a user to perform 'cut and paste' type operations on the database tables to put together new tables. Though there are many different relational database languages, SQL has become the dominant one and is now the international standard.

The main features of relational database languages are illustrated in the next example with the aid of an illustrative SQL statement.

Example 1.13

The following SQL command retrieves from the relational database in Figure 1.8 the names and colours of garments which have been ordered by Super-Brat.

```
SELECT PRODUCT.NAME, COLOUR
FROM PRODUCT, SALES_ORDER, ORDER_LINE, CUSTOMER
WHERE CUSTOMER.NAME = 'Super-Brat'
        AND CUSTOMER.CUSTOMER_NO = SALES_ORDER.CUSTOMER_NO
        AND SALES_ORDER.ORDER_NO = ORDER_LINE.ORDER_NO
        AND PRODUCT.PRODUCT_NO = ORDER_LINE.PRODUCT_NO;
```

When the above SQL is executed with the database in Figure 1.8, the following table of data will be retrieved.

NAME	COLOUR
Pantaloons	khaki
Pinafore	aqua

The detail of the above example SQL instruction is not important at this stage in the book. However, the example does illustrate the following general points.

Relational database languages provides access to *all* data, purely on the basis of the values stored within tables. There is no need to specify any other details relating to the ways in which the tables are physically stored, or the procedures to be used to locate data.

The example SQL specifies:

a) the columns (PRODUCT.NAME and COLOUR) of the table that is to be retrieved;
b) the tables that must be accessed in order to retrieve the new table, i.e. PRODUCT, SALES_ORDER, ORDER_LINE and CUSTOMER;
c) the condition that must be true for the values in each row of the retrieved table, i.e. CUSTOMER.NAME = 'Super-Brat' AND...;

but does not specify how the required product names and colours are to be found. It does not, for example, specify what file structures have been used to implement the tables to be accessed or what access methods are to be used to search those tables.

Relational database languages operate on complete tables of data at a time. This contrasts with conventional programming languages such as COBOL, FORTRAN, Pascal or C, which operate upon one record at a time. The example SQL defines a complete table by specifying its columns and the conditions for values in existing tables to be included in the new table but there is no reference made to individual rows.

Some idea of the power of relational database languages may be gleaned by contrasting the above example SQL instruction with the equivalent file-processing program, written is some conventional programming language. The program would explicitly have to search the CUSTOMER file for the record in which the NAME field value was 'Super-Brat'. It would then have to find related records in the SALES_ORDER file by searching for records where the CUSTOMER_NO field value is the same as that in the retrieved CUSTOMER file records, and so on. The resulting program would be much longer and more complex than the above SQL. Also, if at some later date it is decided to change the ways in which the files are stored, the program would have to be changed accordingly; the SQL is unchanged by changes to the way in which the tables that it uses are physically represented.

To summarise the above introductory discussion of RDBMS features:

a) all information in a relational database is explicitly represented very simply as values in tables;

b) relational database languages operate on whole tables at a time and provide access to all data solely on the basis of data values;

c) relational database systems are based upon a solid theoretical foundation, and so have benefited from the results of the research this has made possible.

1.5 Summary

★ An organisation can be viewed as a system of activities co-ordinated by a flow of information.

★ The information system is the underlying system concerned with maintaining this information flow.

★ Formally communicated information is represented as data. An organisation's database is the set of data which is recorded within the organisation at any one time, but 'database' usually refers specifically to the data that is stored on computers.

★ The conventional file-oriented approach is to build computer systems to support specific information activities or applications. This approach is unstable because of the changing nature of activities, the need to share data, and the dependence of the programs on the structure of the files.

★ The database approach is to treat the database as a central resource in its own right, and to design it to model the organisation. The objectives of the database approach are to store data as a natural representation of information sharable by all applications.

★ The database approach is applied using a special program called a database management system (DBMS). A DBMS is used to provide each user of a database with a logical view of the data that is of interest to them.

★ The database administrator (DBA) is responsible for managing the database.

★ The advantage of applying the database approach is that applications are independent of changes in the representation of the database or of its evolution. Also, central control of data provides better data security and integrity. Investment in both applications and data are preserved.

★ Relational database languages operate on whole tables at a time and provide access to all data solely on the basis of data values.

Exercises

1.1 A database system exists to provide an _____ with the _____ necessary for it to carry out its _____.

1.2 Explain the relationship between an organisation's materials activities and its information activities.

1.3 What is the difference between data and information?

1.4 What is a database?

1.5 A database should be a _____ representation of the data, such that it can be _____ by all relevant applications, without _____.

1.6 What are the main differences between the conventional file-oriented approach and the database approach?

1.7 What is the purpose of a database management system?

1.8 What does the DBA do?

1.9 What is data independence?

1.10 What are the advantages and costs of applying the database approach?

1.11 All data in a relational database is represented in the form of _____.

1.12 What are the main differences between a relational database language and a conventional programming language such as COBOL or PASCAL?

1.13 The directors of a small manufacturing business currently operate conventional file-oriented data processing systems on a minicomputer. They have asked you about the advisability of changing to database technology. Write a short report for them setting out an explanation of the database approach, the costs of changing from file-oriented to database technology, and the likely advantages of doing so.

2 The relational model and relational database management systems

2.1 Introduction

This chapter describes and explains the basic relational model, which is a set of structures, operations and rules that may be used to represent data, relationships between data items, and the ways in which data may be manipulated.

The relational model has two important uses.

★ It may be used to describe and analyse database systems. This facility enables the database designer and the researchers to reason about database systems without actually having to build them.
★ It is the basis for relational DBMSs (RDBMSs). An RDBMS implements the structures, operations and rules of the relational model.

The origins and nature of the relational model are overviewed in Section 2.2. Sections 2.3, 2.4 and 2.5 explain the structures, operations and rules which are the parts of the relational model and illustate how they can be used to describe database systems. Finally, the way in which the model is implemented in actual RDBMSs is described in Sections 2.6 onwards.

2.2 What is the relational model and where did it come from?

The relational model was formulated and first published in the early 1970s by Edgar F. Codd who was then a researcher at IBM's San Jose laboratories in California, USA. He published his proposals for the relational model in a series of research papers in the years 1970 to 1974. Subsequently, the relational model became the major vehicle for research into database systems and is now the basis for current 'state-of-the-art' DBMSs.

The relational model is a theoretical model of databases because with it one can create sets of formulas that represent or model database systems. With such a model a database designer or researcher may study the properties of a database system without actually having to implement it. Having analysed database systems in theory it is then possible to come to conclusions as to what is the best way of achieving a good database design and what are the best ways of using the database.

Theoretical models abound in all branches of science. For instance, the economist may study how the economy of a country will behave, given certain conditions, by constructing a system of definitions and formulas that model the behaviour of the economy. The astronomer may similarly model the behaviour of the solar system. The accuracy and reliability with which a theoretical model mimics the properties and behaviour of that which it attempts to model depend on the assumptions built into the model. If these assumptions are unrealistic or oversimplified then predictions and analyses made by using the model may be naïve or unrealistic. For example, attempts by economists to predict the behaviour of the economy illustrate this problem. Different schools of economic thought will use models based on different and sometimes contradictory assumptions resulting in a wide range of advice on how to create a healthy economy. The quality of a theoretical model must ultimately be determined by how its analyses and predictions coincide with the actual behaviour of that which it models. The relational model must be judged on its ability to model accurately, and to predict the properties and behaviour of database systems.

The relational model has been criticised as being unrealistic and oversimplified in various respects (some of these criticisms are discussed in the final chapter of this book). However, the relational model has been the major vehicle of database research for over a decade; it is the basis for many current DBMSs; and results from the theory of relational databases have found their way into many current computer system design methods. Though the relational model has many known imperfections, it was adopted by most database researchers in the 1970s and 1980s as the best database model available. The search for something which is widely accepted as being better is still in progress.

This position is summed up in the following adaptation of comments made by J.D. Ullman, a prominent researcher in the area of database systems.

> The relational model is like the wave theory of light; it provides lots of insights and fosters useful design methodology even though there may be some technical problems with some of its assumptions when applied in the wrong context.

2.2.1 Data models

The relational model is a particular type of theoretical model: it is a data model. A data model provides a means of representing data and relationships between data items. It also specifies the ways in which the data may be used. A data model will therefore include three parts:

a) a structural part, which is a collection of the types of structures, i.e. the building blocks, with which databases can be constructed,

b) a manipulative part, which is a collection of the types of things that can be done to a database; this will include the operations that are used for retrieving or updating data in the database and for changing the structure of the database,

c) an integrity part, which is a collection of the rules that all valid databases must obey.

Parallels may be drawn between these three parts of a data model and parts of a programming language:

a) the structural part corresponds to facilities for specifying data objects in a programming language,

b) the manipulative part corresponds to executable statements in a programming language which do things with the data,

c) the integrity part corresponds to general rules that apply to programs written in the programming language, such as 'all data objects must be declared'.

2.2.2 Historical context of the relational model

Publication of the relational model in the 1970s was timely. There was then no widely accepted theoretical model of databases suitable both for research into database issues and also as a basis for actual DBMSs. The relational model was suitable for both roles because it has the following properties:

Logical rather than physical. The relational model addresses only the logical properties of database systems. It does not include any rules, structures or operations relating to the physical implementation of database systems.

Other database systems in the 1960s and early 1970s were lacking in the above respects. The major database systems were CODASYL systems, based on the network model, and those such as IBM's IMS, based on the hierarchical model; the network and hierarchical models both represent information as data in the form of collections of interlinked records. Hierarchical and network model-based systems failed to separate clearly the logical (programmer's) view of the database from its physical representation. For instance, the hierarchical and network database programmers were required to know of the physical links between related records, and to know which records could be located by using direct-access techniques such as hashing on the key. This knowledge was needed because the programmer could access records only by using those physical links. If records were logically related but no physical link had been implemented, then the programmer could not retrieve the related records by navigating the logical link.

An objective of the relational model was to introduce a sharp, clear boundary between the physical and logical aspects of databases. Codd called this 'the data independence objective'.

Mathematical rigour. The relational model was defined with mathematical rigour. It provided a means of formally specifying and studying the logical properties of a database system. This facility is a necessary prerequisite to building a sound theoretical foundation for database systems.

Neither the hierarchical nor the network model has a sound theoretical foundation. They were developed pragmatically, with computer efficiency as a priority.

Simplicity. A major appeal of the relational model is its simplicity. All data and relationships are explicitly represented using a single, logical structure called a relation. A relation is a mathematically defined term, but a relation can be represented very simply as a two-dimensional table, or alternatively, as a file of records.

The hierarchical and network models lacked this simplicity because of their orientation towards efficient retrieval, and hence the inclusion of physical aspects such as indexes, pointer chains and random files.

Set-oriented. The relational model's manipulative part, i.e. the types of things that may be done to databases, is set-oriented. The operators may operate on large chunks of the database at a time: a single statement may express the processing of many records.

Hierarchical and network models were record-oriented. The programmer was required to design procedural database programs which accessed the database record by record, using the physical links between records.

In summary, the relational model filled a gap. It was presented at a time when there was no widely accepted theory of databases. The relational model was accepted as a basis for such a theory, because it combined rigour and simplicity, and addressed logical rather than physical properties of databases.

When the relational model was first introduced there was doubt as to its practicability for large databases, but the rapid increase in the power of computer hardware, coupled with a dramatic fall in cost which occurred during the 1970s and 1980s has largely alleviated those fears.

Exercises

2.1 What is a data model?

2.2 Explain the roles of the three parts of a data model.

2.3 What were the advantages of the relational model over other contemporary systems, when it was first published?

2.3 The structural part

2.3.1 Introduction

The superficial view of relational databases given in Chapter 1 was as sets of tables (see Section 1.4). Using the terms of the relational model, the tables are called relations, the columns are called attributes, the column headings are called attribute names and the values in the columns, attribute values. The rows are called *n*-tuples or more usually just tuples.

Alternatively, a relational database may be thought of as being like a set of conventional files, each with just one type of record. Each file corresponds to a relation, its fields to the attributes, and its records to the tuples.

The relational structures and the corresponding part of a table or alternatively of a file are given in Table 2.1.

Table 2.1   Relational structures.

Relational structure	*Tables*	*Files*
Relation	Table	File
Tuple	Row	Record
Attribute	Column	Field
Attribute name	Column heading	Field name
Attribute value	Table entry	Data items

Example 2.1

The three tables in Figure 2.1 depict a small part of a relational database for a children's clothing manufacturer (somewhat larger than Fair-Childs). The database represents information about the products they manufacture, their warehouses and the stock levels of products within each of the warehouses.

PRODUCT

PROD_NO	NAME	COLOUR
P1	Pantaloons	blue
P3	Socks	harebell
P4	Socks	white

data about products

WAREHOUSE

WAREHOUSE_NO	LOCATION
WH1	Leeds
WH2	Bradford

data about warehouses

STOCK

WAREHOUSE_NO	PROD_NO	QUANTITY
WH1	P1	5000
WH1	P3	10000
WH1	P4	10000
WH2	P3	20000
WH2	P4	5000

relationship between product e warehouse

Figure 2.1   *Example relational database*

Table 2.2 lists the components of the relational database in Figure 2.1, and identifies each type of component using the terminology of the relational model, and the corresponding components types in their representation as a set of tables, and as a set of files.

The table and file analogies are useful as an introduction. They provide a simple and familiar way of visualising relational databases. However, there are a number of important differences between files, tables and relations. Those differences should become apparent in the following explanation of the components of relational databases.

The structural part of the relational model, the set of building blocks for constructing databases, comprises the following types of component: domains, attributes, relations and keys. These are each described and explained in the remainder of this section.

In order to make the transition from tables to the components of the relational model which they represent as painless as possible, the following convention is adopted. Relational terms when used (such as relation, tuple, etc.) are followed by the corresponding table representation (e.g. relation (table)). This is so that the reader is not immediately 'bogged down' with new jargon.

Table 2.2   The components of the relational database of Figure 2.1.

Component	Relational structure	Tables	Files
PRODUCT WAREHOUSE STOCK	Relation	Table	File
PROD_NO NAME COLOUR WAREHOUSE_NO LOCATION QUANTITY	Attribute name	Column heading	Field name
P1, P3, P4 Pantaloons, Socks, Leeds, Bradford, harebell, blue, white, 5000, 10000, 20000, 500, WH1, WH2	Attribute value	Column entry	Data item
⟨P1, Pantaloons, blue⟩ ⟨P3, Socks, harebell⟩ ⟨P4, Socks, white⟩ ⟨WH1, Leeds⟩ ⟨WH2, Bradford⟩ ⟨WH1, P1, 5000⟩ ...	Tuple	Row	Record

2.3.2 Domains

Domains are a powerful feature of the relational model. It is with domains that the relationships between objects are represented. Domains have not been mentioned in the table or file analogies above because they have no obvious equivalent.

In order to explain what domains are, let us consider the example relational database (set of tables) given in Figure 2.1. In this example the database is made up of three relations (tables): PRODUCT, WAREHOUSE and STOCK.

Now consider an attribute (column) of a relation (table) in the example. Take, for example, the attribute (column) which is named WAREHOUSE_NO in the relation (table) named WAREHOUSE. This attribute (column) has values 'WH1' and 'WH2'. These values are used to identify warehouses. Any valid warehouse identifier could occur as a value of the WAREHOUSE_NO attribute (as an entry in the WAREHOUSE_NO column).

The set of all valid warehouse identifiers is called the *domain* of warehouse identifiers. In the relational model domains are given names, so let us call this one WAREHOUSE_ID. The WAREHOUSE_NO attribute (column) is said to be *defined on* WAREHOUSE_ID, the domain of warehouse identifiers. The relationship between the WAREHOUSE_NO attribute (column) and the domain of warehouse identifiers, WAREHOUSE_ID, is depicted in the diagram opposite.

Domain - all possible data identifiers for
 a particular field (attribute) or fields

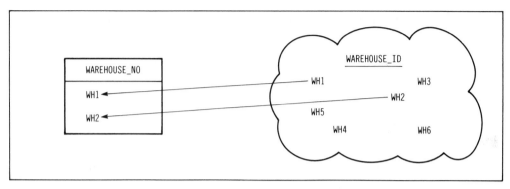

Every attribute (column) in a relational database is defined on a domain. A domain is a set of values from which the values of one or more attributes (columns) are taken. The properties of domains are as follows.

Domains are to do with the meaning of data. A relation (table) in a relational database is used to describe things in the real world, or relationships between things in the real world. These types of things are usually called entities. An entity is a thing about which we wish to store facts. For example, WAREHOUSE describes things of type 'warehouse', PRODUCT describes products, and STOCK describes the relationships between products and warehouses.

Attribute values (values in the columns) represent facts about the things (the entities and relationships) described in the relations (tables). For example, the attribute values in one of the tuples (rows) of the WAREHOUSE relation (table), ⟨WH1, Leeds⟩ say, in the example database represent the following facts about a thing of type WAREHOUSE:

>   the warehouse number of this thing is WH1
>   its location is Leeds.

A domain may therefore be thought of as the set of facts of a particular type that may be represented in the database. For example, the domain on which the LOCATION attribute (column) of the WAREHOUSE relation (table) is defined is the set of all locations at which a warehouse could be sited.

Every value in a database must be a member of some domain. The set of domains on which a database is defined can be viewed as the database's vocabulary. The values in the domains represent all the facts that can be represented within the database. The domain values are therefore collectively all the things that can be said about the world from within the database.

Domain values must be single-valued. Attributes (columns) must be defined on domains of simple values. A value in a domain cannot be split up. The technical way of expressing this restriction is to say domain values must be atomic. The consequences of the above restriction are illustrated in the following two examples.

Example 2.2

The customers of Fair-Childs, a children's clothing manufacturer, are each assigned a customer number. The customer numbers are integers in the range 1 to 9999. The domain of customer numbers, CUST_NO, is therefore the set of all possible customer numbers, i.e. $\{1, 2, 3, \ldots, 9999\}$.

CUST_NO in the above example is an example of a *finite* domain; the elements in a finite domain may be counted. However, some domains are infinite. For example, the domain of customer names is infinite; a new customer could be called anything.

Example 2.3

Previously Fair-Childs used to allocate customer numbers which were composed of a sales area number in the range 1 to 20, followed by a customer number within sales area in the range 1 to 500. Customer 19020 would be the 20th customer in sales area 19.

In this case there was no domain of customer numbers. Such a domain would not be atomic since each value could be split into two other meaningful values. In this case there must be two domains, a sales area domain and a customer number within the sales area domain.

Domains are not about how facts are represented but about which facts may be represented. A domain value may in fact be represented in various ways. The following two examples illustrate this point.

Example 2.4

A domain of dates would include a single entry for the first day of 1990. Though there is only one such value in the domain, there are many ways of representing it. It could, for instance, be represented in any of the following ways:

> 1/1/90
> 1st Jan 90
> 1st January 1990.

They are all representations of the same fact, and so they represent the same domain value.

On the other hand the same symbols may be used to represent different facts and hence elements in different domains, as illustrated in the next example.

Example 2.5

Consider the case where both customer number and product number are represented by integers in the range 1 to 9999. In this case, though the product number domain and the customer number domain both contain exactly the same values, they are still different. Two attribute values (table entries) of 252 will represent different facts if the attributes (columns) are, respectively, defined on the customer number domain and on the product number domain.

Domains are used to represent relationships between the things described by the data within a relational database. This is done by representing the same fact more than once within the database.

Example 2.6

Consider the example database in Figure 2.1. Products are related to the warehouses within which they are stored. To represent this relationship it is necessary to include values from the PROD_NO domain more than once: in both the PRODUCT relation (table) and also in the STORE relation (table). Similarly, it is necessary to store values from the WAREHOUSE_ID domain more than once.

Domains also make possible the representation of relationships between tuples (rows) within the same relation (table).

Example 2.7

In Figure 2.1, product P3 in WH1 and product P4 in WH1 are related in that they are both stored in a quantity of 10000. This relationship is represented in the database by virtue of the fact that when two values of the QUANTITY attribute (column) are the same they must represent the same fact; they both represent the same element in the domain on which the attribute (column) is defined.

More than one attribute (column) of a relation (table) may be defined on the same domain, as illustrated in the following example.

Example 2.8

Consider the following relation (table).

MANAGEMENT

MANAGER	SUBORDINATE
E1	E2
E1	E3
E2	E4

In this relation (table) both attributes (columns) are defined on the same domain, the domain of employee numbers. Each tuple (row) represents a relationship between two employees: the one identified by the value of MANAGER and the one identified by the value of SUBORDINATE. The relation (table) in fact represents the following hierarchy of command:

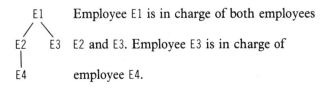

E1   Employee E1 is in charge of both employees

E2 E3 E2 and E3. Employee E3 is in charge of

E4   employee E4.

2.3.3 Relations, attributes and tuples

A relational database is made up of a number of relations (tables). A relation is a structure, somewhat like a table, which contains sets of values taken from domains (see Section 2.3.2). These domain values represent facts about the real world. A relation (table) is made up of tuples (rows) each of which is a set of domain values. Each tuple (row) will contain one value for each type of fact that may be represented in the relation (table). These types of fact are called attributes (columns). Each attribute is given a name, the attribute name (column heading), and actual values in the relation are called attribute values (table entries). Each attribute value (table entry) must be taken from the domain on which the attribute is defined.

A relation and a table are alike, apart from the following three differences.

a) The attributes (columns) of a relation have no ordering. Columns in a table, on the other hand, will always have an ordering; there will always be a first and a last column.

b) The tuples (rows) of a relation have no ordering. There will always be a first and a last row in a table, but there is no such thing as a first, second or last tuple.

c) No two tuples (rows) in a relation may be identical. Rows in a table may contain the same values but still be different because they occupy different positions in the table, but if a table representing a relation has two identical rows then these both represent the same tuple. There is nothing to distinguish between tuples except their values.

The following example illustrates the above three differences between relations and tables.

Example 2.9

Consider the WAREHOUSE relation in Figure 2.1. The three tables given below are each different in detail, but they are all representations of the same relation.

WAREHOUSE

WAREHOUSE_NO	LOCATION
WH1	Leeds
WH2	Bradford

WAREHOUSE

LOCATON	WAREHOUSE_NO
Leeds	WH1
Bradford	WH2

WAREHOUSE

LOCATION	WAREHOUSE_NO
Bradford	WH2
Leeds	WH1
Leeds	WH1

A more accurate, though less readable representation of the WAREHOUSE relation is that given in the diagram opposite.

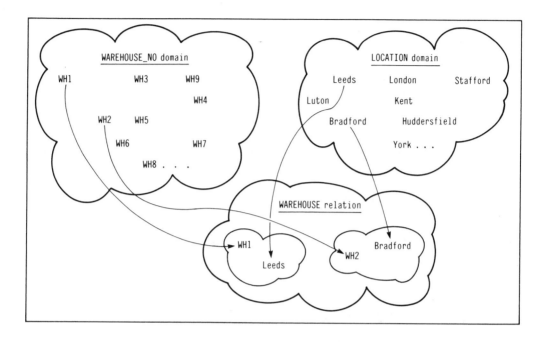

2.3.4 The meaning of relations, attributes and tuples

The domains on which the attributes (columns) are defined represent all the facts that could be represented in the database (see Section 2.3.2); each domain represents a set of facts of a particular type. Relations (tables), attributes (columns) and tuples (rows) provide structures within which domain values may be grouped together so as to represent information about the real world. In fact, each tuple (row) represents a proposition or assertion about one or more things of interest. An example of a proposition is, 'The cat sat on the mat.' This is a proposition about 'cat', 'mat' and the 'sat on' condition which relates them. The condition or predicate 'sat on' – let us call this condition just ON – is applied to the values 'cat' and 'mat'. The proposition is true if the ON condition is true for the two values 'cat' and 'mat'; otherwise it is false.

Another way of writing the example proposition is,

> ON (cat, mat)

In this form the correspondence between propositions and relations (tables) becomes apparent. A relation (table) in a relational database represents propositions of a particular type. The relation name (table name) is the predicate name and the attribute names (column names) are variable names for the values to which the predicate is applied. The tuples (rows) are the actual propositions.

Example 2.10

Consider the situation where we have a lot of pets and we wish to represent information about where each pet is sitting. This may be done by representing propositions of the type:

> ON (pet, seat)

There are four pets, a cat, a dog, a pig and a rat, and they are sitting respectively on the mat, the lap, the wall and the dustbin. This information may be represented by the following set of propositions, each of which is true.

ON (cat, mat)
ON (dog, lap)
ON (pig, wall)
ON (rat, dustbin)

These four propositions may be represented as the relation (table) which is shown below.

ON

PET	SEAT
cat	mat
dog	lap
pig	wall
rat	dustbin

Example 2.11

The example database in Figure 2.1 represents propositions about products, warehouses and stocks. For instance, the tuples (rows), ⟨P1, Pantaloons, blue⟩ and ⟨WH1, Leeds⟩ and ⟨P1, WH1, 5000⟩ in relations (tables) PRODUCT, WAREHOUSE and STOCK, respectively, represent the propositions: 'There exists a product with product number P1, name of Pantaloons which is blue in colour' or

PRODUCT (P1, Pantaloons, blue);

'There exists a warehouse that has been assigned number WH1 and is located in Leeds' or

WAREHOUSE (WH1, Leeds);

'There is a stock of the product numbered P1 in the warehouse numbered WH1 of quantity 5000' or

STOCK (P1, WH1, 5000).

2.3.5 Keys

Keys are an important part of the relational model because they are used to represent the names of the things about which the propositions are made.

A key is one or more attributes (columns) of a relation (table) such that their value will be different for each tuple (row) in the relation (table). Also, every attribute (column) of a key must be necessary for its values to be unique for every tuple (row).

If three attributes (columns) together are a key, then it is not possible to form a key from just two of those attributes (columns). The values of a key uniquely identify each tuple (row) in a relation (table) and the key does not contain any more values than is necessary for that purpose.

The definition of key given above is similar to that of a key for a conventional file but there is an important difference: duplicate keys cannot occur in a relation (table), whereas records in a conventional file may have the same record key.

Note also that there may be many groups of attributes that satisfy the above condition, and so a relation (table) may have many keys.

Example 2.12

In the database in Example 2.1 there are three relations (tables): PRODUCT, WAREHOUSE and STOCK. These represent propositions about products, warehouses and the stocks of products in the warehouses. Keys provide a unique name for each product, for each warehouse, and for each stock of a particular product within a particular warehouse. If we assume a product number uniquely identifies a product, a warehouse number uniquely identifies a warehouse, and that no two warehouses may be at the same location, the keys are then as shown in Table 2.3.

Table 2.3   The keys in the database of Example 2.1.

Relation	Keys
PRODUCT	PROD_NO
WAREHOUSE	WAREHOUSE_NO LOCATION
STOCK	(WAREHOUSE_NO, PROD_NO)

Note that the key of the STOCK relation in the above example is made up of two attributes (columns), WAREHOUSE_NO and PROD_NO. There will be only one tuple (row) for each product stored within a particular warehouse and so this combination of WAREHOUSE_NO value and PROD_NO value will be different for every tuple (row).

The attributes (columns) WAREHOUSE_NO, PROD_NO and QUANTITY also uniquely identify each tuple (row); for example, there can be only one tuple (row) ⟨WH1, P3, 10000⟩ in STOCK. However, WAREHOUSE_NO, PROD_NO and QUANTITY is not a key because QUANTITY can be removed and what is left, i.e. (WAREHOUSE_NO, PROD_NO) is a key. The attributes (columns) (WAREHOUSE_NO, PROD_NO, QUANTITY) form an example of a *superkey*, i.e. a key plus other attributes.

A relational (table) may have many keys. For example, since there may be only one warehouse at each location, the LOCATION attribute (column) could also be used as a key to WAREHOUSE. Either the value of WAREHOUSE_NO or the value of LOCATION could be used uniquely to identify tuples (rows) in the WAREHOUSE relation (table). WAREHOUSE_NO and LOCATION are called *candidate* keys. Every relation (table) has at least one candidate key; this must be the case since duplicate tuples (rows) are not allowed.

For any relation (table) one candidate key will be selected as the *primary* key. The candidate keys not selected as the primary key are called *alternate* keys. If we choose WAREHOUSE_NO to be the primary key then LOCATION is an alternate key.

A primary key is selected so that we can make sure that each tuple (row) has some unique identifier. The attributes which form the primary key are not allowed to have no value at all. (No value at all is called a null value.) Primary key values are used to cross-reference tuples (rows) in one relation (table) with tuples in another in order to represent relationships between the objects about which the data represents information.

An example of cross-referencing of tuples (rows) using primary key values is given in the STOCK relation (table) in Figure 2.1 where WAREHOUSE_NO is the primary key in the WAREHOUSE relation (table) and is also an attribute (column) in the STOCK relation (table). Values of WAREHOUSE_NO in STOCK are used to cross-reference tuples (rows) in the WAREHOUSE relation (table). WAREHOUSE_NO in STOCK is an example of a *foreign* key.

A foreign key is one or more attributes (columns) whose values are used elsewhere as primary key values. For example, PROD_NO is a primary key in PRODUCT and a foreign key in STOCK. The foreign key and the primary key attributes (columns) will be defined on the same domain (they will represent the same set of facts) but they need not necessarily have the same attribute names (column names).

Example 2.13

The database in Figure 2.1 is reproduced below with the primary keys underlined with continuous lines, the foreign keys underlined with dots and the alternate keys underlined with dashes.

PRODUCT

PROD_NO	NAME	COLOUR
P1	Pantaloons	blue
P3	Socks	harebell
P4	Socks	white

WAREHOUSE

WAREHOUSE_NO	LOCATION
WH1	Leeds
WH2	Bradford

STOCK

WAREHOUSE_NO	PROD_NO	QUANTITY
WH1	P1	5000
WH1	P3	10000
WH1	P4	10000
WH2	P3	20000
WH2	P4	500

Example 2.14

The database below describes the management structure within a company. This management structure is such that an employee may have more than one manager, and a manager may manage many employees. The same convention for identifying keys as was used in Example 2.13 is used here.

EMPLOYEE

EMPLOYEE_NO	NAME	DEPARTMENT
E1	B J Brown	Accounts
E2	R M Thomas	Accounts
E4	L Grace	Accounts
E6	M Bainbridge	Packing
E9	B J Brown	Packing

MANAGEMENT_STRUCTURE

SUPERIOR	SUBORDINATE
E1	E2
E1	E4
E9	E6

(handwritten annotation: different attribute names, but same values (ic employee no).)

In this database there are two foreign keys and they both cross-reference the same primary key but have different names.

In both above examples the foreign keys are contained within a primary key but this is not always the case. Attributes which are not part of a candidate key may also be foreign keys.

2.3.6 Summary of the structural part

The components of the structural part of the relational model are depicted in Figure 2.2 and summarised below.

Database. A relational database comprises a set of table-like structures called relations.

Relation. A relation is like a table of values, except that neither the rows nor the columns have any ordering, and there can be no two rows that are identical.

Attribute. A relation is defined on a number of attributes. Attributes are like the columns of a table. Each attribute has an attribute name, which is like the column heading, and attribute values, which are like the column entries. The attribute values represent facts of a particular type.

Domain. A domain is a set of values that represent all the facts of a particular type that may be represented in the database. Each attribute takes values from a particular domain. Domain values must represent single facts; they must be atomic. Domains are used to represent relationships between things described in the database.

Tuple. A relation is a set of tuples. If we think of a relation as being like a table, then a tuple is like a row of that table. Each tuple is a set of attribute values, one for each attribute of the relation. A tuple represents a proposition. The relation name is the predicate or condition, and there is an attribute of each type of value to which the predicate is applied.

Key. A key is a set of attributes whose values uniquely name each tuple of a relation. A superkey is a key plus some other attributes. A relation may have many keys, called candidate keys. One will be chosen to be the primary key and the others are alternate keys. Attributes used to cross-reference tuples using the tuples' primary key values are called foreign keys.

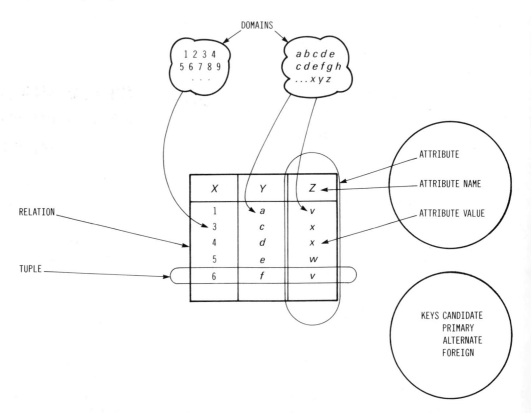

Figure 2.2   *Components of the structural part of the relational model*

Exercises

2.4 Consider the following relational database

EMPLOYEE

EMP_NO	NI_NO	NAME	DEPT_NO
E1	123	J Smith	D1
E2	159	J Smith	D1
E3	5432	R Brown	D2
E5	7654	M Green	D2

DEPARTMENT

DEPT_NO	NAME	MANAGER
D1	Accounts	E1
D2	Stores	E2
D3	Sales	null

EMPLOYEE_EXTENSION

EMP_NO	OFFICE	EXTENSION
E1	R101	811
E1	R102	813
E2	R10	111
E3	R35	123
E5	R35	123

which represents information about an organisation's employees, departments, offices and telephone extensions.

a) A tuple of EMPLOYEE represents a unique employee number (EMP_NO), a unique national insurance number (NI_NO), the name of an employee (NAME), and also the department to which that employee belongs (DEPT_NO).
b) A tuple of DEPARTMENT represents a unique number (DEPT_NO) and name (NAME) for a department, and also the number of the employee who is manager (MANAGER).

c) A tuple of EMPLOYEE_EXTENSION represents the number of an employee (EMP_NO), the employee's office number (OFFICE), and the telephone extension on which they can be contacted (EXTENSION).

Note that employee names are not unique and that an employee may share or have more than one office. Also employees may share or have more than one telephone extension; there is at most one extension per office. Note also that a department will have only one manager and an employee may not manage more than one department.

Identify the following within the above database:

a) relations
b) attribute names and attribute values
c) tuples
d) domains
e) candidate, primary, alternate and foreign keys.

The manipulative part

2.4.1 What is the manipulative part?

The manipulative part of the relational model defines the set of things that can be done to relational databases. It includes operators with which it is possible to describe operations on relational databases. For instance, the manipulative part can be used to describe the things that have to be done in order to retrieve certain items of data from a database, or to change the contents of a database, or to alter the structure of the database.

The manipulative part is expressed in the form of a branch of mathematics called *relational algebra*. Relational algebra is to relations (tables) what conventional algebra is to numbers. There are alternative ways of expressing the manipulative part. One is *relational calculus*, but here only the relational algebra is described. However, the alternative relational calculus is the basis of QUEL, a relational database language, and is briefly described in Chapter 3.

Whereas in conventional algebra we can write expressions to define numbers, relational algebra can be used to write expressions which define relations (tables). For example, in conventional algebra we may write the expression,

$$x + y - (x/20)$$

In this expression there are the following components:

variables, x and y
a *constant* number, 20
arithmetic *operators*, +, − and /.

The above expression defines a number that results from applying the operators (+, − and /), to the numbers represented by the variables x and y, and the number 20. If x and y are assigned values 40 and 20, respectively, then the expression defines the number 58.

Similarly, using relational algebra we may write expressions. The difference is that an expression in relational algebra defines not a number, but a relation (table). The operators in relational algebra are applied to relations (tables) which are represented by variables, and constant relations (tables), i.e. relations (tables) of constant attribute values.

For example, consider the following relational algebra expression.

$$X \text{ union } (\langle 1, 3, 4 \rangle, \langle 1, 4, 6 \rangle)$$

This expression includes:

a) a variable, X, which represent a relation (table) (let us give the attributes (columns) of both relations (tables) arbitrary names, A, B and C),
b) a constant relation (table)

A	B	C
1	3	4
1	4	6

c) an operator, union.

The effect of the union operator is described in detail later in this chapter. For the present we shall simply note that the above expression defines a relation (table) which contains all of the tuples (rows) in X and also the tuples (rows) in the constant relation (table), i.e. ⟨1, 3, 4⟩ and ⟨1, 4, 6⟩. Duplicate (tuples) rows will of course be removed from the result relation (table). So, for instance, if the variable X represents the relation (table) given below,

A	B	C
1	6	9
1	3	4

then the relation (table) defined by the expression is

A	B	C
1	4	6
1	6	9
1	3	4

2.4.2 What use is relational algebra?

Relational algebra has two important roles:

★ It can be used to model and analyse the ways in which relational databases may be used. For instance, expressions in relational algebra may be used to describe data retrieval and data update operations on relational databases, or to describe a reorganisation of a relational database. Once those models have been created it is then possible to use them as a basis for reasoning about the consequences of those database operations.

★ Relational algebra provides a basis for designing languages for relational database systems. A relational database language should be capable of expressing at least that which can be expressed in relational algebra. A relational database language that has this capability is said to be *relationally complete*.

Relational algebra is not a database language. The meaning of an expression in relational algebra is not always easy to understand and so some clearer and 'friendlier' form of relational database language is desirable. (Some such languages are described later in this book, in Chapter 3.) Relational algebra does, however, define the things that it should be possible to do using a relational database language. As such, relational algebra may be considered to be a yardstick by which the power of relational database languages may be judged.

2.4.3 Relational algebra

In the following section the operators of relational algebra are explained and illustrated, with the aid of example operations, mainly on the relational database given below in Figure 2.3. The database represents information about Fair-Childs' customers, products and the sales orders placed by customers for the purchase of products. Each sales order has one or more lines on which quantities of different products are ordered. (It is left as an exercise for the reader to identify the candidate keys, the primary and alternate keys, and the foreign keys.) Note that the example database is scaled down and simplified for clarity. A real database will have many more relations, tuples and attributes.

2.4.4 A non-mathematical view of relational algebra

Relational algebra operations are simple to understand, but this simplicity can be obscured by the use of mathematical symbols which are often used to represent expressions in the algebra. A simple non-mathematical way to imagine relational algebra is in terms of 'cut' and 'paste' operations, similar to those that users of word processors will encounter.

If we imagine that the relational database in Figure 2.3 comprises a set of sheets of paper on which the tables are printed, the algebra then provides us with the equivalent of a pair of scissors for cutting out columns and rows from the tables, and also some glue and a photocopier with which we may duplicate cuttings. In this way, the algebra can be used to piece together new tables from existing ones.

PRODUCT

PROD_NO	NAME	COLOUR
P1	Pantaloons	blue
P2	Pantaloons	khaki
P3	Socks	harebell
P4	Socks	white
P5	Pinafore	white

CUSTOMER

CUST_NO	NAME	ADDRESS
C1	Nippers Ltd	25 High St, Leeds
C2	Tots-Gear	5 Low St, Oxford
C3	Super-Brat	30 New St, Luton
C6	Tiny-Togs	1 Old Rd, Luton

SALES_ORDER

ORDER_NO	DATE	CUST_NO
01	1/9/87	C1
02	2/5/87	C3
09	1/9/87	C6
010	1/9/87	C6

SALES_ORDER_LINE

ORDER_NO	PROD_NO	QUANTITY
01	P1	100
02	P1	100
02	P4	200
09	P1	50
010	P1	50

Figure 2.3   *An example database*

Example 2.15

Consider the following problem: 'Extract from the database in Figure 2.3 the names of customers who have placed orders on 1/9/87'. This problem may be solved in the following way, using the imaginary scissors, glue and copier.

a) Search through the SALES_ORDER table and cut out each row where the date is 1/9/87 and stick these on a new piece of paper to form a new table of sales orders on 1/9/87. This operation will produce the table below.

ORDER_NO	DATE	CUST_NO
01	1/9/87	C1
09	1/9/87	C6
010	1/9/87	C6

The above operation corresponds to applying the 'restrict' operator in relational algebra.

b) Search through the CUSTOMER table and cut out each row where the value in the CUST_NO column is the same as one of the values in the CUST_NO column in the table formed in a). Whenever this happens, take a copy of the two respective rows and combine them to form a row in a new table. This produces the following table:

CUST_NO	NAME	ADDRESS	ORDER_NO	DATE
C1	Nippers Ltd	25 High St, Leeds	01	1/9/87
C6	Tiny-Togs	1 Old Rd, Luton	09	1/9/87
C6	Tiny-Togs	1 Old Rd, Luton	010	1/9/87

This corresponds to applying the 'join' operator of relational algebra.

c) Cut out the NAME column in the table formed in b) and cut out and throw away any duplicate rows. The table below is created.

NAME
Nippers Ltd
Tiny-Togs

This corresponds to applying the 'project' operator in relational algebra. The table created by c) is the required list of customer names.

There is a wide range of database queries that may be satisfied by applying the notional scissors, glue and copier. This range of queries can also be expressed using the corresponding relational algebra expressions.

2.4.5 Relational algebra operators and expressions

Relational algebra includes a set of operators which, when applied to relations (tables), define new relations (tables). These operators may be combined within expressions, in the same way that in conventional algebra, for instance, + and − and / are combined in the expression $(x + (y − z)) / (x − z)$. Relational algebra operators may each be applied to one or two relations (tables) to define one relation (table) as its result. The relations (tables) may be represented by variables or may be specified as constants.

A complete set of relational algebra operators is one with which it is possible to express all the operations on relational databases which are expressible in relational algebra as a whole. One such complete set consists of the following operators:

RESTRICTION
PROJECTION
PRODUCT
UNION
DIFFERENCE

Each of these operators is described and illustrated in the following sections. Also described are other useful operators which may be derived from the above set of operators, namely:

INTERSECTION
DIVISION
JOIN

A variety of notations has been used to represent expressions in relational algebra. Most notations include conventional mathematical symbols and Greek letters. They can be cryptic in appearance and off-putting to the non-mathematician. In this book an English-like notation is used so as to make the meaning of expressions as clear as possible to the non-mathematician. Note, however, that the algebra described below is not a database language. Relational algebra is a means of modelling database usage, e.g. for research purposes, and the basis for database languages. It prescribes what a relational language should be able to express, but not how it expresses operations.

2.4.6 RESTRICT

RESTRICT is an operator which operates on a single relation (table). Such operators are called *unary* operators. Operators that operate on two relations (tables) are called *binary* operators. RESTRICT is sometimes called SELECT, but the name RESTRICT is used here so as to avoid any confusion when the SELECT instruction of the SQL relational database language is introduced later in this book.

The RESTRICT operator is used to define a new relation (table) that contains only those tuples (rows) of a relation (table) for which some condition is true.

A RESTRICT may be thought of as a logical pair of scissors for snipping out a selection of tuples (rows) from a relation (table) as illustrated in Figure 2.4. A RESTRICT could, for instance, be used to model a retrieval operation such as 'Retrieve all tuples (rows) in the SALES_ORDER relation (table) describing sales orders placed by customer C6'. The relational algebra equivalent of this operation is

RESTRICT SALES_ORDER **WHERE** CUST_NO = 'C6'

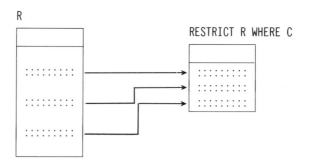

Figure 2.4   *RESTRICTION*

If this expression is applied to the example database in Figure 2.3, it defines the following relation (table).

ORDER_NO	DATE	CUST_NO
09	1/9/87	C6
010	1/9/87	C6

In general, a RESTRICT which defines a relation (table) of tuples (rows) of a relation (table) R, for which a condition C is true, is denoted:

RESTRICT R WHERE C

The condition C is called the restriction predicate. A restriction predicate is an expression which, when evaluated, will return either 'true' or 'false'. It is constructed in a way similar to the way that a condition in an IF statement in a programming language such as Pascal, COBOL, BASIC or FORTRAN is constructed. A restriction predicate is made up of:

> attribute names (column headings)
> constants
> the comparison operators, $<$, $>$, $=$, ...
> logical operators such as AND, OR and NOT
> brackets.

Two other examples of RESTRICT expressions are:

RESTRICT PRODUCT WHERE (COLOUR = 'white' OR COLOUR = 'blue')

which defines the relation:

PROD_NO	NAME	COLOUR
P1	Pantaloons	blue
P4	Socks	white
P5	Pinafore	white

and

RESTRICT PRODUCT WHERE NOT (COLOUR = 'blue') AND (NAME = 'Socks' OR NAME = 'Pantaloons')

which defines the relation (table):

PROD_NO	NAME	COLOUR
P2	Pantaloons	khaki
P3	Socks	harebell
P4	Socks	white

Note that each tuple (row) in the result relation (table) satisfies the condition that the colour of the product described is *not* blue, *and* also the product is either socks *or* pantaloons.

A detailed explanation of conditions, such as the predicates in the above example restrict operations, and how they are evaluated, is given later in Chapter 3 (see Section 3.10.3.1) when the query language SQL is described.

2.4.7 PROJECTION

PROJECT is another unary operator. PROJECT defines a relation which comprises only specified attributes of a relation.

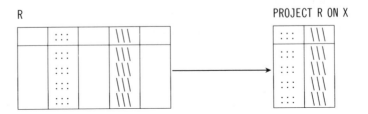

Figure 2.5   *PROJECTION*

PROJECT may be thought of as a logical pair of scissors for cutting out the attributes (columns) of a relation (table). This is illustrated in Figure 2.5. A PROJECT operator may be used to model retrieval operations such as 'Find the colours of all products described in the PRODUCT relation (table)'. This query is represented in relational algebra by the expression:

PROJECT PRODUCT ON COLOUR

When applied to the relational database in Figure 2.3, the relation (table) defined by this expression is as follows:

COLOUR
blue
khaki
harebell
white

Note that duplicates have been removed in the above example; in the PRODUCT relation (table), white occurs in two tuples, but only once in the result relation (table). This is because, by definition, a relation (table) may not have duplicate tuples (rows).

In general, a PROJECT operation which defines a relation consisting of the attributes (columns) X, of a relation (table) R, is denoted:

PROJECT R ON X

X must be one or more of the attributes (columns) of the relation (table) R.

The project operator is further illustrated by the following example.

PROJECT PRODUCT ON PROD_NO, NAME

defines the relation:

PROD_NO	NAME
P1	Pantaloons
P2	Pantaloons
P3	Socks
P4	Socks
P5	Pinafore

Note that the above example illustrates that it is possible to project on more than one attribute (column).

2.4.8 UNION

UNION is a binary operation: it takes two operand relations (tables). The UNION of two relations (tables), illustrated in Figure 2.6, is a relation (table) comprising all the distinct tuples (rows) in the two operand relations (tables).

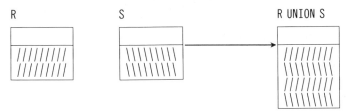

R   S   R UNION S

Figure 2.6   *UNION*

UNION can only combine relations (tables) with the same number of attributes (columns), and where corresponding attributes (columns) are defined on the same domain. UNION can be used to model the insertion of new tuples into a relation (table). For example, 'Add the tuple (row), ⟨011, 3/7/87, C4⟩ to the SALES_ORDER relation (table)' may be expressed by the following expression in the relational algebra:

SALES_ORDER UNION ⟨011, 3/7/87, C4⟩

When applied to the database in Figure 2.3, the above expressions define the relation:

ORDER_NO	DATE	CUST_NO
01	1/9/87	C1
02	2/5/87	C3
09	1/9/87	C6
010	1/9/87	C6
011	3/7/87	C4	⟵ new tuple

Note that the last row in the table above represents the tuple (row) that has been inserted. However, there is no sequence in a relation (table) and so it could just as well have been shown as, say, the first or second row. In general, the union of two relations (tables), *R* and *S*, is denoted:

R UNION *S*

2.4.9 DIFFERENCE

This is another binary operation. The difference (MINUS) of relation S from the relation R is a relation with tuples of R which are not also in S. This is illustrated in Figure 2.7.

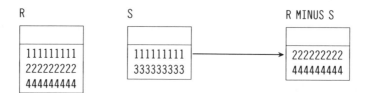

Figure 2.7 *DIFFERENCE*

As with UNION, the relations (tables) upon which DIFFERENCE operates must have the same number of attributes (columns) and corresponding attributes (columns) must be defined on the same domain. DIFFERENCE may be used to model the deletion of tuples from a relation (table).

For example, DIFFERENCE may be used to model, 'Delete the tuple (row), $\langle$02, 2/5/87, C3$\rangle$ from the SALES_ORDER relation (table)'. This is expressed in relational algebra as follows:

SALES_ORDER MINUS $\langle$02, 2/5/87, C3$\rangle$

When applied to the database in Figure 2.3, the above expressions define the relation (table):

ORDER_NO	DATE	CUST_NO
01	1/9/87	C1
09	1/9/87	C6
010	1/9/87	C6

In general the difference of two relations (tables), S from R, is denoted:

R MINUS S

2.4.10 Cartesian product

Cartesian product is a binary operation. The Cartesian product (TIMES) of two relations (tables) is a relation (table) comprising every tuple (row) of one of the relations (tables) combined with every tuple (row) of the other. This is illustrated in Figure 2.8.

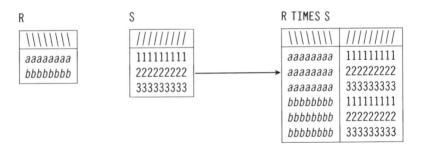

Figure 2.8   *Cartesian product*

Cartesian product may be used to represent queries such as, 'What are all the possible combinations of product and colour?' For example, imagine that there are two relations (tables), PRODUCT_NAME and PRODUCT_COLOUR, as shown below.

PRODUCT_NAME

NAME
Pantaloons
Socks

PRODUCT_COLOUR

COLOUR
blue
khaki
harebell
white

The above example query is then represented by the following expression in relational algebra.

PRODUCT_NAME TIMES PRODUCT_COLOUR

Given the example PRODUCT_NAME and PRODUCT_COLOUR relations (tables), the expression defines the following relation (table).

NAME	COLOUR
Pantaloons	blue
Pantaloons	khaki
Pantaloons	harebell
Pantaloons	white
Socks	blue
Socks	khaki
Socks	harebell
Socks	white

Note that the result includes all pairs of tuples (rows) where one is taken from each of the relations (tables). In general, the Cartesian product of two relations (tables), R and S say, is denoted:

R TIMES S

2.4.11 Derived operators

The set of operators described in the preceding sections form one of a number of *complete* sets of operators with which it is possible to define all relations that are definable with relational algebra as a whole. Other useful operators which may be derived from this complete set are described in the following sections.

2.4.12 INTERSECT

INTERSECT is a binary operator. INTERSECT defines a relation (table) composed of all the tuples (rows) which exist in *both* of the two relations (tables) to which it is applied. This is illustrated in Figure 2.9.

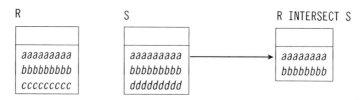

Figure 2.9   *INTERSECTION*

As with UNION and DIFFERENCE the relations (tables) must have the same number of attributes (columns) and corresponding attributes (columns) must be defined on the same domain. INTERSECT can be used to model queries, such as: 'Which products currently on order are also in stock?' If two relations (tables), PROD_IN_STOCK and PROD_ON_ORDER, respectively store numbers of products in stock and products on order, then the above query may be expressed by the following relational algebra.

      PROD_IN_STOCK **INTERSECT** PROD_ON_ORDER.

Given the following instances of the PROD_IN_STOCK and PROD_ON_ORDER relations (tables),

PROD_IN_STOCK

PROD_NO
P1
P2
P3
P4

PROD_ON_ORDER

PROD_NO
P3
P5

the above expression defines the following relation (table)

PROD_NO
P3

because the tuple (row) ⟨P3⟩ occurs in both relations (tables).

In general, the intersection of two relations (tables), R and S, is denoted,

   R INTERSECT S

INTERSECT is a derived operator because the same operation can be expressed with the basic operators. The expression

   R INTERSECT S

is equivalent to the expression

   $((R$ UNION $S)$ MINUS $(R$ MINUS $S))$ MINUS $(S$ MINUS $R)$

It is left as an exercise for readers to satisfy themselves of this equivalence.

2.4.13 DIVIDE

DIVIDE is another binary operator. Its meaning and use are harder to put into words than is the case with the previous operators. However, the effect of a division should become clear through examination of the following examples.

Consider the following relation (table):

SALESMAN_LANG

EMPLOYEE_NO	LANGUAGE
E1	French
E3	English
E3	French
E4	English
E4	French
E4	German
E5	English
E5	German
E5	Swedish

SALESMAN_LANG represents information concerning the linguistic abilities of salesmen. It identifies which languages each salesman speaks. The company wishes to send salesmen to a new sales office in Canada. The candidates for this post are those salesmen who are fluent in both French and English. The relation (table) below represents the required set of language.

LANGS

LANGUAGE
French
English

The following division models the retrieval of the employee numbers of each salesman who speaks all the necessary languages.

DIVIDE SALESMAN_LANG BY LANGS

The above expression defines the following relation (table).

EMPLOYEE_NO
E3
E4

The effect of the DIVIDE operator is to define a new relation (table) containing values taken from the first of the relations (tables) on which it operates. Each tuple (row) of this new relation (table) must also be associated with all of the information in the second relation (table). In the example, salesman numbers are taken from the first relation (table), SALESMAN_LANG, where the employee number is associated with every single language in the second relation (table), LANGS.

In general, the division of a relation (table) R by a relation (table) S is denoted:

DIVIDE R BY S

The relation (table) S must be defined on attributes (columns) which are also attributes (columns) of R. The relation (table) defined has attributes (columns) which are in R but not in S. The tuples (rows) of this relation (table) must occur in R in combination with *each* of the tuples (rows) of S. This is illustrated in Figure 2.10.

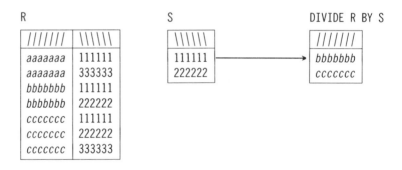

Figure 2.10   *DIVISION*

To further illustrate the divide operator, consider the following relations (tables) each of which represents a set of languages.

LANGS 1

LANGUAGE
English

LANGS 2

LANGUAGE
German
English

LANGS 3

LANGUAGE
English
French
German
Swedish

The results of the following three expressions

DIVIDE SALESMAN_LANG BY LANGS1
DIVIDE SALESMAN_LANG BY LANGS2
DIVIDE SALESMAN_LANG BY LANGS3

are, respectively, the following three relations (tables).

EMPLOYEE_NO
E3
E4
E5

EMPLOYEE_NO
E4
E5

EMPLOYEE_NO

DIVIDE is used to model the retrieval of data objects which are associated with every member of a set of properties. It can model queries such as 'Which products are available in red, green and amber?' and 'Which warehouses have stocks of all of the following products?'

2.4.14 JOIN

The JOIN is an important type of operator as it provides a means of using the relationships between the different relations (tables) of a database in order to construct a new relation (table) representing related information.

A JOIN operation on two relations (tables) defines a third relation (table) in which each tuple (row) is a combination of one tuple (row) taken from the first relation (table) and one tuple (row) taken from the second relation (table). Also, there must be some specific similarity between the tuples (rows) that are combined.

To illustrate the use of the JOIN operator, consider once again the database in Figure 2.3. The four relations (tables), CUSTOMER, PRODUCT, SALES_ORDER and SALES_ORDER_LINE are all interrelated.

A tuple (row) in SALES_ORDER_LINE relates information about a product, represented in PRODUCT, to information about a sales order represented in SALES_ORDER. A tuple (row) in SALES_ORDER includes a customer number and this cross-references information represented in CUSTOMER about the customer who has placed the order.

The JOIN operator may be used to combine information represented in the database in Figure 2.3 in the following ways:

a) to combine information about customers and information about the sales order that they have placed,
b) to combine information about sales orders with information about the sales order lines of which they are made,
c) to combine information about sales order lines with information about the ordered products.

JOINs may be of the following types:

NATURAL JOIN
EQUI-JOIN
THETA-JOIN
SEMI-JOIN
OUTER JOIN

Each of these is described and discussed below.

2.4.14.1 NATURAL JOIN

The NATURAL JOIN is used to combine two relations (tables) on the basis of all the attributes (columns) which occur in both of them. Tuples (rows) are combined where the common attributes (columns) have the same value. This is illustrated in Figure 2.11.

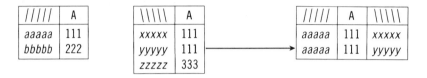

Figure 2.11 *NATURAL JOIN*

For example, consider the SALES_ORDER and CUSTOMER relations (tables) in Figure 2.3. The following expression defines the natural join of these two relations (tables).

JOIN SALES_ORDER AND CUSTOMER

Given the Figure 2.3 database, the above expression defines the relation (table) given below

ORDER_NO	DATE	CUST_NO	NAME	ADDRESS
01	1/9/87	C1	Nippers Ltd	25 High St, Leeds
02	2/5/87	C3	Super-Brat	30 New St, Barnet
09	1/9/87	C6	Tiny-Togs	1 Old Rd, Luton
010	1/9/87	C6	Tiny-Togs	1 Old Rd, Luton

The effect of the above natural join is as follows.

a) The resulting relation (table) is defined on all the attributes of SALES_ORDER and all the attributes of CUSTOMER. The attribute, CUST_NO, which is common to both relations (tables), occurs only once in the result.

b) A tuple in the resulting relation is formed from each pair of tuples, one from SALES_ORDER and one from CUSTOMER, where the value of the common attribute is the same.

c) Any tuple (row) in either SALES_ORDER or CUSTOMER for which there is no matching tuple (row) in the other relation is lost.

In general, a NATURAL JOIN of two relations (tables), R and S, is written

JOIN R AND S

The resulting relation (table) is defined on the attributes (columns) of *R* and the attributes (columns) of *S*. Where the same attribute (column) occurs in both *R* and *S* it occurs only once in the result. Tuples (rows) of *R* and *S* are combined to form a tuple (row) in the resulting relation (table) whenever all the values of the attributes (columns) which are common to both *R* and *S* are identical in the two tuples (rows).

A second example of the NATURAL JOIN is given below.

> JOIN PRODUCT AND SALES_ORDER_LINE

Here the NATURAL JOIN is used to combine information represented in SALES_ORDER_LINE with information represented in PRODUCT. The NATURAL JOIN combines this information on the basis of the values of the attribute (column), PROD_NO, which is common to both relations (tables).

Given the Figure 2.3 database, the relation (table) defined by this expression is as follows:

ORDER_NO	PROD_NO	QUANTITY	NAME	COLOUR
01	P1	100	Pantaloons	blue
02	P1	100	Pantaloons	blue
02	P4	200	Socks	white
09	P1	50	Pantaloons	blue
010	P1	50	Pantaloons	blue

2.4.14.2 EQUI-JOIN

The EQUI-JOIN is a more flexible type of join operator than the NATURAL JOIN (previously described). The EQUI-JOIN defines a relation (table) of tuples (rows) which is a combination of pairs of tuples (rows) taken from two relations (tables), one from each, and where specified attributes (columns) have the same value in each of the pairs of tuples (rows). This is illustrated in Figure 2.12.

Figure 2.12   *EQUI-JOIN*

The EQUI-JOIN and the NATURAL JOIN are both used for the same purpose, i.e. to combine related information that is represented in different relations (tables). The difference between these two types of join is to do with the conditions that must be satisfied when two tuples (rows) are combined. The NATURAL JOIN combines tuples on the basis of the values of *all* attributes of the same name but the EQUI-JOIN joins on the basis of *specified* attributes. This difference is illustrated by the following example.

The two relations (tables) below represent information about the management structure of a business. Information about the department to which employees are attached can be represented by DEPT_EMPLOYEE. MANAGER represents the management structure, i.e. who is in charge of whom.

DEPT_EMPLOYEE

DEPARTMENT	EMPLOYEE_NO	GRADE
D1	E1	II
D1	E2	IB
D1	E3	IB
D1	E4	IA
D2	E5	III
D2	E9	II

MANAGEMENT

MANAGER	SUBORDINATE
E1	E2
E1	E3
E2	E4
E5	E9

DEPT_EMPLOYEE represents the information:

a) department D1 comprises employees E1, E2, E3 and E4 who are employed on grades II, IB, IB and IA, respectively;
b) department D2 comprises employees E5 and E9 who are employed on grades III and II, respectively.

MANAGEMENT represents the information:

a) employee E1 is in charge of employees E2 and E3,
b) employee E2 is in charge of employee E4,
c) employee E5 is in charge of E9.

Note that EMPLOYEE_NO, MANAGER and SUBORDINATE are all defined on the same domain, the domain of employee numbers.

It is not possible to combine the information in the two relations (tables) using a NATURAL JOIN. This is because there are no attributes (columns) which occur in both relations (tables), so that there is no overlap. However, the information in the two relations (tables) is strongly interrelated, and it is possible to combine the information using an EQUI-JOIN. Two example EQUI-JOINS are given in the following two expressions:

> JOIN DEPT_EMPLOYEE AND MANAGEMENT
> WHERE DEPT_EMPLOYEE.EMPLOYEE_NO = MANAGEMENT.MANAGER

> JOIN DEPT_EMPLOYEE AND MANAGEMENT
> WHERE DEPT_EMPLOYEE.EMPLOYEE_NO = MANAGEMENT.SUBORDINATE

The above two expressions will result in the following relations (tables), respectively:

DEPARTMENT	EMPLOYEE_NO	GRADE	MANAGER	SUBORDINATE
D1	E1	II	E1	E2
D1	E1	II	E1	E3
D1	E2	IB	E2	E4
D2	E5	III	E5	E9

DEPARTMENT	EMPLOYEE_NO	GRADE	MANAGER	SUBORDINATE
D1	E2	IB	E1	E2
D1	E3	IB	E1	E3
D1	E4	IA	E2	E4
D2	E9	II	E5	E9

Note that the condition for joining tuples (rows) is explicitly stated in the two example EQUI-JOINS. The join conditions are as follows.

a) The first joins tuples (rows) where the value of EMPLOYEE_NO in DEPT_EMPLOYEE is equal to the value of MANAGER in MANAGEMENT.

b) The second joins tuples (rows) where EMPLOYEE_NO in DEPT_EMPLOYEE is equal to SUBORDINATE in MANAGEMENT.

The EQUI-JOIN is so called because the condition for joining tuples (rows) is always equality of values. Note also that the resulting relation includes *all* the attributes (columns) of the joined relation (table). This contrasts with the NATURAL JOIN, where any attributes (columns) which occur in both of the joined relations (tables) occur only once in the resulting relation (table).

The EQUI-JOIN of relations (tables) R and S on equality of values of A in R and B in S is denoted by

JOIN R AND S WHERE $R.A = S.B$

The above EQUI-JOIN combines tuples (rows) in R and S where the values of specified attributes (columns), A in R and B in S, are equal. The specified attributes (columns) must be defined on the same domain. The result relation (table) is defined on attributes (columns) of R and S.

The third example of an EQUI-JOIN, given below, illustrates what happens where attributes (columns) in the joined relations (tables) have the same attribute (column) names. This example joins the PAYMENT and INVOICE relations (tables) shown below.

PAYMENT

INVOICE_NO	DATE
I1	880101
I4	880901

INVOICE

INVOICE_NO	DATE	AMOUNT
I1	880101	1000
I3	880101	150
I4	880301	200

JOIN PAYMENT AND INVOICE WHERE PAYMENT.DATE = INVOICE.DATE

defines the following relation:

PAYMENT. INVOICE_NO	PAYMENT. DATE	INVOICE. INVOICE_NO	INVOICE. DATE	AMOUNT
I1	880101	I1	880101	1000
I1	880101	I3	880101	150

Note that all attributes (columns) of PAYMENT and INVOICE exist in the result relation (table). Attribute (column) names are qualified by the relation (table) name where they would otherwise be ambiguous. The effect of the above EQUI-JOIN is to retrieve details of invoices that were paid on the same date that an invoice was issued.

The EQUI-JOIN is much more versatile and realistic than the NATURAL JOIN because, unlike the NATURAL JOIN, it does not assume that attributes (columns) with the same name have the same meaning. In practice relational database languages directly support EQUI-JOIN and other more general forms of join, but not the NATURAL JOIN.

2.4.14.3 THETA-JOIN

A THETA-JOIN is a more general version of the EQUI-JOIN. In the EQUI-JOIN tuples (rows) are joined where the values of specified attributes (columns) are equal. In a THETA-JOIN, the condition is not restricted to equality. Any comparison operator may be used.

The THETA-JOIN defines a relation (table) of tuples (rows) which are a combination of pairs of tuples (rows) taken from two relations (tables), one from each, and where specified attributes (columns) have values which are related in some specified way. This is illustrated in Figure 2.13.

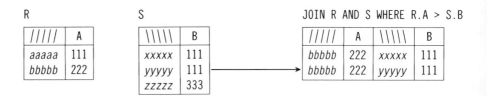

Figure 2.13   *THETA-JOIN*

Consider again the two relations (tables), PAYMENT and INVOICE, in the previous example. The following THETA-JOIN will define a relation (table) which details invoices and payments, where the payment was on a date later than the date on which an invoice w issued.

JOIN PAYMENT AND INVOICE WHERE PAYMENT.DATE > INVOICE.DATE

The above expression defines the following relation (table):

PAYMENT. INVOICE_NO	PAYMENT. DATE	INVOICE. INVOICE_NO	INVOICE. DATE	AMOUNT
I4	880901	I1	880101	1000
I4	880901	I3	880101	150
I4	880901	I4	880301	200

Note, the result contains all combinations of a tuple (row) from PAYMENT and a tuple (row) from INVOICE where DATE in INVOICE is less than DATE in PAYMENT, regardless of whether they are to do with the same invoice.

The next example expression in relational algebra models the query, 'What are the details of invoices which have been paid on a date later than the date on which the invoice was issued?' This is modelled by the following expression:

> JOIN PAYMENT AND INVOICE WHERE (PAYMENT.DATE > INVOICE.DATE
> AND PAYMENT.INVOICE_NO = INVOICE.INVOICE_NO)

The relation (table) defined by the above expression is as follows:

PAYMENT. INVOICE_NO	PAYMENT. DATE	INVOICE. INVOICE_NO	INVOICE. DATE	AMOUNT
I4	880901	I4	880301	200

Note that to represent this query it is necessary further to restrict the join conditions so as to ensure that tuple (row) pairs are joined only when they represent information about the same invoice.

The general form of a theta-join on two relations (tables), R and S, where the join condition is C, is denoted

> JOIN R AND S WHERE C

The result relation (table) is defined on attributes (columns) of R and attributes (columns) of S (all are assumed to be distinct). Each tuple (row) is formed from a tuple (row) of R and a tuple (row) of S such that the condition C is true.

2.4.14.4 SEMI-JOIN

The semi-join of two relations (tables) is the set of all the tuples (rows) of the first, which will join with tuples (rows) of the second. This is illustrated in Figure 2.14.

SEMI-JOINS can be SEMI-NATURAL JOINS, SEMI-EQUI-JOINS or SEMI-THETA-JOINS. As an illustration, consider the following example SEMI-NATURAL JOIN applied to the Figure 2.3 database.

> SJOIN CUSTOMER AND SALES_ORDER

The above expression models the query, 'What are the details of customers who have placed sales orders?' The relation (table) defined by this expression is as follows:

CUSTOMER

CUST_NO	NAME	ADDRESS
C1	Nippers Ltd	25 High St, Leeds
C3	Super-Brat	30 New St, Barnet
C6	Tiny-Togs	1 Old Rd, Luton

Note that the tuple (row) for C2 is missing because there is no corresponding sales order tuple (row).

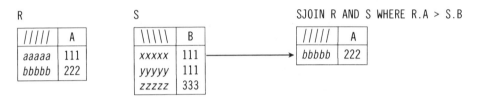

Figure 2.14   *SEMI-THETA-JOIN*

In general, the semi-join of two relations (tables), *R* and *S*, on condition *C* is denoted:

SJOIN *R* AND *S* WHERE *C*

The result relation (table) is defined on the attributes (columns) of *R*, and includes the tuples (rows) of *R* for which, when paired with some tuple (row) of *S*, the condition *C* is true.

SEMI-JOINS are important in the design of distributed database systems (see Chapter 6).

2.4.14.5 OUTER JOIN

Tuples (rows) may be lost in the course of a JOIN. This occurs when there is a tuple (row) in one of the joined relations (table), but no tuple (row) in the other relation (table) with which it can combine and satisfy the join condition.

The OUTER JOIN is an information-preserving version of the join. An OUTER JOIN preserves the tuples (rows) which would have been lost by other types of join. For these tuples (rows), the attribute (column) values which would normally be supplied by the other relation (table) are set to null. Null represents no value at all. This is illustrated in Figure 2.15.

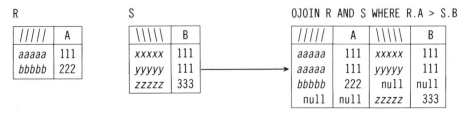

Figure 2.15   *OUTER EQUI-JOIN*

An OUTER JOIN may be an OUTER NATURAL JOIN, an OUTER EQUI-JOIN or an OUTER THETA-JOIN. To illustrate the OUTER JOIN, consider again the example database in Figure 2.3. The following expression in relational algebra is the OUTER NATURAL JOIN of the relations (tables) SALES_ORDER and CUSTOMER. The effect is to define a relation (table) which contains details of all customers and also of all sales orders.

OJOIN SALES_ORDER AND CUSTOMER

The above expression defines the following relation (table):

ORDER_NO	DATE	CUST_NO	NAME	ADDRESS
01	1/9/87	C1	Nippers Ltd	25 High St, Leeds
null	null	C2	Tots-Gear	5 Low St, Oxford
02	2/5/87	C3	Super-Brat	30 New St, Barnet
09	1/9/87	C6	Tiny-Togs	1 Old Rd, Luton
010	1/9/87	C6	Tiny-Togs	1 Old Rd, Luton

Note that there are nulls in the second tuple (row) because there is no sales order tuple (row) with which the tuple (row) for customer C2 can join.

In general, the outer join between two relations (tables), R and S on a condition C, is denoted:

OJOIN R AND S WHERE C

The result relation (table) is defined on the attributes of R and of S. Each tuple (row) is formed either by joining a tuple (row) of R with a tuple (row) of S for which C is true; or by joining other tuples (rows) of R or of S with null values.

2.4.15 Complex expressions in relational algebra

Expressions in relational algebra may include combinations of any or all of the operators described above. This ability to form complex expressions makes relational algebra a very expressive language. There is a wide range of database operations that may be modelled using relational algebra. The following examples, also based on the Figure 2.3 database, illustrate ways in which complex expressions may be formed.

To model the query, 'What are the names of products ordered by Super-Brat?' it is necessary to define the following:

a) Customer details of Super-Brat: this may be defined by the following RESTRICT operation:

RESTRICT CUSTOMER WHERE NAME = 'Super-Brat'

b) Sales orders placed by Super-Brat. This may be defined by joining the relation (table) defined in a) above with the SALES_ORDER relation, i.e.

JOIN (RESTRICT CUSTOMER WHERE NAME = 'Super-Brat') AND SALES_ORDER

c) Details of the order lines of the sales order placed by Super-Brat. This may be defined by joining the relation (table) defined in b) with the SALES_ORDER_LINE relation (table), i.e.

JOIN
(JOIN (RESTRICT CUSTOMER WHERE NAME = 'Super-Brat') AND SALES_ORDER)
AND
SALES_ORDER_LINE

d) Details of products ordered by Super-Brat. This may be defined by joining the relation (table) defined in c) above with the PRODUCT relation (table) where the product numbers are the same. This is represented by the following expression:

JOIN
    (JOIN
        (JOIN (RESTRICT CUSTOMER WHERE NAME = 'Super-Brat')
        AND SALES_ORDER)
    AND SALES_ORDER_LINE)
    AND
    PRODUCT WHERE PRODUCT.PROD_NO = SALES_ORDER_LINE.PROD_NO)

e) Names of the products ordered by Super-Brat. This may be defined by projecting the relation (table) defined in d) above, on the product name attribute (column), i.e.

PROJECT
    (JOIN
        (JOIN
            (JOIN (RESTRICT CUSTOMER WHERE NAME = 'Super-Brat')
            AND SALES_ORDER)
        AND SALES_ORDER_LINE)
        AND
        PRODUCT WHERE PRODUCT.PROD_NO = SALES_ORDER_LINE.PROD_NO)
    ON PRODUCT.NAME

As can be seen, the algebra is not a very friendly language. It is not a database language and would not be used by a database user, and so the reader need not become proficient in using relational algebra to model database operations. The importance of relational algebra is that it can be used as a language for research, and also it defines what it should be possible to do using a relational database language.

2.4.16 Summary of the manipulative part of the relational model

The manipulative part of the relational model is the set of operators that may be applied to a relational database. These form a type of mathematics called relational algebra. Expressions in relational algebra define relations (tables), derived from the attribute values (column entries) of other relations (tables).

A basic set of relational algebra operators is as follows:

RESTRICT	Extracts tuples (rows) that satisfy a condition
PROJECTION	Extracts specified attributes (columns)
UNION	Merges two relations
DIFFERENCE	Removes tuples (rows) that occur in one relation (table) from another
CARTESIAN PRODUCT	Produces all possible pairs of tuples (rows), one taken from the first relation (table) and the other from the second.

Using the above operators, other useful operators may be derived. These are:

INTERSECT	Extracts tuples (rows) that occur in both of two relations (tables)
DIVIDE	Extracts attribute values (column entries) in one relation (table) which occur with all of the attribute values (column entries) of another
NATURAL JOIN	Combines tuples (rows) in two relations (tables) where the common attributes (columns) have common values
EQUI-JOIN	Combines tuples (rows) where specified attributes (columns) have common values
THETA-JOIN	Combines tuples (rows) where the values of specified attributes (columns) satisfy some specified condition
SEMI-JOIN	Selects tuples (rows) that will join with tuples (rows) of another relation (table)
OUTER JOIN	Combines tuples (rows) in two relations (tables) where some join condition is true. Tuples (rows) for which there is no match are combined with a tuple (row) of null values.

Exercises

2.5 Consider the following relational database:

EMPLOYEE

EMP_NO	NI_NO	ENAME	DEPT_NO
E1	123	J Smith	D1
E2	159	J Smith	D1
E3	5432	R Brown	D2
E5	7654	M Green	D3

DEPARTMENT

DEPT_NO	DNAME	MANAGER
D1	Accounts	E1
D2	Stores	E2
D3	Sales	E5

EMPLOYEE_EXTENSION

EMP_NO	OFFICE	EXTENSION
E1	R101	811
E1	R102	813
E2	R10	111
E3	R35	123
E5	R35	123

The above database represents information about an organisation's employees, departments, offices and telephone extensions.

i) A tuple (row) of EMPLOYEE represents a unique employee number (EMP_NO), a

unique national insurance number
(NI_NO), and the name of an employee
(ENAME), and also the department to
which that employee belongs (DEPT_NO).

ii) A tuple (row) of DEPARTMENT represents a
unique number (DEPT_NO) and name
(DNAME) for a department, and also the
number of the employee who is manager
(MANAGER).

iii) A tuple (row) of EMPLOYEE_EXTENSION
represents the number of an employee
(EMP_NO), the employee's office number
(OFFICE), and the telephone extension on
which that employee can be contacted
(EXTENSION).

Note that employee names are not unique,
and that an employee may share or have
more than one office. Also employees may
share or have more than one telephone
extension; there is at most one extension per
office. Note also that a department will have
only one manager and an employee may not
manage more than one department.

Identify the relations defined by the following
expressions in relational algebra, when
applied to the above database.

a) RESTRICT DEPARTMENT WHERE MANAGER
= 'E1'

b) RESTRICT EMPLOYEE WHERE NOT
(ENAME = 'J Smith' AND DEPT_NO = D2)
OR EMP_NO = E1

c) PROJECT EMPLOYEE ON ENAME

d) PROJECT EMPLOYEE_EXTENSION ON
OFFICE, EXTENSION

e) PROJECT (RESTRICT EMPLOYEE
WHERE DEPT_NO = D1) ON ENAME

f) EMPLOYEE UNION ⟨E4,2222, 'R Grey', D3⟩

g) (PROJECT DEPARTMENT OVER MANAGER)
UNION (PROJECT EMPLOYEE_EXTENSION
ON EMP_NO)

h) (PROJECT EMPLOYEE ON EMP NO) MINUS
(PROJECT DEPARTMENT ON MANAGER)

i) EMPLOYEE TIMES DEPARTMENT

j) (PROJECT EMPLOYEE_EXTENSION ON
EMP_NO) INTERSECT (PROJECT
EMPLOYEE ON EMP_NO)

k) DIVIDE EMPLOYEE_EXTENSION BY ROOMS
where ROOMS is as follows:

ROOMS

OFFICE
R101
R102

l) DIVIDE (PROJECT EMPLOYEE_EXTENSION
ON EMP_NO, OFFICE) BY ROOMS

m) JOIN EMPLOYEE AND DEPARTMENT

n) JOIN EMPLOYEE AND DEPARTMENT WHERE
EMP_NO = MANAGER

o) OJOIN EMPLOYEE AND DEPARTMENT
WHERE EMP_NO = MANAGER

p) SJOIN EMPLOYEE AND DEPARTMENT

q) SJOIN EMPLOYEE AND DEPARTMENT
WHERE EMP_NO = MANAGER

r) PROJECT (JOIN DEPARTMENT AND
(JOIN EMPLOYEE AND (RESTRICT
EMPLOYEE_EXTENSION WHERE OFFICE =
R35))) ON DNAME

2.5 The integrity part of the relational model

2.5.1 What is the integrity part?

The integrity part of the relational model is the set of rules that all valid relational
databases must obey. The purpose of these rules is to ensure that relational databases
are at least self-consistent and complete.

There are just two general integrity rules: these are called the entity integrity rule and the referential integrity rule, and are explained below. There are also a number of other types of integrity rule, but these are specific to individual databases and will be discussed later in this book (see Chapters 3 and 4).

2.5.2 Entity integrity

The effect of enforcing the entity integrity rule is to ensure that each tuple (row) includes a unique name or identifier for the object about which it represents information. The entity integrity rule is that in every tuple (row), attributes (columns) that belong to a primary key must have a non-null value.

A null value is a way of representing that no value at all has been assigned to an attribute (column). It may be likened to a vacuum within the database. There are many reasons why a tuple (row) may have an attribute (column) for which no value has been assigned. For example, the value may be unknown or inapplicable. A primary key, however, has a special purpose. The primary key uniquely identifies each tuple (row) within a relation (table), thus providing a name for the objects about which the tuples (rows) represent information, and so a null primary key value would not make sense. It would result in an object without a name, and there is then no way of distinguishing between different objects without names.

PRODUCT

PROD_NO	NAME	COLOUR
P1	Pantaloons	blue
P2	Pantaloons	khaki
P3	Socks	harebell
P4	Socks	white
P5	Pinafore	white

Figure 2.16   *Example PRODUCT relation*

For example, consider the PRODUCT relation (table) in Figure 2.16. The primary key there is PROD_NO. Imagine there are two new products, both blue socks, but made to different patterns. However, they have not yet been assigned product numbers. It would be a breach of the entity integrity rule to then insert two new tuples (rows):

⟨null, Socks, blue⟩

which represents the first of the new products and

⟨null, Socks, blue⟩

which represents the second. It would be nonsense to do so because the two tuples (rows) are not uniquely identifiable. In fact, in this case the tuples (rows) are indistinguishable, even though the null values will eventually be replaced by different product numbers, and a relation (table), by definition, may not have identical tuples (rows).

2.5.3 Referential integrity

The effect of enforcing the referential integrity rule is to ensure that all objects that are cross-referenced from within the database are also described within the database. In this way it is possible to avoid, for instance, recording a sales order placed by customer C9 when there is no record of customer C9, or orders for products which are not described in the database.

The referential integrity rule is as follows. The domain of a single attribute (column) primary key may be designated as a primary domain. If a relation (table) contains a foreign key on a primary domain, then every tuple (row) of that relation (table) must satisfy the constraints that the foreign key value is either null or a value which occurs elsewhere in the database as a primary key. To illustrate referential integrity, consider the two relations (tables), CUSTOMER and SALES_ORDER in Figure 2.17.

CUSTOMER

CUST_NO	NAME	ADDRESS
C45	Boys	Newsome
C46	Girls	Honley

SALES_ORDER

ORDER_NO	DATE	CUST_NO
011	1/7/89	C45
012	1/8/89	null
013	2/5/88	C47
null	1/1/89	C45

Figure 2.17   *Example CUSTOMER and SALES__ORDER relations*

The primary key of CUSTOMER is CUST_NO. It is a single attribute (column) primary key and so its domain may be designated a primary domain. CUST_NO in SALES_ORDER is a foreign key as it is defined on the same domain as is CUST_NO in CUSTOMER. It is therefore a foreign key on a primary domain.

Now, consider the instances of CUSTOMER and SALES_ORDER in Figure 2.17. This database instance is illegal because it violates both integrity rules. The tuple (row) represented as the first row in SALES_ORDER represents the following information: 'Customer C45 placed sales order 011 on 1/7/89'. That is an acceptable proposition and the corresponding tuple (row) satisfies both integrity rules. The primary key (ORDER_NO) value is not null and so the entity integrity rule is satisfied and the foreign key (CUST_NO) value cross-references a tuple (row) in the CUSTOMER relation (table) which satisfies the referential integrity rule.

The tuple (row) represented as the second row of SALES_ORDER represents 'Sales order 012 was placed on 1/8/89 but we have no record of the customer's number'. Under certain circumstances this may also be an acceptable proposition. For example, it may be the case that a new customer has placed an order, but the customer has not yet been assigned a customer number. The corresponding tuple (row) satisfies both integrity rules. Entity integrity is satisfied because the primary key (ORDER_NO) value is not null. The foreign key (CUST_NO) value is null, but this is allowed by the referential integrity rule.

On the other hand, the two tuples (rows) represented by the last two rows of SALES_ORDER are both unacceptable. The first of them represents the information 'Customer C47 placed sales order 013 on 2/5/88'. That is unacceptable because there is no record of a customer C47 in the database and so referential integrity is violated.

The second of the two unacceptable tuples (rows) represents 'Customer C34 placed an order on 1/1/89 but we have no record of the order number'. That is unacceptable because ORDER_NO is the primary key of SALES_ORDER and so a null value violates entity integrity. The result of accepting this tuple (row) would be a tuple (row) within the database which may not always be uniquely addressable.

2.5.4 Summary

The integrity part is a set of two rules, the entity and the referential integrity rules, which, respectively, ensure that all data objects have names and do not cross-reference other non-existent data objects.

Exercises

2.6 State the two integrity rules.

2.7 Explain the anomalies that may occur when the two integrity rules are violated.

2.8 For each of the following tuples (rows), state which, if any, of the integrity rules are

violated when they are added to the SALES_ORDER relation in Figure 2.17.

a) ⟨014, 1/1/91, C45⟩
b) ⟨015, 1/4/90, null⟩
c) ⟨016, 2/4/92, C52⟩
d) ⟨017, null, null⟩
e) ⟨null, 1/1/91, C45⟩

2.6 Relational database management systems

The parts of a computer system and the relationships between them are called its architecture. Most database systems, including relational ones, have the same general architecture. The following sections describe the general database systems architecture and explains how it applies to relational database systems. Within this context, the main features of relational database management systems (RDBMSs) are reviewed, and the link between these features and the theoretical model of relational databases, described earlier in this chapter and in Chapter 3, is explained.

2.7 Overview of a general database system architecture

A system consisting of a DBMS, a database, and applications programs which use the database is called a database system. Figure 2.18 represents a general architecture, i.e. the component parts of a system and relationships between them, to which most database systems conform.

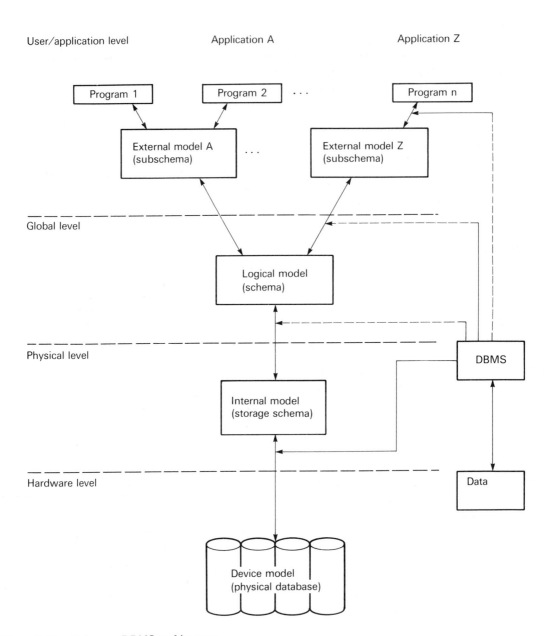

Figure 2.18   *Reference DBMS architecture*

Levels
The architecture in Figure 2.18 includes components within a framework of four levels. The purpose of each level is as follows.

a) The user/application level is the level at which database applications programs, usually just called applications, access the database. Applications are given a selective view of the database; they are only allowed to access the logical data structures which are relevant to them.

b) The global level is where the logical structure of the database as a whole is described.

c) The physical level is where the physical data structures which are used to represent the logical data structures of the database are described. It is here that the ways in which the database is actually stored, i.e. as files, indexes, linked lists, hashing algorithms, and the like, are described.

d) At the hardware level, the database exists as 1s and 0s, stored on storage devices such as disks.

Within this layered framework, there are three types of component. These are models, programs, and the data dictionary.

Models

The models in Figure 2.18 are the external models, the logical model, the internal model, and the device model. Each model is all or part of the database, in a form appropriate to the level at which it resides.

a) The logical model is the complete database as a set of logical data structures.

b) An external model is part of the database relevant to some application, as a set of logical structures.

c) The internal model is the database as a set of storage structures such as files and indexes.

d) The device model is the database as the 1s and 0s stored on storage devices, such as disks.

Figure 2.18 includes arrows between models to indicate that there is a correspondence between objects at the different levels. For example, storage structures in the internal model will implement logical structures in the logical model; the logical structures in an external model correspond to structures in the logical model.

Each model has a description called a schema, or subschema in the case of an external model. A schema describes the database as it exists within a particular model and also includes details of the correspondences between the data within that model and those within some adjacent model. For example, the subschema for an external model will describe logical structures relevant to some application, and also how they relate to logical structures in the logical model; the internal model schema will describe the structure of the files, indexes, etc. in the internal model, and also identify the structures in the logical model that they implement.

Programs

The computer programs are the applications programs that use the data stored in the database, and the DBMS itself. The DBMS is a special program that allows the models at each level to be defined, and implements the mappings between them when the database is used. (The control of the mappings is represented in Figure 2.18 by the arrows with broken lines.)

The DBMS uses the schemas to implement the mappings between the different levels of the database system in the following way. An application may access only the portion of the database which is contained in a specific external model. That external model will include only the logical data structures which represent information relevant to that application. The subschema for that external model describes these logical data structures. An application may use a special database language to access data in its external model.

To access specific data, it must refer to the appropriate logical data structures described in the subschema.

The DBMS will translate an instruction which accesses specific external model data into equivalent instructions which access the corresonding data in the logical model. The translated instruction will refer to the appropriate logical data structures described in the logical model schema.

The DBMS will then translate the instructions which access data in the logical model into equivalent instructions which access the corresponding storage structures in the internal model. The storage structures are described in the internal model schema.

Finally, the DBMS will translate the instructions which access storage structures in the internal model into equivalent instructions which access the corresponding stored data (in the device model). The DBMS will usually cause the actual data to be accessed by issuing appropriate file read and write instructions to the computer's operating system.

Data dictionary

The data dictionary (sometimes called the system catalogue) is a database of information about the organisation's computer systems, and its database system in particular. It is the repository for metadata, i.e. data about the data, and will describe files, programs, database schemas, users, applications, and so on.

In addition to containing descriptions of the models of a database system (depicted in Figure 2.18), a data dictionary will sometimes describe the real world information represented in the database. For example, a typical dictionary system for an RDBMS will describe the physical representation of the database, i.e. the files, indexes, storage devices, etc.; the logical data structures, i.e. the relations, attributes, etc.; and may also describe the real world objects, their properties, and relationships between them, represented in the database. This real world description is called a conceptual model.

Whereas the structures of a database must be designed and defined by the DBA, a data dictionary system comes ready-structured. The data dictionary has a default design, including the structures necessary to describe any database system. Some data dictionary systems also include an extensibility feature which allows the DBA to define additional structures within which to store additional information about the database and other computer systems, and programming languages with which the DBA may create data dictionary processing programs. Using these, DBAs can tailor the dictionary system to suit their own local and specific needs.

Data dictionary systems can be either active or passive. An active system automatically updates the data dictionary when changes are made to the database system, but in a passive system all updates to the data dictionary must be initiated by the DBA.

A data dictionary system may also be integrated with a DBMS, or it may be a stand-alone system. An integrated system uses the DBMS to access the data dictionary, whereas a stand-alone system includes its own specialised DBMS.

A comprehensive data dictionary is a powerful tool for documenting and controlling the database system throughout its life. It can be used during the application of systems analysis and design methods, programming methods, data analysis and database design.

Three specific data dictionary roles are as follows. The data dictionary provides an important feature of a fourth generation environment. Fourth generation environments provide the user with a very high-level set of interfaces for creating applications. A user can typically create an application by describing what that application is to do, rather than how it is to be done. The data dictionary contains information which is needed to turn that description of *what* into a program which describes *how*. Fourth generation environments are described in some detail in Chapter 3.

The data dictionary system includes facilities to provide the DBA with information on the state and usage of the database system. For example, the DBA may use these facilities to make ad hoc on-line queries to extract a report which lists specified database structures, and details of applications programs which use each of them.

The data dictionary can also be used as a help system for the database user. A user may search the data dictionary in order to find out about the database structures. This may be useful, for example, when the user requires help in formulating a database query. The data dictionary may be used to determine the correct names to be included within a query.

2.8 Relational database system architecture

Relational database systems mainly conform to the architecture in Figure 2.18. An RDBMS presents to the user the 1s and 0s, which are the stored data (in the device model), in the form of the structures of the relational model, i.e. as relations (in the logical model and external models), and allows the user to manipulate these relations (at the user/application level) using languages which have the power of relational algebra.

Global level

The global level is where the logical structures of the database as a whole are described. The structures at the global level are those of the data model on which the database is based. In the case of an RDBMS, the logical structures are all relations (see Section 2.3).

RDBMS suppliers do not always use the terminology of the relational model within their products. For example, some RDBMS manuals and interfaces refer to relations as files or tables. The documents and interfaces of the UNIFY system, for example, consistently refer to relations and tuples as files and records. The International Standards Organisation (ISO) definitions of SQL, the standard relational database language, refer to relations and tuples as tables and rows. However, regardless of the terms used by the supplier, the structures of the logical model should be relations and tuples. (The distinction between relations, files and tables has been previously explained in Section 2.3.3).

The global level should not include details of how the relations are physically represented. It should not for instance include details of where the data is physically located, or which file structures are used to implement relations.

The data objects at the global level, i.e. the relations, tuples, and attribute values, may be thought of as representing objects, their properties, and relationships between them, that exist in the part of the real world that is of interest to the organisation which the database system serves.

★ A relation represents information about a set of objects or relationships of a
particular type.
★ A tuple represents information about one of those objects or relationships.
★ An attribute value represents a fact about one of those objects or relationships.

In this way, the logical model at the global level, i.e. the set of relations, may be thought
of as being a model of the part of the real world that the database serves; it is a natural
representation of information as data as prescribed by the database approach (see
Chapter 1).

The relations at the global level are called *base relations*. This is because they are the
basic building blocks of a relational database. They are not constructed from other
lower-level logical relations.

The RDBMS system should ensure that when the base tables are altered the integrity
rules of the relational model (see Section 2.5) are still adhered to. Entity integrity forbids
null values in a primary key, and referential integrity forbids a cross-reference, via
foreign key values, to non-existent tuples. However, current RDBMSs do not
automatically enforce both of these general integrity rules for the following reasons.

a) Referential integrity is expensive to enforce. This is because, whenever a new tuple is
added within which there are non-null foreign key values, it is necessary to search the
database for the tuples that are cross-referenced by the foreign keys. Accordingly, the
database must be accessed many times for a single insert, and this does of course
slow the system down. For this reason, referential integrity is either not supported at
all, or is optional within current RDBMSs.
b) Entity integrity is usually supported. Either the user or the database administrator
identifies the primary key when a new relation is described to the system or,
alternatively, constraints may be explicitly specified which prohibit duplicate attribute
values and/or null values for specified attributes.

User/application level
This is the level at which the database is used by those who want to do something with
the information represented by the data. The external models at this level are created for
applications so that only the information that is relevant to an application can be
accessed by the programs which implement that application, or by the users who access
the database using query languages.

An RDBMS will typically support a number of languages and tools for processing the
information represented within the database. These languages and tools include:

special database languages
extensions to conventional programming languages
fourth generation languages and tools.

Special database languages are programming languages designed especially for a database
system. They will include facilities for:

a) retrieving and updating data in the database,
b) defining the structure of the database,
c) making sure that invalid data is not entered into the database,
d) controlling who is allowed to use the database system and how they use it,
e) defining external models.

For the special programming language to be used on its own, it must also include basic features of a conventional programming language. It must also be able to perform:

f) some input and output, other than to and from the database, e.g. for input from a terminal or output to a report,

g) some control facilities to make decisions and to perform processing loops,

h) definition and manipulation of variables within the program.

There are now many special relational database languages. However, the industry is currently standardising on a language called SQL. It is likely that in the near future all major RDBMS products will support all or part of the standard SQL language. SQL is relationally complete, by which we mean that it has the expressive power of relational algebra (see Sections 2.4).

Conventional languages are extended in some systems by providing a means of embedding instructions in some special database languages within programs. A programmer may write in a conventional language such as Pascal, COBOL, FORTRAN or C and, when access to the database is required, the programmer may insert special database language instructions.

Fourth generation languages and tools in their purest form provide a means of creating applications programs from a description of what the program must do, rather than how it is to do those things. They typically include facilities for creating programs to:

> write reports
> produce graphics
> manipulate spread sheets
> process transactions.

Special database languages, extended conventional languages and fourth generation languages and tools are described in some detail in Chapter 3.

An external model is a view of just part of the database. External models are defined so that an applications program or a user will only have access to the data that is relevant. Providing an external model for an application can be likened to putting blinkers on a horse; by removing from sight all irrelevancies and distractions, life becomes simpler.

Not all RDBMSs support an external model facility. If this facility is omitted, then all programs must directly process the base relations in the logical model. However, some external model facility is very desirable when a database becomes large and complex, because it hides the complexity of the database as a whole from the programs. Also, external model facilities can be used to shield programs from some of the effects of changes to the structure of a database. A third advantage is that by hiding irrelevant information from a program the chance of information being inadvertently or maliciously accessed and perhaps modified is reduced.

On a comprehensive RDBMS an external model is a collection of base relations, and virtual relations. A virtual relation is a relation which appears to the user and the programmer to exist but does not actually exist. Instead, it is derived from base relations and other virtual relations by applying some expression in relational algebra. The expression in relational algebra is expressed in a special database language such as SQL.

This concept of virtual relations should become clearer with the aid of an example.

Below are represented two base relations of a database. PRODUCT describes the products produced by a children's clothing manufacturer; STOCK describes the amount of each product in stock at each of their warehouses.

PRODUCT

PROD_NO	NAME	COLOUR
P1	Pantaloons	blue
P3	Socks	harebell
P4	Socks	white

STOCK

WAREHOUSE_NO	PROD_NO	QUANTITY
WH1	P1	5000
WH1	P3	10000
WH1	P4	10000
WH3	P3	20000
WH2	P4	500

The warehouse manager at the Leeds warehouse, WH1, is interested only in the parts of these relations which represent information about the stocks at WH1. Using relational algebra (described in Section 2.4), we may define a relation that contains just that information, as follows.

JOIN PRODUCT AND (RESTRICT STOCK WHERE WAREHOUSE_NO = 'WH1')

In SQL this relational algebra could be expressed as

```
SELECT PRODUCT.PROD_NO, PRODUCT.NAME, PRODUCT.COLOUR,
STOCK.WAREHOUSE_NO, STOCK.QUANTITY
FROM PRODUCT, STOCK
WHERE PRODUCT.PROD_NO = STOCK.PROD_NO AND
  WAREHOUSE_NO = 'WH1';
```

(The detail of the SQL examples is not important at this stage of the book, as SQL is covered in detail later in Chapter 3.)

The relational algebra expression (and the SQL) defines the relation below.

PROD_NO	NAME	COLOUR	WAREHOUSE_NO	QUANTITY
P1	Pantaloons	blue	WH1	5000
P3	Socks	harebell	WH1	10000
P4	Socks	white	WH1	10000

The above result relation does not exist as a base relation but is derived from base relations. A user view mechanism makes it possible to create the illusion for a user or applications program that the above relation does actually exist in the same way that base relations exist. A relation such as this which is so derived is a virtual relation.

In SQL, the above relation could be created as a virtual relation by the following instruction.

```
CREATE VIEW WH1_STOCK
AS SELECT PRODUCT.PROD_NO, PRODUCT.NAME, PRODUCT.COLOUR,
STOCK.WAREHOUSE_NO, STOCK.QUANTITY
FROM PRODUCT, STOCK
WHERE PRODUCT.PROD_NO = STOCK.PROD_NO AND
  WAREHOUSE_NO = 'WH1';
```

The result of executing the above SQL is that a user or application may then access WH1_STOCK, a virtual relation, in much the same way that it would access a base relation such as PRODUCT or STOCK. In fact, the RDBMS will provide this facility by modifying SQL instructions which access WH1_STOCK so that instead they perform the appropriate access to the relations, PRODUCT and STOCK, from which WH1_STOCK is derived.

Physical level
The storage model describes how the logical structures in the logical model are actually implemented. It will include descriptions of the file structures and access techniques used to implement each base relation (in the logical model).

The physical level should be hidden from the user. It is the job of the database administrator to select the appropriate physical data stuctures that will ensure that the database system performs with adequate speed while not requiring excessive resources.

A relation is often mistakenly thought of as a file. A relation is not a physical structure and there are many ways that a relation may be physically implemented. One way is to implement it as a conventional disk file with appropriate access mechanisms such as indexes and hashing functions but there are other ways.

A database administrator will have utility programs or special privileged instructions in the database language or a special data definition language for specifying how relations are to be physically implemented.

It is common for a system physically to implement relations as conventional disk files with optional indexes, though some systems, such as INGRES, also provide hashing facilities. It is also sometimes possible to cluster related records together; clustering is the technique whereby records that are likely to be retrieved together are stored close to each other so as to reduce the number of disk accesses.

The way in which relations are physically represented will not affect applications, apart from making them execute faster or slower. Also, changes in the way a relation is represented should not affect applications. This independence of an application from the way in which logical data structures are physically stored is called data independence. Physical representation of relational databases is discussed in detail in Chapter 4.

Hardware level
The hardware level of an RDBMS includes the device model, which is the stored data; it is the 1s and 0s stored on storage devices such as disks.

Data dictionary
The data dictionary is a database of information about the database. In a relational database system the dictionary will normally exist as a set of special relations, often called the system catalogue, which is automatically created when the RDBMS is

installed and is automatically updated to reflect any alterations to the database structures. The contents of the data dictionary relations may be retrieved in the same way as data stored in other relations, e.g. using a relational database language such as SQL.

2.9 Summary

★ The parts of a computer system and the relations between them are called its architecture. A database system is made up of the database, the DBMS, and the programs which use the database, and will typically have the architecture shown in Figure 2.18.

★ A relational database management system (RDBMS) is a DBMS which supports structures, operations and integrity rules of the relational model (described in this chapter and Chapter 3).

★ A relational database system will usually conform to the architecture in Figure 2.18. The RDBMS makes possible the definition and creation of the models, and implements the mapping between the levels when the database is used.

★ The logical model comprises the base relations of the database.

★ The external models are sets of relations relevant to specific applications. An external model will be made up of base relations, and also virtual relations or views. A virtual relation is one which appears to the user to exist but which is actually derived from other relations.

★ The internal model describes how relations are actually implemented, e.g. which file structures and which access techniques are used.

★ The device model is the stored data.

★ Users and the database administrator (DBA) use an RDBMS by one or more of the following means:
   a) using special database languages, such as SQL,
   b) through the use of conventional programming languages with embedded statements in a special database language,
   c) through a fourth generation language and tools,
   d) through special utility programs.

★ An RDBMS will usually include relations which contain a description of the database. These are called the data dictionary or system catalogue.

Exercises

2.9 What is meant by the term, 'the architecture of a computer system'?

2.10 What information is there represented at each of the following levels of the database system architecture in Figure 2.18?

a) application/user level
b) logical level
c) physical level
d) device level.

2.11 What form does the database take in each of the following models?

  a) external model
  b) logical model
  c) internal model
  d) device model
  e) conceptual model.

2.12 What is a schema and subschema?

2.13 How are schemas and subschemas used when an application accesses the database?

2.14 Identify the contents of the subschema, schema and storage schema, as shown in Figure 2.18 within an RDBMS.

2.15 How are the structures of the relational model used to represent information about the real world?

2.16 What role does relational algebra play in an RDBMS?

2.17 What are the contents of the data dictionary and what is it used for?

2.18 Name three ways of creating database applications.

2.19 An external model comprises base relations and views. Explain the terms 'base relation' and 'view'.

2.20 The head of the accounts department of a small manufacturing organisation has decided that her department should purchase two or three personal computers. She has read various articles in the computer trade magazines about relational databases and is also considering purchasing RDBMSs to run on the computers. However, she feels that her reading so far has given her only a superficial understanding of what a relational database is. You are asked to write her a report explaining the foundations of relational database technology.

3 Database languages

3.1 Introduction

This chapter discusses the process of creating applications programs for a database system. The software development life-cycle is described and the range of tools for developing database applications is reviewed.

3.2 Developing applications

The process of producing an applications program for a database system follows the same steps as are necessary for producing any other type of computer program. This sequence of steps is called the software life-cycle.

The software life-cycle is as follows.

a) *Requirements analysis and definition*. The requirements of the software system (the programs) to be produced must be analysed. This involves identifying the services that the software must provide and the constraints under which the software is to be developed and under which it will operate.

b) *Software specification*. Having defined what the software is required to do, the next stage is to specify programs which will satisfy those requirements.

c) *Software design*. The programs must be designed in detail. First the structures of the programs are defined, and then each part or program module is designed in detail.

d) *Software implementation*. The program modules must be coded and tested, and then combined to form the required programs.

e) *System testing*. The programs must be tested to ensure that they satisfy the requirements defined in step a).

f) *Operation and maintenance*. Once the system is installed and put into practical use, errors must be corrected and improvements may be made.

Computer professionals (analysts, programmers, and software engineers) are traditionally responsible for different stages of the software life-cycle.

Systems analysts are responsible for the requirements analysis. They must translate what the people who have requested the computer system say they *need* into a definition of *what* the requested computer system is required to do.

Systems analysts are also responsible for software specification. They must specify one or more programs which, when correctly implemented, will satisfy the specified requirements.

Programmers will decide how the specified programs are to work. They will design, code and test the specified program.

Systems analysts will oversee the system testing.

If software engineers are involved in the development of the software they will be involved with all of these stages. The software engineer is involved where the required system is large and complex and its implementation involves teams of implementors. The software engineer then applies computing, management and communications skills

74

to manage the progression of the project. The software engineer will apply techniques that are necessary to assure the quality of the implemented system, and to ensure that the system produced corresponds to that expected by the requester of the system.

Operation and maintenance may involve systems analysts to design enhancements, and will involve programmers to implement them. Alternatively, software engineers may be involved with both design and programming.

Software tools may exist to provide support for each of the stages of the software life-cycle. These tools aid the implementors in the various tasks they have to perform, and in some cases tools may fully automate a task. For instance, fourth generation languages are tools with which applications programs may be automatically generated from specifications of what they must do. Using these the implementation phase of the life-cycle may be completely automated, thus removing the need for professional programmers to be involved.

3.3 Software development in a database environment

Database environments are particularly blessed with powerful tools which ease the task of creating applications programs. The power and simplicity of the software tools is such that it is sometimes possible for users to take an active role in the production of the applications that they require. In cases where the application is straightforward, it may be possible for the user to create the required programs without any aid from computer professionals, or with computer professionals acting solely in an advisory role.

The database environment software tools for creating applications typically include the following.

Database languages. An RDBMS will include software for inputting and executing instructions in one or more database languages. The international standard relational database language is SQL and it is likely that most proprietary RDBMSs will soon support a version of SQL.

Relational database languages can be used to access and alter data stored in a database. Also, database languages will often include facilities for defining and modifying the structure of the database, but this facility is not always available; there are sometimes separate languages or programs for defining or modifying database structures. The reason for separating these two facilities is that defining database structures is sometimes seen as the sole responsibility of the database administrator.

Database languages + third generation languages. Software is usually provided that enables a programmer to include instructions of a database language within programs written in conventional programming languages, such as COBOL, PL/1, FORTRAN, Pascal or C. These languages are called third generation languages (3GLs), first generation languages being machine code, and second generation languages being assembler languages.

3GLs may be necessary when a database language does not include all of the facilities necessary to implement the application required by a user. The database language, for instance, may not include sufficient facilities for screen handling, input validation, or report generation. The application may require access to conventional files as well as to the database, and the database language may have insufficient facilities for this. It may then be necessary to embed the database language statements within programs written in a 3GL.

The use of a 3GL is a task for computer professionals as it requires programming skills. The implementor must define the applications in procedural logic, i.e. as operations controlled by loops, decisions, sequences and procedure calls. This environment has a number of disadvantages:

a) procedural programming is a time-consuming task for all but the most trivial problem;
b) the resulting programs are likely to contain undetected bugs; this is an inevitable consequence of the complexity of the task;
c) a person who requests a new application program may have to wait months while professional analysts and programmers design, implement and test the required program.

The remoteness of the requester and user from the analysts and programmers, and the length of time it takes for a working program to appear may result in an unacceptable program. The program may implement an application which differs from the one the requester had in mind. Subsequent alterations, modifications and corrections to the program will similarly involve expert programmers and be time-consuming and error-prone.

Fourth generation language environments. RDBMSs usually support software that creates applications programs automatically from high-level descriptions, mainly of what the applications are to do, rather than how they are to do it. These high-level tools are called fourth generation languages (4GLs) or applications generators.

The production of applications using 4GLs is made very much speedier and simpler, because the 4GL largely eliminates the program design and development stages of the software life-cycle. Using 4GLs the requester and the future user may be involved with specifying what the system is to do, and the system may then be prototyped from that specification.

Prototyping is the rapid and often automatic translation of a specification into an applications program. Sometimes it is necessary to ignore or relax some of the requirements of the application in order to achieve this rapid implementation. This faster implementation time makes possible greater involvement of the user. In fact with some fourth generation products it is possible for the users themselves to generate their own applications, or to sit with and direct the computer professionals as they implement the required applications. This closer involvement of the user ensures that the system is more likely to do what the user wants, as opposed to what the computer professional thinks the user wants. Also, the rapid implementation from specification makes possible an iterative mode of application development, where the developer designs the system, creates the system, assesses it, modifies it, creates the modified version, assesses it, modifies it, and so on. The user may be involved at each stage and thus the product may home in on the desired application. In fact, it may be only after trying out ideas that other requirements and problems come to mind.

There are two general methods of prototyping. The prototype may be be taken as a first version of the required system, and refined until it is sufficiently well produced to be handed over to the user for operational use.

Alternatively, once the prototype has served its purpose and the requirements have been established to the satisfaction of both requester and implementor, it may be 'thrown away' and a high-quality version of the application may be constructed from scratch, perhaps using third generation languages with embedded database language instructions, in order to produce a more comprehensive and efficient version.

The range of applications addressed by 4GLs usually includes, report generation, database querying and updating, graphics generation and spreadsheet facilities.

PURE 4GLs are non-procedural applications generators. This means that the application may be constructed purely from a user-provided description of what is to be done, rather than how to do it. This is possible because built into the 4GL is the knowledge of how certain types of problems may be solved. The user then defines a problem of a type known to the 4GL and the 4GL creates code that will solve the problem.

Pure 4GLs have two limitations. A 4GL is limited by the range of problem solutions that the designer has built into it. The more versatile a 4GL, the more complex it becomes and consequently the more a user must learn in order to use it. In a number of 4GLs the casual users are offered a simple and easy-to-use subset of the facilities of the 4GL so as to shield them from the full complexity of the system as a whole. These may be available through a subset of the language or through a completely separate 'naïve user's' language. This makes it possible for users to generate their own straightforward applications, while retaining the power for experts to create more sophisticated applications.

Another limitation is that, however many types of problem the 4GL is able to solve, there are always other problems which are not catered for. The 4GL will lack the flexibility to solve all types of problem. This second limitation is often overcome by providing access from within the 4GL to more conventional procedural programming facilities, such as are available in third generation languages. These 4GLs with facilities for procedural programming are called hybrid 4GLs. They allow the implementor to use conventional programming within the 4GL environment when some aspect of the required application is new to the 4GL.

The above three classes of application development tools, database languages, database languages + third generation languages, and fourth generation languages, are described and illustrated in the remainder of this chapter.

3.4 Summary

★ Developing relational database applications follows the conventional software life-cycle, i.e. requirements analysis and definition, software specification, software design, software implementation, system testing, operation and maintenance.
★ Relational database applications are implemented using one or more of the following.
   a) Special database languages, such as SQL.

b) Third generation languages with embedded database language statements.
c) Fourth generation languages (4GL) environments. Pure 4GLs create applications from a description of what is required, but are limited by the range of problem solutions built into them. Hybrid 4GLs also allow the user to specify procedural logic to solve problems which are non-standard to the 4GL.

★ High-level database languages and 4GLs reduce the role of the computer professional and make possible requirements definitions and fast implementation through prototyping. In this way the user is given greater say in the design of applications.

Exercises

3.1 Identify the stages of the software life-cycle.

3.2 What are the roles of the systems analyst, programmer and software engineer in conventional software development?

3.3 Identify three types of tool for creating database applications.

3.4 Why is it sometimes necessary to use 3GLs to program database applications?

3.5 What are the advantages of using 4GLs?

3.6 What is the difference between a pure 4GL and a hybrid 4GL?

3.5 SQL

In the following sections the international standard relational database language SQL is described in detail. The features of SQL are described and illustrated in a tutorial fashion with the aid of examples. This book concentrates on SQL because other relational database languages are likely to become increasingly of historic and academic interest only.

This description of SQL should not be skipped over, even by the reader who has an RDBMS which does not support SQL. This is because SQL is used here as a vehicle for describing many important features of relational database languages in general. In particular, the section covers the following characteristics which are general to relational database languages.

★ There are two parts of a relational database language, the schema definition language (SDL) for defining the database structures, and the data manipulation language (DML) for using the data stored in the database.
★ The SDL includes facilities for defining relations, for defining integrity constraints, for specifying the ways in which relations are to be physically stored, for defining the external model, and for authorising users to access the database.
★ The DML may be used both for accessing data stored within relations, and also for accessing information about the database stored in the data dictionary.
★ Using a relational database language it is possible to create all of the relations that may be defined in relational algebra.

★ The result of executing a data retrieval statement in a relational database language is presented as a table of data within which there may be duplicate rows and in which the ordering of rows and columns may be significant. A relation does not have any attribute or tuple sequence and may not have duplicates, but the table retrieved by the relational database language statement may be thought of as a convenient representation of a relation.
★ Many relational database language statements may be executed together as a single transaction. A transaction is the unit of recovery: either the effect of executing all of the instructions in a transaction are made permanent within the database, and known to other database users, or none of them are.

3.6 History of SQL

SQL sometimes pronounced Sequel, is an acronym for Structured English Query Language, and comes from the IBM stable. It was invented in the IBM San Jose research laboratories by D. Chamberlin and others. The prototype IBM RDBMS, System R, built at San Jose, used SQL as its language, and System R later became the basis of the IBM RDBMS products, DB2 and SQL/DS. SQL and SQL-like languages have also been adopted by many other RDBMS suppliers, including, for example, INGRES (formerly Relational Technology Inc.) who supply the INGRES RDBMS, and ORACLE Corporation Ltd who supply the ORACLE RDBMS. SQL is also incorporated into the extended OS/2 personal computer operating system. SQL has now been adopted as the basis of the standard relational database language (RDL) approved by many standards organisations, e.g. ASCII, ISO and BSI, and it is likely that in the near future, all major RDBMS products will support SQL.

There are variations in the different implementations of SQL, as there are in other 'standard' computer languages. The language described here is mainly consistent with the proposed standard SQL published by the International Standards Organisation (ISO) in 1987, but also includes some additional features of other SQL implementations where facilities are undefined in the standard.

(Note: new releases of RDBMSs are likely to move closer to the standard SQL and so the non-standard SQL examples given in this chapter may be valid only for the release of the RDBMS at the time of writing this book; e.g. all INGRES SQL examples are valid only for INGRES Version 5.)

3.7 Stand-alone SQL, embedded SQL and 4GL SQL

SQL is used in three contexts.
a) As a stand-alone database language. Using stand-alone SQL, complete database applications may be expressed purely in SQL statements. These applications may be executed interactively, statement by statement, or alternatively sequences of SQL statements may be stored and executed as programs.

b) As an embedded database language. Embedded SQL statements may be included within computer programs written in other conventional third generation programming languages.

c) Integrated into fourth generation languages (4GLs) and tools. A number of products integrate SQL into their 4GL environment tools, making it possible, for example, for SQL instructions to be executed from within a report generator, spreadsheet or graphics generator.

In the following sections stand-alone SQL is described. Embedded SQL is described later in Sections 3.21 to 3.26, and 4GL SQL in Section 3.27 onwards.

3.8 Schema definition language and data manipulation language

A database system includes two parts: a description of the database, and the database itself.

The database description, sometimes called the intension, is encoded as the database schema. In Chapter 2, a multi-level database systems architecture was described. This architecture consists of external, logical and internal models, and descriptions of these models are stored in the subschemas, schema and storage schema, respectively. However, in an RDBMS there is typically a single schema in which all description of the database is stored. A relational database schema describes the relations, their attributes, the domains, the integrity constraints, user privileges, views, and also details of how relations are physically implemented. The relational database itself is the set of relations that the user sees as tables of data values.

SQL includes statements with which to define or modify the database schema. These statements, for instance, enable the user to create new relations or to add new attributes to existing relations. SQL also includes statements with which to access or modify the data values within a database. These two sets of statements are respectively called the SQL Schema Definition Language (SDL) and the SQL Data Manipulation Language (DML).

3.9 SQL schema definition language (SDL)

The SDL includes statements to declare the following:

> the database structures,
> its integrity constraints,
> constraints on the use of the database,
> details of its physical implementation.

All of this information is stored in the database schema; the database schema gives a complete description of the database. From the user's point of view this schema exists as the data dictionary, sometimes called the system catalogue. The data dictionary is usually stored as a set of relations which contain data about the database, and is often accessible using the same database languages that are used to access the database itself, though not always (see Sections 2.7 and 2.8). For example, in some RDBMSs, schema information is available only through the use of an extended 'help' facility or through the use of special programs which generate reports from the data dictionary.

3.9.1 Creating a new database

Before a user is able to create relations and populate them with data, a SCHEMA must be created within which the description of the database may reside. Standard SQL includes a CREATE SCHEMA instruction for this purpose. The following example illustrates this instruction.

```
CREATE SCHEMA AUTHORISATION Fair_Childs;
```

The above instruction creates a new schema, named Fair_Childs. The ISO standards also indicate that it should be possible to specify within this instruction the range of facilities available to the users of this schema, but the details of how these privileges are specified is left to the database implementor.

In practice, the above CREATE SCHEMA instruction is not yet widely implemented. More often a new database schema is created through the use of special programs which are run at the operating system level. For example, a new INGRES database is created by running the CREATEDB program. The following operating system level instruction will create a schema for a new INGRES database called 'Fair-Childs'.

```
CREATEDB Fair_Childs
```

3.9.2 Creating a new base relation

The following SQL example, when executed, will create the ORDER_LINE relation shown immediately below it.

```
CREATE TABLE ORDER_LINE
(ORDER_NO      CHARACTER (5) NOT NULL,
 PRODUCT_NO    CHARACTER (5) NOT NULL,
 QUANTITY      INTEGER,
 UNIQUE (ORDER_NO, PRODUCT_NO));
```

ORDER_LINE

ORDER_NO	PRODUCT_NO	QUANTITY

This statement includes examples of all the features of the CREATE TABLE statement in SQL.

a) The CREATE TABLE adds an empty relation to the database.

b) The new empty relation is given a name, ORDER_LINE in the example.

c) Each attribute of the relation is defined. An attribute is given a name, a type, and optionally certain integrity constraints may be defined. In the example, two types have been used, CHARACTER and INTEGER. Other data types that may be specified in standard SQL are:

> NUMERIC, DECIMAL, SMALLINT (small integer), FLOAT (floating point), REAL, and DOUBLE PRECISION.

Variations in the set of types and in the notation for declaring them exist between different implementations of SQL. In the INGRES system (Version 5) for example, the types listed in Table 3.1 may be specified in a CREATE TABLE instruction.

Table 3.1   Types that may be specified in CREATE TABLE in INGRES.

Notation	Type and range
c1–c255	a string of 1 to 255 characters
vchar(1)–vchar(2000)	a string of 1 to 2000 characters
integer1	1-byte integer (-128 to $+127$)
integer2 (smallint)	2-bytes integer ($-32,768$ to $+32,767$)
integer4 (integer)	4-byte integer ($-2,147,483,648$ to $+2,147,483,647$)
float4	4-byte floating point ($-10**38$ to $+10**38$ with 7 decimal precision)
float8 (float)	8-byte floating point ($-10**38$ to $+10**38$ with 17 decimal precision)
date	12-byte date (1–jan–1582 to 31–dec–2382 and -800 to $+800$ years for time intervals)
money	8 bytes (-99999999999999.99 to $+99999999999999.99$)

Note that SQL allows the specification of attribute data types, but not domains (see Section 2.3.1). The distinction is that a type defines a range of values that an attribute may have and the operators that may be applied to them, but a domain is to do with the meaning of attribute values. In the above example CREATE TABLE statement, both ORDER_NO and PRODUCT_NO have the same type, i.e. CHARACTER (5), but are defined on different domains.

Integrity rules may be specified to make it invalid for specific attributes to contain NULL values, and to ensure that specific attributes and combinations of attributes are unique for each tuple.

In the example neither ORDER_NO nor PRODUCT_NO may have NULL values and there may be no two tuples in which the combined value of the ORDER_NO and PRODUCT_NO are identical. This constraint is necessary because ORDER_NO and PRODUCT_NO together form the primary key of the relation, and the entity integrity rule forbids duplicate or null values in a primary key (see Section 2.4).

3.9.3 Removing a base relation from the database

The following SQL statement will remove from the database the relation ORDER_LINE, created by the previous example.

```
DROP TABLE ORDER_LINE;
```

Obviously DROP TABLE has a rather dramatic effect. Later in this chapter we will describe statements for restricting the use of DROP TABLE (see Section 3.9.7).

3.9.4 Creating an index

The following SQL statement creates an index on the PRODUCT_NO attribute of the ORDER_LINE relation. The effect of this index is to reduce the time taken to access a tuple of ORDER_LINE given the PRODUCT_NO value of the required tuple.

```
CREATE INDEX PROD_INDEX
ON ORDER_LINE (PRODUCT_NO DESC) CLUSTER;
```

DESC specifies that the index entries are in descending sequence. The other option is ASC for ascending sequence. The CLUSTER option means that PROD_INDEX is a clustering index. Clustering is the technique of placing logically related records physically close together so that many related records may be retrieved with a single disk access. When a new tuple is inserted the clustering index is used to find the location of other tuples with the same values for certain attributes, i.e. those on which it is 'cluster' indexed. The new tuple is then stored near to those tuples. In this way, a clustering index reduces the number of disk accesses necessary to execute certain applications, and thus makes them run faster. Obviously there may be only one clustering index for a base relation. If there were more than one cluster index, multiple copies of tuples would be necessary so that they could be placed close to a number of different related tuples. The effect of the CLUSTER option in the example is to cluster together tuples with the same PRODUCT_NO value. This will make it faster, for instance, to retrieve all ORDER_LINE tuples for orders of some specific product.

Indexes are physical rather than logical structures. They are to do with how data is accessed and not to do with the logical structure of that data. For this reason indexes are out of place in a relational database language. The reason that they are there and visible to the user is purely pragmatic. If a user creates an index then certain database operations will execute faster, other operations will be slower, and the database will use more store. By experimentation with indexes the user may find the combination of relations and indexes which provides a satisfactory performance within acceptable storage costs.

A second example of CREATE INDEX is given below:

```
CREATE UNIQUE INDEX NA_INDEX
ON CUSTOMER (NAME,ADDRESS);
```

The above will create an index to the CUSTOMER relation on the combined NAME and ADDRESS attributes. Neither ASC nor DESC have been specified and so ASC (the default) is assumed. UNIQUE specifies that no index entry may reference more than one tuple. It has been specified in this example because (NAME,ADDRESS) is a candidate key; CUSTOMER_NO is the primary key.

3.9.5 Removing an index

The following SQL statement removes from the database the NA_INDEX created in the previous example. The only noticeable effect of this action will be a change in the speed of certain database operations.

```
DROP INDEX NA_INDEX;
```

3.9.6 Adding attributes to an existing relation

The following SQL statement will add an extra attribute, named LINE_NO, of type INTEGER, to the relation ORDER_LINE.

```
ALTER TABLE ORDER_LINE
ADD LINE_NO INTEGER;
```

The values of this new attribute will be initialised to null for every existing tuple of the relation. Integrity constraints, NOT NULL or UNIQUE, cannot be specified for the new attribute. The reason is obvious – the new attribute will be initialised to NULL.

ALTER TABLE is not supported in a number of current products. In the absence of ALTER, it is necessary to create a new version of a relation, and then to copy tuples from the old version to the new.

3.9.7 Restrictions on database use

The following SQL illustrates some of the facilities for restricting what database users are allowed to do.

```
GRANT SELECT, INSERT, UPDATE(QUANTITY)
ON ORDER_LINE
TO WAREHOUSE_MAN, DELIVERIES
WITH GRANT OPTION;
```

The above SQL restricts the ways in which the two database users, identified by WAREHOUSE_MAN and DELIVERIES, may access the ORDER_LINE relations. They are only allowed to use SQL SELECT instructions to retrieve information from ORDER_LINE, to use SQL INSERT instructions to add new tuples into ORDER_LINE, and to use the SQL UPDATE instruction to alter the values of the QUANTITY attribute. The 'WITH GRANT' clause means that WAREHOUSE_MAN and DELIVERIES are allowed to grant the same privileges to other users.

Some RDBMSs also provide extensions to the above GRANT facility which enable the database administrator to restrict the times at which users may use the system, the terminals from which they may use the system, and the applications through which they may use the database.

3.9.8 SDL summary

The above set of SQL statements are sufficient to create and modify a set of relation structures. The statements described above enable us to:

> create a database schema
> add a relation to the database schema
> remove an existing relation from the database schema
> add attributes to an existing relation
> add or remove indexes
> restrict the use of the above structures.

There are other SDL statements to do with the external model and to do with the physical model, but these are described later in the book (see Section 3.11).

3.10 SQL data manipulation language

The data manipulation language (DML) statements are used to retrieve, alter, insert or delete data values.

A DML statement operates on relations and defines a new relation derived from them. In this way a DML statement is similar to an expression in relational algebra. In fact all the statements which may be expressed in relational algebra may also be expressed as SQL DML statements. A language with the ability to express that which can be expressed in relational algebra is said to be relationally complete.

A relation produced as a result of executing SQL DML instructions is presented to the user in the form of a table. The table will represent rows and columns in some sequence and may even include duplicate rows, but it should be remembered that the table is a convenient representation of a relation, and there can be no ordering of tuples or attributes and no duplicate tuples in a relation that is being represented.

3.10.1 Basic structure of a DML statement

The basic structure of a DML statement is

```
SELECT target_list
FROM list_of_relations
WHERE condition;
```

The meaning of this form of statement is 'Retrieve a table containing the columns specified in the target list, taking values FROM those combinations of tuples in the relations specified in the list_of_relations, WHERE the condition is true'. The target_list may simply be a list of attribute names, or it may indicate that various computations are to be applied to the retrieved values.

In general the above type of SQL statement is evaluated in the following way:

a) the Cartesian product of the relations in the list_of_relations is created (see Section 2.4.10);
b) the relation created in a) above is restricted (see Section 2.4.6) so as to include only the tuples for which the condition is true;
c) The attributes specified in the target_list are projected (see Section 2.4.7) from the relation created in b).

The following example illustrates the evaluation of this basic type of SQL statement.

```
SELECT A, B, C
FROM X, Y
WHERE D = E;
```

If the relations X and Y are as follows,

X

A	B	D
1	2	3
1	3	2

Y

C	E	F
1	2	3
9	2	3

then the SQL will cause the following operations to take place. The Cartesian product of the relations in the list_of_relations is formed. The Cartesian product, X TIMES Y, is the relation containing all possible pairs of tuples, one from X and one from Y.

X TIMES Y

A	B	D	C	E	F
1	2	3	1	2	3
1	2	3	9	2	3
1	3	2	1	2	3
1	3	2	9	2	3

Tuples are then restricted to those for which the condition, D = E is true, giving

RESTRICT (X TIMES Y) WHERE D = E

A	B	D	C	E	F
1	3	2	1	2	3
1	3	2	9	2	3

The A, B and C attributes, i.e. those in the target_list, are then projected out, giving

PROJECT (RESTRICT (X TIMES Y) WHERE D = E) ON A, B, C

A	B	C
1	3	1
1	3	9

We now have the result relation.

3.10.2 Retrieval of attributes from a single relation

The following SQL statement will retrieve a unary relation (i.e. a relation with a single attribute). The attribute of the resulting relation is named COLOUR and its values are all the values of the COLOUR attribute in the base relation, PRODUCT.

    SELECT COLOUR
    FROM PRODUCT;

Given the following instance of the PRODUCT relation,

PRODUCT

PRODUCT_NO	NAME	COLOUR
P1	Pantaloons	blue
P2	Pantaloons	khaki
P3	Socks	white
P4	Socks	harebell
P7	Socks	blue

the above SQL produces the following table.

Note that the resulting table includes duplicate values, though of course there can be no duplicates in the relation that the table represents. There are two `blue` rows in the table, because there are two tuples in PRODUCT for which the COLOUR attribute value is 'blue'. It is often desirable to keep these duplicates within the result table for the following reasons.

a) The user may actually wish to know if there is more than one blue product.
b) It takes additional time to remove duplicates and the user may want speedy results.

It is possible to remove duplicate rows from the table which represents the result of the SQL instruction, by using the DISTINCT option. For example,

```
SELECT DISTINCT COLOUR
FROM PRODUCT;
```

produces the following table

The result is the same as that of the previous statement with the exception that the DISTINCT clause has caused the duplicate 'blue' row to be removed.

The above examples are equivalent to the relational algebra expression

PROJECT PRODUCT ON COLOUR

SQL has all the versatility of PROJECT in relational algebra. For example it is possible to project on more than one attribute.

```
SELECT DISTINCT NAME, COLOUR
FROM PRODUCT;
```

produces the following table

NAME	COLOUR
Pantaloons	blue
Pantaloons	khaki
Socks	white
Socks	harebell
Socks	blue

The above SQL is equivalent to the relational algebra expression

PROJECT PRODUCT ON NAME, COLOUR

In the examples in the remainder of this chapter duplicate rows have been omitted from the result tables for reasons of clarity. However, in practice the DISTINCT clause must be used in order to achieve this removal.

To retrieve a complete relation, all attributes must be specified in the target_list. For example, the following SQL will retrieve all tuples of PRODUCT.

```
SELECT PRODUCT_NO, NAME, COLOUR
FROM PRODUCT;
```

A shorter way of expressing the same query is as follows:

```
SELECT *
FROM PRODUCT;
```

The * means 'all the attributes in the relation'.

3.10.3 Retrieval of selected tuples from a single relation

The SQL SELECT instruction may be used to express the function of the RESTRICT operator in relational algebra. For example,

```
SELECT *
FROM PRODUCT
WHERE COLOUR = 'blue';
```

has the same effect as the relational algebra expression

RESTRICT PRODUCT WHERE COLOUR = 'blue'

Given the following instance of the PRODUCT relation

PRODUCT

PRODUCT_NO	NAME	COLOUR
P1	Pantaloons	blue
P2	Pantaloons	khaki
P3	Socks	white
P4	Socks	harebell
P7	Socks	blue

execution of the above SQL statement will produce the following table.

PRODUCT_NO	NAME	COLOUR
P1	Pantaloons	blue
P7	Socks	blue

3.10.3.1 Evaluation of the WHERE condition

The WHERE condition clause in an SQL SELECT can be complex and it is this which gives the SQL SELECT much of its power. The components of a WHERE condition are as follows.

a) The condition, or predicate as it is called, is constructed from terms, each of which may be true or false or unknown for any given tuple. Examples of terms are COLOUR = 'blue', NAME = 'Socks', and NAME = 'Pantaloons'.
b) Terms may be combined using the usual logic operators, i.e. AND, OR and NOT.
c) Brackets may also be used.

For instance, the following SQL SELECT includes all of the above components.

```
SELECT *
FROM PRODUCT
WHERE NOT (COLOUR = 'blue') AND
      (NAME = 'Socks' OR NAME = 'Pantaloons');
```

The effect of this SQL is to select all the tuples of PRODUCT that describe either Socks or Pantaloons, but excluding those which are blue. Given the above instance of PRODUCT, execution of the SQL statement will produce the following table.

PRODUCT_NO	NAME	COLOUR
P2	Pantaloons	khaki
P3	Socks	white
P4	Socks	harebell

The rules for evaluating a condition expression against a tuple are:

an expression is evaluated from left to right
subexpressions in brackets are evaluated first
NOTs are evaluated before ANDs and ORs.

The effect of the logical operators AND, OR and NOT is shown in Table 3.2.

Table 3.2 Truth tables for AND, OR and NOT.

X	Y	X AND Y	X OR Y	NOT X
true	true	true	true	false
true	false	false	true	false
true	unknown	unknown	true	false
false	true	false	true	true
false	false	false	false	true
false	unknown	false	unknown	true
unknown	true	unknown	true	unknown
unknown	false	false	unknown	unknown
unknown	unknown	unknown	unknown	unknown

The rows of this truth table show the values of the expressions X AND Y, X OR Y and NOT X for given values of X and Y. For instance, the first row shows that when X and Y are both true, then X AND Y and X OR Y are both true, but NOT X is false.

The following example illustrates the application of the WHERE condition evaluation rules. The condition

NOT (COLOUR = 'blue') AND (NAME = 'Socks' OR NAME = 'Pantaloons')

is evaluated against the tuple

PRODUCT_NO	NAME	COLOUR
P1	Pantaloons	blue

The evaluation proceeds in the following manner. The expressions in brackets are evaluated first (left to right).

(COLOUR = 'blue') is true

To evaluate the subexpression

(NAME = 'Socks' OR NAME = 'Pantaloons')

we first evaluate the terms.

NAME = 'Socks'   is false
NAME = 'Pantaloons' is true

This subexpression therefore becomes

(false OR true)

which has the value true (see line 4 of Table 3.2).

Having evaluated the expressions in brackets the condition

NOT (COLOUR = 'blue') AND (NAME = 'Socks' OR NAME = 'Pantaloons')

becomes

NOT true AND true

The NOTs are evaluated before ANDs and ORs.

'NOT true' has the value 'false'

(see line 1 or 2 or 3 of Table 3.2). The condition

'NOT true AND true'

therefore becomes

'false AND true'

which returns the value false (see line 4 of the Table 3.2). Thus the condition returns the value false.

In general the meanings of the logical operators AND, OR and NOT, are similar to the meaning of the corresponding words in the English language. However, care should be taken. For instance, a person may say 'Tell me about your red and green coats', meaning that he requires details of coats which are red and of coats which are green. However, the stated request is ambiguous. A valid interpretation of the request is 'Retrieve details of coats which are both red and green', but that is not what the requester meant. Though there is no such ambiguity in logic, it is common for users who are new to SQL to use AND in the same ambiguous way that they use it in speech. It would not be unusual, for instance, for a novice user to express the above query using the following SQL

```
SELECT *
FROM PRODUCT
WHERE NAME = 'trousers' AND
      (COLOUR = 'red' AND COLOUR = 'green');
```

This SQL does not correctly express the intended query, and will always retrieve an empty relation; there cannot be a tuple of PRODUCT where the value of COLOUR has both the value 'red' and also the value 'green'. The correct SQL is

```
SELECT *
FROM PRODUCT
WHERE NAME = 'trousers' AND
      (COLOUR = 'red' OR COLOUR = 'green');
```

3.10.3.2 Arithmetic comparisons

As well as equality, =, the other usual comparison operators may be used in a WHERE condition. The condition may include any of the following.

- != (not equal),
- < (less than),
- \> (greater than),
- <= (less than or equal to), and
- \>= (greater than or equal to).

For example

```
SELECT *
FROM ORDER_LINE
WHERE QUANTITY > 1000;
```

will retrieve order line details where the quantity ordered is over 1000. Given the following instance of ORDER_LINE

ORDER_LINE

ORDER_NO	PRODUCT_NO	QUANTITY
01	P1	100
01	P2	20000
01	P6	20
02	P2	1000
02	P6	10000

the above SQL statement will produce the following table

ORDER_NO	PRODUCT_NO	QUANTITY
01	P2	20000
02	P6	10000

3.10.3.3 Range checks

It is possible to select on the basis of a value being within a specific range. For example the following SQL expression

```
SELECT *
FROM ORDER_LINE
WHERE QUANTITY BETWEEN 20 AND 1000;
```

will select order line details for orders of between 20 and 1000 items. Given the above instance of ORDER_LINE, the example SQL statement will produce the following table.

ORDER_NO	PRODUCT_NO	QUANTITY
01	P1	100
01	P6	20
02	P2	1000

It is also possible to select on the basis of values which are not within a specified range. For example,

```
SELECT *
FROM ORDER_LINE
WHERE QUANTITY NOT BETWEEN 100 AND 200;
```

will select order line details where the quantity ordered is not between 100 and 200. Given the above instance of ORDER_LINE this statement would produce the following table.

ORDER_LINE

ORDER_NO	PRODUCT_NO	QUANTITY
01	P2	20000
01	P6	20
02	P2	1000
02	P6	10000

3.10.3.4 Value set tests

The IN comparison may be used to test for membership of a set of values. The set of values may be explicitly stated, as in the example below, or it may be retrieved from the database using a 'nested' SELECT instruction (uses of 'nested' SELECTs are described later in section 3.10.6). For example,

```
SELECT *
FROM ORDER_LINE
```

```
WHERE PRODUCT_NO IN ('P1', 'P2', 'P3') AND
ORDER_NO NOT IN ('01', '05');
```

will select order line details for products P1, P2 and P3, but not order lines of orders 01 or 05. Given the above instance of ORDER_LINE this would produce the following table.

ORDER_NO	PRODUCT_NO	QUANTITY
02	P2	1000

3.10.3.5 String matching

The LIKE comparison is used for 'fuzzy' matching, i.e. matching values that are similar in some aspect, but not necessarily exactly alike. An example is

```
SELECT *
FROM CUSTOMER
WHERE NAME LIKE 'S%';
```

The above selects details of order lines where the customer name starts with the letter S. The right hand side of the comparison expression defines a *pattern* of characters. The expression is true for a particular tuple if that pattern exists in the left hand side attribute value. In the example the pattern 'S%' represents the letter S followed by anything.

Given the following instance of CUSTOMER

CUSTOMER

CUSTOMER_NO	NAME	ADDRESS
C1	Nippers Ltd	25 High St, Leeds
C2	Tots-Gear	5 Low St, Oxford
C3	Super-Brat	30 New St, Luton

the example SQL statement will produce the following table

CUSTOMER_NO	NAME	ADDRESS
C3	Super-Brat	30 New St, Luton

A pattern definition consists of a character string which may include a number of characters with special meaning.

%   represents an arbitrary string, i.e. any string of characters. In the example, S% represents S followed by any other characters, e.g. Smith, Small, ...

_   represents a single arbitrary character, e.g. B_OWN represents BROWN, BLOWN, BOOWN, ...

[]   square brackets may contain any number of letters, each of which is tested individually in the specified position. For example, B[RLO]OWN represent either BROWN or BLOWN or BOOWN.

To select details of all customers whose names begin with T, followed by something, followed by t, and then the rest, we would use the following SQL expression

```
SELECT *
FROM CUSTOMER
WHERE NAME LIKE 'T_t%';
```

Given the above instance of CUSTOMER, this example SQL statement will produce the following table.

CUSTOMER_NO	NAME	ADDRESS
C2	Tots-Gear	5 Low St, Oxford

The next two examples illustrate the use of square brackets for specifying sets of characters that may occur in a specified position.

```
SELECT * FROM CUSTOMER WHERE NAME LIKE '[NT]%';
```

will retrieve tuples where the name started with either N or T. Given the above CUSTOMER relation, this retrieves the following.

CUSTOMER_NO	NAME	ADDRESS
C1	Nippers Ltd	25 High St, Leeds
C2	Tots-Gear	5 Low St, Oxford

The next SQL example specifies a range of characters which may be the first character of the value of NAME.

```
SELECT * FROM CUSTOMER WHERE NAME LIKE '[N-P]%';
```

The above would retrieve tuples where the name started with any letter in the range N to P. In the case of the above CUSTOMER relation, this would produce:

CUSTOMER_NO	NAME	ADDRESS
C1	Nippers Ltd	25 High St, Leeds

In some cases we may wish to retrieve tuples in which a special character such as % or _ actually occurs. For example, we may wish to retrieve details of all products with a name starting with the characters S%_. To specify this, a method of saying that in this case % and _ are to be themselves and not special characters, is required. This can be done with the use of ESCAPE characters.

```
SELECT *
FROM PRODUCT
WHERE NAME LIKE 'S/_/%%'
      ESCAPE /;
```

specifies the above retrieval. The slash (/) character has been nominated as the escape character. In the pattern definition any character that is preceded by / is taken as itself and not as some special character. The above SQL will retrieve an empty relation, since there are no names beginning 'S_%' in the example PRODUCT relation.

3.10.3.6 Testing for null values

A tuple typically represents information about some entity. The attribute values represent facts about that entity but sometimes facts about a particular entity that we wish to represent in the database are unknown or not applicable. When this is the case the corresponding attribute is assigned a null value.

Nulls are not the same as spaces or zeros. A null value represents the fact that no value has been specified, whereas spaces or zeros are specific values. SQL include facilities for selecting tuples where specified attribute values are null and also for selecting tuples where specified attributes have non-null values. This facility is illustrated in the following SQL.

```
SELECT *
FROM PRODUCT
WHERE COLOUR IS NULL;
```

will retrieve details of products for which no colour has been represented. Give the PRODUCT relation below

PRODUCT

PRODUCT_NO	NAME	COLOUR
P1	Pantaloons	blue
P2	Pantaloons	khaki
P3	Socks	white
P4	Socks	harebell
P7	Socks	blue
P9	Socks	null

the SQL statement will produce the following table.

PRODUCT_NO	NAME	COLOUR
P9	Socks	null

In the above example nulls have been explicitly represented in the tables with the word 'null'. In a typical RDBMS the nulls will be invisible in the same way that a string of space characters is.

Note, the above SQL is not the same as

```
SELECT *
FROM PRODUCT
WHERE COLOUR = '        ';
```

which selects product details for which the colour has been recorded as spaces. Given the above instance of PRODUCT this would produce an empty relation. Similarly, a null value in a numeric field is not the same as zero.

It is also possible to test for values which are not null. For example, given the above instance of PRODUCT,

```
SELECT *
FROM PRODUCT
WHERE COLOUR IS NOT NULL;
```

will retrieve all customer details where a colour has been recorded, i.e.

PRODUCT_NO	NAME	COLOUR
P1	Pantaloons	blue
P2	Pantaloons	khaki
P3	Socks	white
P4	Socks	harebell
P7	Socks	blue

There are a number of current RDBMSs that do not support null values. When this is the case it is necessary to use default values to represent the absence of a data value. Typically, in the absence of support for null values, spaces are used for character attributes and zero for numeric attributes.

3.10.3.7 Computation

Using SQL, it is possible to retrieve values which are computed from the values of a relation. This is done by specifying the appropriate formula in the target_list of the SELECT statement. The usual arithmetic operators may be used within the formula, i.e.

+	add
–	subtract
*	multiply
/	divide
**	to the power of

Some RDBMSs also provide a set of mathematical functions. For example, INGRES provides the following.

abs	(expr)	the absolute value of
atan	(expr)	arctangent
cos	(expr)	cosine
exp	(expr)	exponential
log	(expr)	natural logarithm
mod	(expr1, expr2)	expr1 modulo expr2
sin	(expr)	sine
sqrt	(expr)	square root

The above may be useful for statistical and graphical applications. The next example illustrates the SQL facility for performing computations.

```
SELECT PRODUCT_NO, QUANTITY, value = PRICE * QUANTITY
FROM INVOICE_LINE;
```

Given the following INVOICE_LINE relation

INVOICE_LINE

ORDER_NO	PRODUCT_NO	QUANTITY	PRICE
01	P1	100	2.99
01	P2	20000	2.99
01	P6	20	14.98
02	P2	1000	14.98
02	P6	10000	14.98

the above SQL will produce the following relation.

PRODUCT_NO	QUANTITY	value
P1	100	299.00
P2	20000	59800.00
P6	20	299.60
P2	1000	14980.00
P6	10000	149800.00

Note that the third column of the result contains values computed from values within the database. Also, note that the computed values are assigned to an attribute named value. Normally, a column in the result table takes its name from the attributes of the database relations from which it has been retrieved, but any column may be renamed in the manner illustrated in the above example.

3.10.3.8 Summarising functions

It is possible to retrieve summary information about sets of values by using summarising functions. The following set functions are usually supported, but some systems also support many more.

AVG   which is used to average the values of an attribute.
MAX   which returns the largest value of an attribute.
MIN   which returns the minimum value of an attribute.
SUM   which returns the total of the values of an attribute.
COUNT which counts the number of values in an attribute or the number of tuples in a relation.

The use of these is illustrated by example SQL expressions applied to the following STOCK relation.

STOCK

WAREHOUSE_NO	BIN_NO	PRODUCT_NO	QTY
WH1	1	P1	300
WH1	2	P2	50
WH2	1	P2	250

The following SQL,

```
SELECT AVG (QUANTITY)
FROM STOCK;
```

will retrieve the average stock quantity. The result is NULL rather than zero if there are no values to average. Given the example STOCK relation, it produces the result below.

The following SQL,

```
SELECT MAX (QUANTITY)
FROM STOCK
WHERE PRODUCT_NO = 'P2';
```

will retrieve the recorded largest quantity of product P2. The table produced is

The following SQL,

```
SELECT low = MIN (QTY), high = MAX (QTY), average = AVG (QTY)
FROM STOCK
WHERE PRODUCT_NO = 'P2';
```

will select the minimum, maximum and average quantity of product P2 held in stock, and will produce

low	high	average
50	250	150

The following SQL,

```
SELECT COUNT (*)
FROM STOCK;
```

will count the number of tuples in the STOCK relation. This will produce the same result as counting the occurrences of any particular attribute, e.g. COUNT (NAME), and so * (the whole tuple) is used. The table produced is,

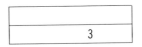

Sometimes it is required to know the number of distinct values, rather than the number of tuples. To do this the DISTINCT clause is used. For example, the following SQL,

```
SELECT COUNT (DISTINCT PRODUCT_NO)
FROM STOCK;
```

will count the number of different types of product in stock, rather than the number of bins – two bins may hold the same type of product. This will produce the following table.

2

3.10.3.9 GROUP BY

In addition to the SELECT, FROM and WHERE clauses, an SQL SELECT instruction may also include a GROUP BY clause. The GROUP BY clause may be used to apply built-in functions to specific groupings of tuples. For example, the following SQL,

```
SELECT PRODUCT_NO, IN_STOCK = SUM (QTY)
FROM STOCK
GROUP BY PRODUCT_NO;
```

will produce the total quantity ordered for each product. The resulting table, given the above example STOCK relation, is

PRODUCT_NO	IN_STOCK
P1	300
P2	300

The GROUP BY clause may be thought of as creating a number of relations, one for each distinct value of the attributes specified in the GROUP BY clause. So, in the example, there will be one relation for product P1, another for product P2, and so on. The select statement is then applied to each of these subrelations.

The GROUP BY clause may be qualified by the HAVING clause which states additional conditions that tuples of a subrelation must satisfy. For example, the SQL

```
SELECT PRODUCT_NO, IN_STOCK = SUM (QTY)
FROM STOCK
GROUP BY PRODUCT_NO
HAVING COUNT (*) > 1 AND
SUM (QTY) > 100;
```

will report only those products contained in more than one warehouse bin, and where the total quantity stored is in excess of 100. The result of this SQL with the above STOCK relation is as follows.

PRODUCT_NO	IN_STOCK
P2	300

Note that P1 has been excluded because there is only one bin of P1s.

3.10.3.10 ORDER BY

Another clause that may be included in a SELECT statement is ORDER BY. ORDER BY is used to specify that the rows of a retrieved table are to be in a specific ordering. For example,

```
SELECT *
FROM PRODUCT
ORDER BY COLOUR;
```

will retrieve a table which represents the PRODUCT relation, and the rows of that table will be in ascending alphabetical order of COLOUR, as shown below.

PRODUCT_NO	NAME	COLOUR
P1	Pantaloons	blue
P7	Socks	blue
P4	Socks	harebell
P2	Pantaloons	khaki
P3	Socks	white

Many 'sort keys' may be specified, and the ordering may be either ascending or descending. For example,

```
SELECT *
FROM PRODUCT
PRODUCT
ORDER BY COLOUR ASC, PRODUCT_NO DESC;
```

will retrieve the following table.

PRODUCT_NO	NAME	COLOUR
P7	Socks	blue
P1	Pantaloons	blue
P4	Socks	harebell
P2	Pantaloons	khaki
P3	Socks	white

The rows in the result are ordered in ascending COLOUR order, and for each colour they are ordered in descending PRODUCT_NO order. If a sort key is specified, but neither ASC or DESC is specified, ASC is assumed.

The above example is restated in an alternative form below. Note that the redundant ASC has been removed, and instead of using column names in the ORDER BY clause, the position of the column within the column list following the SELECT is used.

```
SELECT PRODUCT_NO, NAME, COLOUR
FROM PRODUCT
PRODUCT
ORDER BY 3, 1 DESC;
```

If there is no ORDER BY clause in a SELECT statement, then the rows of the resulting table will depend upon how the query is evaluated, and how the queried relations are physically stored.

3.10.4 Retrieval from two relations

The join operator of relational algebra makes it possible to define a relation which is made up of data taken from more than one relation. This is an important facility because it makes it possible to extract information about related entities. For example, a join may be used to define a relation representing information about customers and also sales orders placed by them, even when customer and sales order information are stored in separate relations. In the following subsections we describe how join operations are expressed in SQL.

Here, SQL is related to relational algebra in order to demonstrate the ways in which the theoretical relational model (see Chapter 2) is implemented in actual database systems. However, SQL is generally simple to use at a direct and intuitive level, or by trial and error. In practice a user will formulate queries directly into SQL, and will certainly not first formulate the relational algebra and then translate that into SQL.

3.10.4.1 Equi-join

The equi-join combines tuples in two relations when specified attributes have the same value. SQL expresses the equi-join operation as in the following example.

```
SELECT PRODUCT.*, ORDER_LINE.*
FROM PRODUCT, ORDER_LINE
WHERE PRODUCT.PRODUCT_NO = ORDER_LINE.PRODUCT_NO;
```

The above SQL will produce a table which has all the attributes of the PRODUCT relation and also all the attributes of the ORDER_LINE relation. Each tuple in this result table will comprise the values of one tuple in PRODUCT and the values of one tuple in ORDER_LINE. The two component tuples will be such that the condition in the WHERE clause is true, i.e. the values of the PRODUCT_NO attribute in the two tuples will be equal. Executing the above SQL with the following two relations

PRODUCT

PRODUCT_NO	NAME	COLOUR
P1	Pantaloons	blue
P2	Pantaloons	khaki
P3	Socks	white
P4	Socks	harebell
P7	Socks	blue

ORDER_LINE

ORDER_NO	PRODUCT_NO	QUANTITY
01	P1	100
01	P2	20000
01	P6	20
02	P2	1000
02	P6	10000

gives the result table below.

PRODUCT. PRODUCT_NO	NAME	COLOUR	ORDER_NO	ORDER_LINE. PRODUCT_NO	QUANTITY
P1	Pantaloons	blue	01	P1	100
P2	Pantaloons	khaki	01	P2	20000
P2	Pantaloons	khaki	02	P2	1000

There are several points to note with respect to the above example. The FROM clause must list the names of all relations accessed in order to retrieve the specified table, i.e. both the PRODUCT and the ORDER_LINE relations in the example. It must even list those relations accessed but whose data is not included in the resulting table, for example when only certain attributes are projected out.

Sometimes the same attribute name will occur in two or more relations, e.g. PRODUCT_NO occurs in both PRODUCT and ORDER_LINE. It is therefore necessary to qualify attribute names used in the SQL by preceding them with the appropriate relation name. This avoids any ambiguity. That is why PRODUCT_NO is prefixed by either PRODUCT or ORDER_LINE when it is used within the example.

Not all the tuples of PRODUCT and ORDER_LINE occur in the result. For example, the PRODUCT tuple, ⟨P7, Socks, blue⟩ does not occur because there are no orders for that product. Similarly, the tuple of ORDER_LINE, ⟨02, P6, 10000⟩, does not occur because there is no description of a part P6 in PRODUCT (the latter situation should not arise because it is a violation of the referential integrity rule (see Section 2.4)).

The equivalent relational algebra is:

> JOIN PRODUCT AND ORDER_LINE where PRODUCT.PRODUCT_NO =
>   ORDER_LINE.PRODUCT_NO.

The equi-join includes all attributes of both of the joined relations. This means that attributes which are common to both relations occur twice. In the example, PRODUCT_NO occurs twice.

3.10.4.2 Correlation names

It is desirable that relation names should be chosen so as to be meaningful. That is why we choose to call the relation which represents information about products by the name PRODUCT or PROD, rather than P or FRED, say. However, where a relation name is long it is often convenient to be able to use some alternative shorter name, e.g. with which to qualify attributes when formulating an SQL query. It is possible to do this by specifying correlation names in the FROM clause. For example, the above SQL could be rewritten as:

```
SELECT P.*, O.*
FROM PRODUCT P, ORDER_LINE O
WHERE P.PRODUCT_NO = O.PRODUCT_NO;
```

In the FROM clause both the relations that must be accessed are named, but they are also assigned correlation names. PRODUCT and ORDER_LINE are respectively assigned the correlation names P and O. The correlation name may be used instead of the full relation name, and so we may write P.PRODUCT_NO instead of PRODUCT.PRODUCT_NO. The correlation names are valid only within the SQL statement in which they are declared.

Correlation names are sometimes not just a convenience (to avoid excessive typing) but are necessary. This is the case when a relation is joined with itself (see Section 3.10.4.7).

3.10.4.3 Natural join

The natural join combines tuples of relations where, for each attribute that is common to the two relations, the attribute values in the two tuples are the same. However, unlike the result of an equi-join, the common attributes occur only once within the resulting relation.

To produce the same results as the natural join

JOIN PRODUCT AND ORDER_LINE

the SQL is as follows

```
SELECT P.*, O.ORDER_NO, QUANTITY
FROM PRODUCT P, ORDER_LINE O
WHERE P.PROD_NO = O.PROD_NO;
```

The result of executing this SQL with the above PRODUCT and ORDER_LINE relations is the following table

PRODUCT_NO	NAME	COLOUR	ORDER_NO	QUANTITY
P1	Pantaloons	blue	01	100
P2	Pantaloons	khaki	01	20000
P2	Pantaloons	khaki	02	1000

Points to note in this example are that all attributes of PRODUCT are included in the result (CUSTOMER.*), but the attributes of ORDER_LINE are explicitly listed so as to avoid duplicating the PRODUCT_NO attribute in the result.

Once an attribute name in the target_list is qualified by its relation name, then attribute names that follow are implicitly qualified by the same relation name. In the example, QUANTITY did not require qualification; it was not necessary to write O.QUANTITY because it automatically inherited the qualification of the preceding attribute, O.PRODUCT_NO.

3.10.4.4 Theta-join

The equi-join combines tuples where specified attributes have equal values. The theta-join is a generalisation of the equi-join in which join relationships other than equality can be specified. SQL may be used to execute various forms of theta-join (see Section 2.4.14.3) by using other comparison operators in the WHERE clause condition. For example, one form of the theta-join is the less-than join. The following example of the less-than join,

JOIN ORDER_LINE AND STOCK_TOTAL
WHERE ORDER_LINE.QUANTITY < STOCK_TOTAL.QUANTITY

can be expressed in SQL as follows.

```
SELECT S.*, O.*
FROM STOCK_TOTAL S, ORDER_LINE O
WHERE O.QUANTITY < S.QUANTITY;
```

Executing the SQL with the following two relations,

STOCK_TOTAL

PRODUCT_NO	QUANTITY
P1	20000
P2	10000
P3	1500
P4	20
P7	0

ORDER_LINE

ORDER_NO	PRODUCT_NO	QUANTITY
01	P1	100
01	P2	20000
01	P6	20
02	P2	1000
02	P6	10000

gives the result table below.

STOCK_TOTAL. PRODUCT_NO	STOCK_TOTAL. QUANTITY	ORDER_LINE. ORDER_NO	ORDER_LINE. PRODUCT_NO	ORDER_LINE. QUANTITY
P1	20000	01	P1	100
P1	20000	01	P6	20
P1	20000	02	P2	1000
P1	20000	02	P6	10000
P2	10000	01	P1	100
P2	10000	01	P6	20
P2	10000	02	P2	1000
P3	1500	01	P1	100
P3	1500	01	P6	20
P3	1500	02	P2	1000

Any of the arithmetical comparison operators, i.e. >, <, <=, >=, !=, =, may be used to express a join condition in a way similar to that illustrated in the above SQL.

The result of the above SQL is probably not a very useful result since it is likely that what we really wanted to know was 'For which order lines is there sufficient stock?' The SQL does not ask this question, because it does not specify that the joined tuples of STOCK and ORDER_LINE must be for the same product. The intended query could be expressed in the relational algebra as

> **RESTRICT (JOIN** STOCK **AND** ORDER_LINE **WHERE** ORDER_LINE.PRODUCT_NO
>   = STOCK_TOTAL.PRODUCT_NO) **WHERE** ORDER_LINE.QUANTITY
>   < STOCK_TOTAL.QUANTITY

That is to say, combine tuples of ORDER_LINE with the corresponding STOCK_TOTAL tuples and then select those where the quantity ordered is less than the quantity in stock.

The above is expressed by the following SQL statements,

```
SELECT S.*, O.*
FROM ORDER_LINE O, STOCK_TOTAL S
WHERE O.PRODUCT_NO = S.PRODUCT_NO AND
      O.QUANTITY < S. QUANTITY;
```

The result from the above SQL when executed with the example STOCK_TOTAL and ORDER_LINE relations above is the following table.

STOCK_TOTAL. PRODUCT_NO	STOCK_TOTAL. QUANTITY	ORDER_LINE. ORDER_NO	ORDER_LINE. PRODUCT_NO	ORDER_LINE. QUANTITY
P1	20000	01	P1	100
P2	10000	02	P2	1000

This result informs us that there is an order for 100 of P1 and that we have a stock of 20000 of P1; and there is also an order for 1000 of P2, of which we have a stock of 10000. All other orders are for quantities equal to or in excess of our stocks.

3.10.4.5 Outer join

The outer join retains tuples which do not satisfy the join condition. These tuples are included in the defined relation, but with null values for the attributes of the tuple to which they are joined. The outer join may be expressed in some implementations of SQL but there is no direct representation of an outer join in standard SQL. ORACLE is one of the current RDBMSs which does support the outer join. Using ORACLE the following relational algebra

> OJOIN STOCK_TOTAL AND ORDER_LINE
>   WHERE STOCK_TOTAL.PRODUCT_NO = ORDER_LINE.PRODUCT_NO

is expressed by the following SQL

```
SELECT S.*, ORDER_LINE.*
FROM STOCK_TOTAL S, ORDER_LINE O
WHERE S.PRODUCT_NO = O.PRODUCT_NO (+);
```

Given the above example of the STOCK_TOTAL and ORDER_LINE relations, this SQL will retrieve the following table.

STOCK_TOTAL. PRODUCT_NO	STOCK_TOTAL. QUANTITY	ORDER_LINE. ORDER_NO	ORDER_LINE. PRODUCT_NO	ORDER_LINE. QUANTITY
P1	20000	01	P1	100
P2	10000	01	P2	20000
P2	10000	02	P2	1000
P3	1500	null	null	null
P4	20	null	null	null
null	null	01	P6	20
null	null	02	P6	10000
P7	0	null	null	null

Points to note are that the outer join retains *all* of the tuples of the joined relations, even when a tuple in one of the relations does not match with any tuples in the other. Where these 'loose ends' occur, they occur once within the result relation with null values for the attributes of the other relation. The outer join is specified in ORACLE SQL by suffixing the join condition with (+).

It is also possible to express the outer join in standard SQL but it requires the use of a UNION operator, which is described later in this chapter (see Section 3.11).

3.10.4.6 Mixed queries on two relations

The examples of join operations expressed in SQL given in the previous section follow the general pattern,

```
SELECT target_list
FROM list_of_relations
WHERE condition;
```

where the target_list specifies the columns of the table representing attributes of the joined relation; the list_of_relations specifies the relations involved in the join; and the condition is the join condition.

Complex expressions in the relational algebra, including join, project and restrict, may also be expressed in SQL by judicious use of the target_list, list_of_relations, and condition. This facility is illustrated by the next example.

The following SQL retrieves order lines for 'Pantaloons'.

```
SELECT O.*
FROM   PRODUCT P, ORDER_LINE O
WHERE P.PRODUCT_NO = O.PRODUCT_NO AND
        P.NAME = 'Pantaloons';
```

Given the following instance of PRODUCT and of ORDER_LINE,

PRODUCT

PRODUCT_NO	NAME	COLOUR
P1	Pantaloons	blue
P2	Pantaloons	khaki
P3	Socks	white
P4	Socks	harebell
P7	Socks	blue

ORDER_LINE

ORDER_NO	PRODUCT_NO	QUANTITY
01	P1	100
01	P2	20000
01	P6	20
02	P2	1000
02	P6	10000

the above SQL would produce the following result table.

ORDER_NO	PRODUCT_NO	QUANTITY
01	P1	100
01	P2	20000
02	P2	1000

Note that the above example implements the following relational algebra,

```
PROJECT (JOIN ORDER_LINE AND
    (RESTRICT PRODUCT where NAME = 'Pantaloons'))
        ON ORDER_LINE.ORDER_NO, PRODUCT_NO, QUANTITY
```

The target_list is used to specify projections, the list_of_relations specifies relations to be joined or multiplied (applying the Cartesian product), and the WHERE condition may be used to qualify the joins, or to specify restrictions.

3.10.4.7 Comparing rows in the same relation

On occasions it may be necessary to join a relation with itself. This is possible with the use of correlation names. For example, to retrieve pairs of products which share the same name, we could use the following SQL statement.

```
SELECT FIRST.PRODUCT_NO, SECOND.PRODUCT_NO, NAME
FROM PRODUCT FIRST, PRODUCT SECOND
WHERE FIRST.NAME = SECOND.NAME
AND FIRST.PRODUCT_NO > SECOND.PRODUCT_NO;
```

The result of this SQL when applied to the following PRODUCT relation,

PRODUCT

PRODUCT_NO	NAME	COLOUR
P1	Pantaloons	blue
P2	Pantaloons	khaki
P3	Socks	white
P4	Socks	harebell
P7	Socks	blue
P9	Socks	null

is as follows.

FIRST. PRODUCT_NO	SECOND. PRODUCT_NO	SECOND. NAME
P2	P1	Pantaloons
P4	P3	Socks
P7	P3	Socks
P9	P3	Socks
P7	P4	Socks
P9	P4	Socks
P9	P7	Socks

Note that it was not necessary to qualify NAME in the target_list, because it automatically inherits the previously used qualifier. The result is as if there were two copies of the PRODUCT relation, and result relation tuples are formed by comparing each row of the first copy of PRODUCT with each row of the second copy of PRODUCT, and combining them when the WHERE condition is true. The second term of the WHERE condition,

```
FIRST.PRODUCT_NO > SECOND.PRODUCT_NO
```

was included to filter out redundant rows in the result table. It excludes rows from the result table that result from joining a row with itself, and from joining two rows that have already been joined. The rows that have been excluded are as follows.

FIRST. PRODUCT_NO	SECOND. PRODUCT_NO	SECOND. NAME
P2	P2	Pantaloons
P1	P2	Pantaloons
P3	P3	Socks
P3	P4	Socks
P3	P7	Socks
P3	P9	Socks
P4	P4	Socks
P4	P7	Socks
P4	P9	Socks
P7	P7	Socks
P7	P9	Socks
P9	P9	Socks

3.10.5 Queries on more than two relations

The above examples all operate upon either one or two relations. However, it is possible for SQL instructions to operate upon more than two relations. To illustrate this, consider the following example SQL which retrieves the names and colours of products that have been ordered by Nippers Ltd.

```
SELECT P.NAME, COLOUR
FROM CUSTOMER C, SALES_ORDER S, ORDER_LINE O, PRODUCT P
WHERE CUSTOMER.NAME = 'Nippers Ltd'
        AND C.CUSTOMER_NO = S.CUSTOMER_NO
        AND S.ORDER_NO = O.ORDER_NO
        AND O.PRODUCT_NO = P.PRODUCT_NO;
```

When we executed with the following CUSTOMER, SALES_ORDER, ORDER_LINE and PRODUCT relations,

CUSTOMER

CUSTOMER_NO	NAME	ADDRESS
C1	Nippers Ltd	25 High St, Leeds
C2	Tots-Gear	5 Low St, Oxford
C3	Super-Brat	30 New St, Luton

SALES_ORDER

ORDER_NO	CUSTOMER_NO	DATE
01	C1	1/1/90
02	C3	2/1/90
03	C1	20/1/90

ORDER_LINE

ORDER_NO	PRODUCT_NO	QUANTITY
01	P2	50
01	P1	100
02	P1	200
03	P2	100

PRODUCT

PRODUCT_NO	NAME	COLOUR
P1	Pantaloons	blue
P2	Pantaloons	khaki
P3	Socks	white

the above SQL retrieves the following.

PRODUCT. NAME	COLOUR
Pantaloons	khaki
Pantaloons	blue

The execution of the above SQL has the same effect as the following steps.

a) A relation is formed containing tuples which combine one tuple of CUSTOMER, one tuple of SALES_ORDER, one tuple of ORDER_LINE and one tuple of PRODUCT. This table contains all possible combinations of tuples from these four relations, i.e. the Cartesian product of these four relations is formed.

b) A relation is formed which contains only those tuples of the relation created in a) above for which the WHERE condition is true, i.e. a restriction is applied.

c) The result relation is created from the PRODUCT.NAME and COLOUR attributes of the relation created in b) above, i.e. a projection is applied.

In practice, the above execution strategy is somewhat inefficient, and an actual database may use other strategies to execute the SQL in a shorter time. In particular the RDBMS will take advantage of the ways in which the relations are physically represented (see Section 3.11.1).

The above SQL is equivalent to the following relational algebra expression. It is left as an exercise for readers to convince themselves of this equivalence.

```
PROJECT (JOIN (JOIN (RESTRICT (JOIN CUSTOMER AND SALES_ORDER WHERE
    CUSTOMER.CUSTOMER_NO = SALES_ORDER.CUSTOMER_NO) WHERE
    CUSTOMER.NAME = 'Nippers Ltd') AND ORDER_LINE)
    AND PRODUCT) ON PRODUCT.NAME,PRODUCT.COLOUR;
```

3.10.6 Nested SELECTs

Much of the expressive power of SQL is a consequence of the facility by which a SELECT statement may be included within the WHERE clause of another SELECT statement. This nesting of SELECT statements is illustrated in the following example.

Consider the following query: 'Determine the name and colour of all products on order O1'. This query could be expressed in SQL as follows.

```
SELECT P.NAME, COLOUR
FROM PRODUCT P, ORDER_LINE O
WHERE P.PRODUCT_NO = O.PRODUCT_NO
  AND  O.ORDER_NO = 'O1';
```

Given the above PRODUCT and ORDER_LINE relations, this produces,

PRODUCT. NAME	PRODUCT. COLOUR
Pantaloons	blue
Pantaloons	khaki

However, the use of nested SELECTs offers an alternative step-by-step way of forming this query. The query could be pieced together in the following stages. First find out the numbers of all products on order '01'. This may be simply expressed using

```
SELECT PRODUCT_NO
FROM ORDER_LINE
WHERE ORDER_NO = '01';
```

This query may be input and tested. The relation produced is

PRODUCT_NO
P1
P2

The results of the above SQL may now be used to SELECT the required details of the products on order 01, as follows

```
SELECT NAME, COLOUR
FROM PRODUCT
WHERE PRODUCT_NO IN
      (SELECT PRODUCT_NO
       FROM ORDER_LINE
       WHERE ORDER_NO = '01');
```

Note the use of IN within the condition. This tests if a product number is contained IN the set of product numbers retrieved by the nested SELECT (see also Section 3.10.3.4).

As a further illustration of this step-by-step development of an SQL query, consider the query 'Retrieve details of products ordered by Nippers Ltd.' The first attempt is as follows

```
SELECT ORDER_NO
FROM CUSTOMER, SALES_ORDER
WHERE CUSTOMER.NAME = 'Nippers Ltd'
AND CUSTOMER.CUSTOMER_NO = SALES_ORDER.CUSTOMER_NO;
```

This retrieves the following

ORDER_NO
01
03

The result produced by the above SQL is a set of order numbers for orders placed by Nippers Ltd. That is not really what was required, but this relation of order numbers can be used to specify the order lines that are of interest. The above expression is modified as shown below:

```
SELECT PRODUCT_NO
FROM ORDER_LINE
WHERE ORDER_NO IN
      (SELECT ORDER_NO
       FROM CUSTOMER, SALES_ORDER
       WHERE CUSTOMER.NAME = 'Nippers Ltd'
       AND CUSTOMER.CUSTOMER_NO
       = SALES_ORDER.CUSTOMER_NO);
```

This SQL produces the following

PRODUCT_NO
P1
P2

The IN condition tests that order numbers of the order lines are contained in the set of order numbers retrieved above.

The SQL now retrieves the PRODUCT_NO values contained in the ORDER_LINE relation which are also in the list of order numbers placed by Nippers Ltd retrieved by the first attempt. The user is now nearer to a solution to his request but what he really wants to know are the details of the products whose numbers have been listed.

A second and final modification may be made to the SQL to retrieve the information required, i.e.

```
SELECT *
FROM PRODUCT
WHERE PRODUCT_NO IN
      (SELECT PRODUCT_NO
       FROM ORDER_LINE
       WHERE ORDER_NO IN
            (SELECT ORDER_NO
             FROM SALES_ORDER, CUSTOMER
             WHERE CUSTOMER.NAME = 'Nippers Ltd'
             AND CUSTOMER.CUSTOMER_NO = SALES_ORDER.CUSTOMER_NO));
```

This final version retrieves the following.

PRODUCT_NO	NAME	COLOUR
P1	Pantaloons	blue
P2	Pantaloons	khaki

Though the final SQL looks somewhat complicated, the above step-by-step development may make it relatively easy to formulate. The user may develop his SQL statement through experimentation and successive refinement. To this end an SQL system will usually enable the user to edit and execute the current statement again after it has first been input and executed.

3.10.6.1 Qualified comparison

The above SQL examples of nested SELECTs have the following form.

```
SELECT  target__list__1
FROM    list__of__relations__1
WHERE   attribute IN
        (SELECT target__list__2
         FROM list__of__relations__2
         WHERE condition);
```

The inner SELECT retrieves a set of values, and the outer SELECT retrieves tuples where specific attribute values are members of that set.

The IN operator compares attribute values with those in a set defined either explicitly (see Section 3.10.3.4) or by some nested SELECT (as above). IN means 'is equal to any member of the set'. At times however, the user may wish to test for other relationships, such as 'is greater than all members of the set' or 'is less than some member of the set'. This is possible using qualified comparison, as illustrated in the following examples.

```
SELECT *
FROM EMPLOYEE
WHERE AGE > ALL
   (SELECT AGE
    FROM EMPLOYEE
    WHERE DEPT_NO = 'D1');
```

The above SQL will retrieve details of employees who are older than all of the employees in department D1. ALL qualifies the operator > so that is has to be true for every value in the set retrieved by the inner SELECT. Given the following EMPLOYEE relations

EMPLOYEE

EMP_NO	NAME	AGE	DEPT_NO
E1	J Smith	39	D1
E2	J Smith	28	D1
E4	M Fish	37	D3
E6	F Hoyle	23	D4
E7	M Hull	55	D4

the SQL will produce the following,

EMP_NO	NAME	AGE	DEPT_NO
E7	M Hull	55	D4

Comparison operators may alternatively be qualified by ANY in order to specify that the operator must hold for at least one value of the set (standard SQL allows SOME to be used instead of ANY). The following example illustrates this.

```
SELECT *
FROM EMPLOYEE
WHERE DEPT_NO <> 'D1' AND AGE < ANY
         (SELECT AGE
            FROM EMPLOYEE
              WHERE DEPT_NO = 'D1');
```

The above SQL will retrieve details of employees, not in department D1, who are younger than at least one employee in department D1. Given the above EMPLOYEE relations, this produces,

EMP_NO	NAME	AGE	DEPT_NO
E4	M Fish	37	D3
E6	F Hoyle	23	D4

3.10.6.2 Nested SELECTs which always retrieve a single value

IN has been used in previous examples to select details associated with values in a set. Some SQL SELECT instructions will always retrieve a single value. This is the case, for example, when the WHERE condition tests for a particular primary key value. In such cases the comparison operators which operate upon single values may be used. These operators are: =, <, >, !=, <=, >=. This feature is illustrated by the following example SQL.

```
SELECT *
FROM PRODUCT
WHERE NAME =
         (SELECT NAME
            FROM PRODUCT
              WHERE PRODUCT_NO = 'P1');
```

This SQL statement will retrieve details of all products with the same name as product P1. Given the PRODUCT relation

PRODUCT

PRODUCT_NO	NAME	COLOUR
P1	Pantaloons	blue
P2	Pantaloons	khaki
P3	Socks	white

the above SQL will produce

PRODUCT_NO	NAME	COLOUR
P1	Pantaloons	blue
P2	Pantaloons	khaki

The nested SELECT retrieves a relation with the one tuple, ⟨Pantaloons⟩. The outer SELECT then retrieves tuples where the value of the NAME attribute is equal to 'Pantaloons'.

3.10.6.3 Testing for the empty set

The EXISTS operator is used to ask questions such as 'Are there any customers who have not placed a sales order?' EXISTS tests whether a set of tuples defined by a SELECT is empty. The above question can be expressed in SQL as follows,

```
SELECT *
FROM CUSTOMER C
WHERE NOT EXISTS
        (SELECT *
          FROM SALES_ORDER S
          WHERE S.CUSTOMER_NO = C.CUSTOMER_NO);
```

and, given the above CUSTOMER and SALES_ORDER relations it will retrieve the following.

CUSTOMER_NO	NAME	ADDRESS
C2	Tots-Gear	5 Low St, Oxford

The inner SELECT in the above SQL defines the set of sales order tuples which have the same customer number as some customer tuple. If there are no sales order records corresponding to a particular customer tuple then this set is empty and the NOT EXISTS condition is true. In this way the outer SELECT defines the set of tuples of CUSTOMER where there are no corresponding sales order tuples.

Note the use of the correlation names in the condition of the inner SELECT. These provide a means of communication between the inner and outer SELECTs. A way of interpreting the above SQL is as follows.. The outer SELECT looks at each tuple of the CUSTOMER relation and evaluates the inner SELECT against it. Thus, the first time the inner SELECT is evaluated, C.CUSTOMER_NO takes the value C1, the second time C2, and the third time C3.

3.10.7 Set operations on relations

SQL includes facilities for applying the set operator, UNION. The union operator combines the elements of two sets into a single set. In SQL it brings together tuples of two relations into a single relation. This facility is illustrated by the following example.

```
SELECT PRODUCT_NO
FROM STOCK

UNION

SELECT PRODUCT_NO
FROM ORDER_LINE;
```

Given the following STOCK and ORDER_LINE relations,

STOCK

WAREHOUSE_NO	BIN_NO	PRODUCT_NO	QTY
WH1	1	P1	100
WH1	2	P2	50
WH2	1	P2	250

ORDER_LINE

ORDER_NO	PRODUCT_NO	QTY
01	P1	100
01	P6	200
01	P7	20
02	P7	1000
02	P6	10000

the above SQL is evaluated as follows.

The SQL includes two SELECTs. The first SELECT retrieves the product number of all products which are held in stock. The result is the following.

PRODUCT_NO
P1
P2

The second SELECT retrieves the product numbers of all products which have been ordered by customers, giving,

PRODUCT_NO
P1
P6
P7

The union operator combines these two sets of product numbers into a single relation. Duplicate product numbers are automatically removed. This produces the following.

PRODUCT_NO
P1
P2
P6
P7

If the outer join is not supported in a particular implementation of SQL (see Section 3.10.4.4) then it may be expressed using UNION. The outer join,

> OJOIN STOCK_TOTAL **AND** ORDER_LINE
> **WHERE** STOCK_TOTAL.PRODUCT_NO = ORDER_LINE.PRODUCT_NO,

of the following STOCK_TOTAL and ORDER_LINE relations

STOCK_TOTAL

PRODUCT_NO	QUANTITY
P1	20000
P2	10000
P3	1500
P4	20
P7	0

ORDER_LINE

ORDER_NO	PRODUCT_NO	QUANTITY
01	P1	100
01	P2	20000
01	P6	20
02	P2	1000
02	P6	10000

defines the following relation

STOCK_TOTAL. PRODUCT_NO	STOCK_TOTAL. QTY	ORDER_LINE. ORDER_NO	ORDER_LINE. PRODUCT_NO	ORDER_LINE. QUANTITY
P1	20000	01	P1	100
P2	10000	01	P2	20000
P2	10000	02	P2	1000
P3	1500	null	null	null
P4	20	null	null	null
null	null	01	P6	20
null	null	02	P6	10000
P7	0	null	null	null

This outer join contains three types of tuple:

a) tuples which are formed by joining two tuples
b) tuples which are formed from one STOCK_TOTAL tuple
c) tuples which are formed from one ORDER_LINE tuple.

These three sets of tuples may be retrieved using separate select commands and the outer join may then be formed from the union of these sets. In this way the above outer join may be expressed by the following SQL,

```
    SELECT S.PRODUCT_NO, QUANTITY, O.ORDER_NO, PRODUCT_NO, QUANTITY
    FROM   STOCK_TOTAL S, ORDER_LINE O
    WHERE  S.PRODUCT_NO = O.PRODUCT_NO
UNION
    SELECT null, null, O.ORDER_NO, PRODUCT_NO, QUANTITY
    FROM ORDER_LINE O, STOCK_TOTAL S
    WHERE O.PRODUCT_NO NOT IN
      (SELECT PRODUCT_NO
       FROM STOCK_TOTAL)
UNION
    SELECT S.PRODUCT_NO, QUANTITY, null, null, null
    FROM ORDER_LINE O, STOCK_TOTAL S
    WHERE S.PRODUCT_NO NOT IN
      (SELECT PRODUCT_NO
       FROM ORDER_LINE);
```

Note that the three relations produced by the three SELECTs must have union – compatible attributes. This means that corresponding attributes must have the same type.

The target_lists of the SELECT statements do not have to specify the same attribute names. In the above example some of them specify null values. The order in which the target_list attributes are listed indicates which attribute of each of the retrieved relations are to be combined.

3.10.8 Changing values in the database

SQL includes UPDATE, DELETE and INSERT commands for altering the contents of relations. Like the SELECT previously described, these commands operate on sets of tuples. In certain forms they include embedded SELECT statements.

3.10.8.1 Updating values in existing tuples

The following sequence of SQL examples illustrates the facilities for altering the values in tuples. The examples are all illustrated by showing the result of executing them with the PRODUCT relation, given below.

PRODUCT

PRODUCT_NO	NAME	COLOUR	PRICE
P1	Pantaloons	blue	17.00
P2	Pantaloons	khaki	17.00
P3	Socks	white	2.00
P4	Socks	harebell	3.00
P7	Socks	blue	3.00

The following SQL will increase all prices by 10%.

```
UPDATE PRODUCT
SET    PRICE = PRICE * 1.1;
```

The result when applied to the above relation is as follows.

PRODUCT

PRODUCT_NO	NAME	COLOUR	PRICE
P1	Pantaloons	blue	18.70
P2	Pantaloons	khaki	18.70
P3	Socks	white	2.20
P4	Socks	harebell	3.30
P7	Socks	blue	3.30

Note that the UPDATE instruction updates a single relation at a time, but may alter many tuples. Note also that new values may be computed. They may in fact be computed using any of the expressions that may be used in the target_list of a SELECT (see Sections 3.10.3.7 and 3.10.3.8).

The second example SQL alters only selected tuples. It changes the colour of all products which are blue to violet and increases their price by 10p.

```
UPDATE PRODUCT
SET COLOUR = 'violet',
    PRICE = PRICE + .10
WHERE COLOUR = 'blue';
```

The result of applying it to the above relation is the following relation.

PRODUCT

PRODUCT_NO	NAME	COLOUR	PRICE
P1	Pantaloons	violet	18.80
P2	Pantaloons	khaki	18.70
P3	Socks	white	2.20
P4	Socks	harebell	3.30
P7	Socks	violet	3.40

Note that more than one attribute may be altered in a single UPDATE, and that a WHERE condition may be included as in the SELECT command in order to restrict those tuples which are updated.

This final example of the UPDATE command changes the name of product P1 from 'Pantaloons' to 'Shorts'.

```
UPDATE PRODUCT
SET NAME = 'Shorts'
WHERE PRODUCT_NO = 'P1';
```

The effect of applying it to the above example is as follows.

PRODUCT

PRODUCT_NO	NAME	COLOUR	PRICE
P1	Shorts	violet	18.80
P2	Pantaloons	khaki	18.70
P3	Socks	white	2.20
P4	Socks	harebell	3.30
P7	Socks	violet	3.40

Note that in the above example we have updated an individual tuple by specifying its primary key value in the WHERE condition.

The UPDATE command in SQL has the following general form:

```
UPDATE table__name
SET    field = expression
       [, field = expression]
[WHERE   condition];
```

As illustrated by the examples, the strength of this command is its ability to make general changes across a whole relation or to a restricted set of tuples, or, by specifying the primary key value, individual tuples may be updated.

3.10.8.2 Inserting new tuples into a relation

SQL includes an INSERT command for adding new tuples to a relation. The new tuples may be specified by sets of values, or may be created from values already stored in the database. The two examples given below illustrate these two facilities.

The following SQL illustrates the facility for inserting a new tuple into a relation, where the values of the new tuple are specified.

```
INSERT INTO PRODUCT (PRODUCT_NO, NAME, PRICE)
VALUES ('P10', 'Shirt', 4.95);
```

When applied to the above (unupdated) example of the PRODUCT relation, the above INSERT instruction will produce the following PRODUCT relation.

PRODUCT

PRODUCT_NO	NAME	COLOUR	PRICE	
P1	Pantaloons	blue	18.70	
P2	Pantaloons	khaki	18.70	
P3	Socks	white	2.20	
P4	Socks	harebell	3.30	
P7	Socks	blue	3.30	
P10	Shirt	null	4.95	← new tuple

Note that the new tuple includes a null-valued COLOUR attribute. This is because the value of COLOUR is not specified in the INSERT. An RDBMS which does not support nulls would place a default value in COLOUR: spaces for character fields and zero for numeric fields.

The following example illustrates the SQL facility for inserting new tuples that are constructed from values already stored in the database. First, we create a new relation for storing details of 'under-a-fiver' products, i.e. costing less than five pounds.

```
CREATE TABLE UNDER_5_PROD                          .
(PRODUCT_NO       CHARACTER (5) NOT NULL,
 LOW_PRICE        DECIMAL (3,2));
```

Note the use of the NOT NULL constraint for the primary key so as to enforce entity integrity (see Section 2.5.2). Note also the data types used. CHARACTER (5) specifies a fixed-length field 5 characters long. DECIMAL (3,2) specifies a three-digit decimal number with an assumed decimal point two digits from the right.

We now create tuples from the values in the PRODUCT relation. The tuples in which we are interested are those where the condition, PRICE < 5.00, is true, and it is only the PRODUCT_NO and PRICE attributes that are required for the new tuples. The new tuples are created by the following SQL.

```
INSERT UNDER_5_PROD (PRODUCT_NO, LOW_PRICE)
SELECT PRODUCT_NO, PRICE
FROM PRODUCT
WHERE PRICE < 5.00;
```

When applied to the following PRODUCT relation,

PRODUCT

PRODUCT_NO	NAME	COLOUR	PRICE
P1	Pantaloons	blue	18.70
P2	Pantaloons	khaki	18.70
P3	Socks	white	2.20
P4	Socks	harebell	3.30
P7	Socks	blue	3.30
P10	Shirt	null	4.95

the above INSERT produced the following UNDER_5_PROD relation

UNDER_5_PROD

PRODUCT_NO	LOW_PRICE
P3	2.20
P4	3.30
P7	3.30
P10	4.95

Note the use of an embedded SELECT instruction to retrieve the set of tuples to be inserted. Note also that the attribute names of the relation into which the tuples are to be inserted need not be the same as those of the relations from which the tuples are retrieved. For example, we have LOW_PRICE in UNDER_5_PROD which is populated with values taken from the PRICE attribute in PRODUCT.

3.10.8.3 Transfer between files and relations

RDBMSs often include non-standard SQL facilities for inserting tuples supplied in a conventional file, and for outputting tuples to a file. These facilities are used for inserting tuples in batches, for making back-up copies of relations, and for recreating a relation from its back-up copy. The following is an example of this facility as supported in INGRES SQL.

```
COPY TABLE CUSTOMER
    (ORDER_NO = c0tab, PRODUCT_NO = c0tab, QUANTITY = c0nl)
    FROM 'customer.dat';
```

The above will insert tuples read from a (non-database) file called customer.dat into the CUSTOMER relation. This command describes how the tuples are set out in the file. ORDER_NO = c0tab means that the values for order number will exist as character strings, followed by a tab character. QUANTITY = c0nl means that a quantity value is stored as a character string followed by a new line character.

The tuples of a relation may be copied into a file in a similar way, e.g.

```
COPY TABLE CUSTOMER
    (ORDER_NO = c0tab, PRODUCT_NO = c0tab, QUANTITY = c0nl)
    INTO 'customer.dat';
```

3.10.8.4 Deleting tuples

SQL includes a DELETE command with which sets of tuples may be deleted from a relation.

The following SQL will remove from the PRODUCT relation all tuples describing blue products.

```
DELETE FROM PRODUCT
WHERE COLOUR = 'blue';
```

The effect when applied to the above PRODUCT relation is as follows.

PRODUCT

PRODUCT_NO	NAME	COLOUR	PRICE
P2	Pantaloons	khaki	18.70
P3	Socks	white	2.20
P4	Socks	harebell	3.30
P10	Shirt	null	4.95

The power of this delete facility is that it may be used to delete individual tuples, by specifying the primary key value in the WHERE condition, or it may be used to delete sets of related records, as in the above example.

3.11 More elements of the SQL schema definition language

3.11.1 Specifying storage structures

The SQL SDL for specifying storage structures, i.e. the ways in which relations are to be physically represented, is not defined in the standards and differs from system to system. In fact there is variation between RDBMSs in the ways in which relations are physically implemented. Also, in some RDBMSs the database languages do not support specification of storage structures and this task must be done by the database administrator using special programs. INGRES does support specification of storage structures using database languages and is described below to illustrate this type of facility.

INGRES supports both QUEL (see Section 3.15) and SQL. Both languages include a MODIFY command with which the physical representation of a relation may be specified. The instruction is illustrated by the following example.

```
MODIFY CUSTOMER TO ISAM ON CUSTOMER_NO;
```

This instruction represents the CUSTOMER relation as an ISAM (Indexed Sequential Access Method) file, indexed on the CUSTOMER_NO attribute. INGRES supports a number of physical structures for representing relations, including B-trees, ISAM, hashed files and heap files. These and other methods of physical storage are discussed in Chapter 4. When a new relation is created, by default it is represented using a heap file. Its representation may later be changed using the MODIFY instruction illustrated above.

3.11.2 Views

An external model in a database system is a part of the database that is relevant to some particular application. An external model of a relational database system is a set of base relations and virtual relations.

A virtual relation is a relation that appears to the user to exist, and can be manipulated as if it were a base relation, but which does not actually exist. It is a relation retrieved from other relations in the database. Any manipulations of a virtual relation are automatically translated by the RDBMS into manipulations of the relations from which it was derived.

A virtual relation is called a VIEW, and SQL includes CREATE VIEW and DROP VIEW instructions for creating new views and deleting existing views. This facility is illustrated by the following examples.

The following SQL creates views with which a warehouse person may query the contents of a warehouse WH1. We assume that the database included the following PRODUCT and STOCK base relations.

PRODUCT

PRODUCT_NO	NAME	COLOUR
P1	Pantaloons	blue
P2	Pantaloons	khaki
P3	Socks	white
P4	Socks	harebell
P7	Socks	blue

STOCK

WAREHOUSE_NO	BIN_NO	PRODUCT_NO	QTY
WH1	1	P1	100
WH1	2	P2	50
WH2	1	P2	50

The view WH1_STOCK_A is defined by the following SQL

```
CREATE VIEW WH1_STOCK_A
AS SELECT   BIN_NO, PRODUCT_NO, QTY
   FROM STOCK
   WHERE WAREHOUSE_NO = 'WH1';
```

This view will give the illusion that the following relation exists.

WH1_STOCK_A

BIN_NO	PRODUCT_NO	QTY
1	P1	100
2	P2	50

The above view does not include the warehouse number. It is not necessary, because the definition will require it always to have the value of WH1.

When the user submits SQL to manipulate WH1_STOCK_A the RDBMS will modify the SQL so that it operates directly on the corresponding values of STOCK. For example,

```
SELECT BIN_NO, QTY
FROM WH1_STOCK_A
WHERE PRODUCT_NO = 'P1';
```

will be changed to the following before it is executed.

```
SELECT BIN_NO, QTY
FROM STOCK                      ◄────── FROM clause of CREATE VIEW
WHERE PRODUCT_NO = 'P1'
AND WAREHOUSE_NO = 'WH1';        ◄────── WHERE clause of CREATE VIEW
```

The view name in the FROM clause is replaced by the relations from which it is derived (specified in the FROM clause of the CREATE VIEW statement), and the WHERE of the CREATE VIEW statement is ANDed to the WHERE clause of the SELECT.

The second example CREATE VIEW statement has the same effect as the previous one, with the exception that the WAREHOUSE_NO attribute is also included in the view.

```
CREATE VIEW WH1_STOCK_B
AS SELECT *
   FROM STOCK
   WHERE WAREHOUSE_NO = 'WH1';
```

The view created will be as follows.

WH1_STOCK_B

WAREHOUSE_NO	BIN_NO	PRODUCT_NO	QTY
WH1	1	P1	100
WH1	2	P2	50

An important difference between WH1_STOCK_A and WH1_STOCK_B is that the latter includes the primary key (WAREHOUSE_NO BIN_NO) of the base relation from which it is derived, but WH1_STOCK_A does not. The absence of the primary key from the view will make it *unupdatable*. That is to say, the user may not alter the information in the view; he may only retrieve information. This is because in the absence of a primary key value, it is not clear from which base relation tuples the view tuples were derived and so the effect of any update is unclear.

A third example CREATE VIEW statement defines a view which is the same as WH1_STOCK_B with the exception that the product name, taken from the product relation is also included.

```
CREATE VIEW WH1_STOCK_C
AS SELECT WAREHOUSE_NO, BIN_NO, PRODUCT_NO, NAME, QTY
   FROM STOCK, PRODUCT
   WHERE STOCK.PRODUCT_NO = PRODUCT.PRODUCT_NO AND
   WAREHOUSE_NO = 'WH1';
```

The view created will be as follows.

WH1_STOCK_C

WAREHOUSE_NO	BIN_NO	PRODUCT_NO	NAME	QTY
WH1	1	P1	Pantaloons	100
WH1	2	P2	Pantaloons	50

Here the view is created by joining two relations. Some views defined on more than one relation are *in theory* updatable, because the correspondence between tuples in the view and the tuples in the base relations from which they were derived can be unambiguous. This is the case with the above example; it includes the primary key attribute of PRODUCT, i.e. PRODUCT_NO, and also the primary key attribute of STOCK, i.e. WAREHOUSE_NO BIN_NO. However, updates on views formed by joining relations are not supported by current RDBMSs. The fact that there may be many tuples in the view which derive from the same PRODUCT tuple, e.g. there may be two bins with the same product, make the update a complicated process with potential ambiguities.

The standard SQL includes the following rules on view updatability. A view is updatable if and only if:

a) DISTINCT is not specified
b) every item in the target_list is an attribute name, (rather than a constant or function or arithmetical expression)
c) the FROM clause specifies only one relation
d) the WHERE clause does not include any nested SELECTs
e) there is no GROUP BY or HAVING clause in the query part of the VIEW definition.

In addition to the above rules it is also necessary to add that any tuple added to the view does not violate the integrity constraints of the base relation. For example, if a new tuple is added to a view, attributes not included in the view must be given a null value, but this must not violate a NOT NULL integrity constraint.

In practice, the above rules for view updatability mean that a view is updatable, only if each tuple of the view corresponds to a single tuple of the single relation from which the view is derived.

Migrating tuples
Tuples exist within a view because they satisfy the WHERE condition of the view definition. If a tuple is altered, such that it no longer satisfies this condition, then it will disappear from the view. Similarly, new tuples will appear within the view when an update causes them to satisfy the view condition. These tuples that leave or enter a view are called migrating tuples.

A view can be defined such that the user is not allowed to cause any tuple to migrate out of the view. This is done using the WITH CHECK OPTION clause. This is illustrated below.

```
CREATE VIEW WH1_STOCK_B
SELECT *
FROM STOCK
WHERE WAREHOUSE_NO = 'WH1'
WITH CHECK OPTION;
```

The view created will be as follows.

WH1_STOCK_A

WAREHOUSE_NO	BIN_NO	PRODUCT_NO	QTY
WH1	1	P1	100
WH1	2	P2	50

The WITH CHECK OPTION clause has been included in the above SQL, and this means that the user of this view may not alter the values of WAREHOUSE_NO. If the user were able to do so, the altered tuple would migrate out of the view.

3.11.3 Integrity constraints

Integrity constraints are rules that must be obeyed by all tuples in the database. Examples are the NOT NULL, and UNIQUE constraints on attribute values that may be specified when a new relation is created (see Section 3.9.2).

Standard SQL does not include a standard for defining integrity constraints, apart from the NOT NULL and UNIQUE rules which may be specified in a CREATE TABLE instruction. The examples given below are of INGRES SQL and are given to illustrate this type of facility.

INGRES (Version 5) SQL allows the specification of rules which restrict the values that may be stored within a relation. These rules are specified using the CREATE INTEGRITY instruction. For example,

```
CREATE INTEGRITY
   ON ORDER_LINE
   IS QUANTITY > 0 AND QUANTITY <= 1000000;
```

restricts the way in which the ORDER_LINE relation may be updated. Operations which attempt to set a value of QUANTITY which is not in the range 0 to 1 000 000 will not be allowed. Integrity constraints may be any of the WHERE conditions that are allowed in a SELECT statement which operates on a single relation.

An integrity constraint may be listed using the INGRES command HELP INTEGRITY. The command

```
HELP INTEGRITY ORDER_LINE;
```

will list all the integrity constraints which currently constrain the values of the

ORDER_LINE relation. Each integrity constraint is numbered. If the constraint created above is constraint number 6, then it may be removed by,

```
DROP INTEGRITY ON ORDER_LINE 6;
```

3.12 Transactions

A database is a snapshot of the world; it represents information about the world as it is at a particular moment in time. When there are changes in the world, then corresponding changes have to be made to the database. For example, when a customer places an order, that alters the state of the world, and so the database must be altered so as to represent information about that order.

Certain activities in the world require consistent information (information about a single snapshot of the world). For example, if a salesman requires a list of current stocks of a particular product, then the rows of that table should not be distorted by transfers of stock which are taking place in between accessing each tuple.

A transaction is the name given to a sequence of SQL instructions which either alter the database so as to represent some single change in the world, or which retrieve information about a single snapshot of the world, to support some task.

For example, recording a new order is a transaction which will necessitate retrieving details of the customer, so as to ascertain his or her credit worthiness, and then insertion of tuples into the ORDER and ORDER_LINE relations.

A transaction is a unit of recovery. By this we mean that either all of the instructions of the transaction are executed, or none of them are. All SQL instructions of a transaction execute a single task, and if for any reason it is decided that the task should not be completed, then the effects of any of those SQL instructions which have already been executed must be removed from the database. Similarly, other users should not be affected by, or be able to affect, the data used by a transaction until it has been completed or has been abandoned.

A transaction is completed when the following SQL is executed.

```
COMMIT WORK;
```

A transaction is abandoned, and the effects of instructions already executed are undone, by the SQL instruction,

```
ROLLBACK WORK;
```

The mechanisms by which many transactions may occur simultaneously is described in Chapter 5.

Many RDBMSs work on the assumption that as one transaction ends, so the next one starts. However, some RDBMSs do include explicit START TRANSACTION instructions.

3.13 Data dictionary

The data dictionary, sometimes called the system catalogue, of a relational database system (see Sections 2.7 and 2.8) exists usually as a set of relations which are automatically populated with details of the database system. When a user creates a new relation, or a new integrity constraint or a new database application, the RDBMS will automatically add tuples to these special relations, so as to represent information about it. Thus the data dictionary provides an automatically maintained description of the database system.

It is usually possible to use relational database languages to retrieve information about the database system from the relations which are in the data dictionary, but some systems also include a 'help' facility for this purpose and programs with which the database administrator may generate reports from the data dictionary. For example the DB2 catalogue, (DB2 is an IBM RDBMS), includes relations

> SYSTABLES   which represents information about relations
> SYSCOLUMNS which represents information about attributes.

A user, Barry, wishing to retrieve details of his relations could execute the following SQL,

```
SELECT T.NAME, C.NAME, COLTYPE
FROM SYSTABLES T, SYSCOLUMNS C
WHERE T.CREATOR = 'Barry' AND
      T.NAME = C.NAME;
```

Alternatively, as well as providing for access of data dictionary relations through the database languages, some systems enable the above information to be retrieved using a 'help' facility. For example, INGRES (Version 5) supports two relational database languages, SQL and QUEL, but also has a help facility for retrieving information from the data dictionary. The INGRES instruction,

```
HELP;
```

will retrieve a list of the current user's relations and views. Further details of a specific object may be retrieved using 'HELP object-name'. For example, further informations about a relation named PRODUCT is retrieved using,

```
HELP PRODUCT;
```

3.14 Summary

★ SQL is the international standard relational database language.

★ SQL is a relationally complete database language because it has the expressive power of the manipulative part of the relational model, relational algebra.

★ SQL may be used as a stand-alone language or its statements may be embedded within 3GL programs or used within a 4GL environment.

★ SQL has two parts:
  a) the schema definition language (SDL) is used to define the logical and physical database structures, integrity constraints, and constraints on the use of the database (see Sections 3.9 and 3.11).
  b) the data manipulation language (DML) is used to access and alter the values stored in the database (see Section 3.10).

★ The SDL and DML of SQL includes instructions for creating, destroying, accessing and updating views; views are virtual relations derived from the base relations. A problem with view is that it is not always possible unambiguously to translate updates into the corresponding updates on the base relations. SQL in fact allows updates to only a subset of the views which are known to be theoretically updatable.

★ The DML of SQL can be used to specify the start and end of transactions. At the end of a transaction it is COMMITted, in which case the changes made during that transaction are made permanent or alternatively a ROLLBACK will undo those changes.

★ SQL may also be used to access the relations which store the data dictionary or system catalogue.

Exercises

Most of the following exercises involve writing SQL expressions. The reader is advised to work through the problems using an actual RDBMS if one is available, but to be wary of the differences which exist between different implementations of SQL.

SQL – general problems

3.7   SQL is relationally complete. Explain the significance of this.

3.8   Who invented SQL, and where?

3.9   Identify three environments from within which SQL may be used.

3.10 What are the two parts of SQL and what function do they serve?

SQL schema definition language problems

3.11 a) Write the SDL CREATE TABLE statements to define the relations (create empty relations) in Figure 3.1. Make sure that you specify the integrity constraints necessary to ensure entity integrity, and that you choose appropriate data types.

   b) If you are using an actual RDBMS, fill the relations created in a) with the data given in Figure 3.1 (using the INSERT instruction).

3.12 Define indexes on the primary keys of the relations in Figure 3.1 opposite.

SQL data manipulation language problems
Retrieval from a single relation

3.13.1 Retrieve employee number, NI number, employee name, age and department number for all employees.

3.13.2 Retrieve the names of all employees.

3.13.3 Retrieve the name and NI numbers for all employees.

3.13.4 Retrieve a list of all the distinct employee names.

3.13.5 Retrieve NI numbers of all employees called J Smith.

EMPLOYEE

EMP_NO	NI_NO	NAME	AGE	DEPT_NO
E1	123	J Smith	21	D1
E2	159	J Smith	31	D1
E3	5432	R Brown	65	D2
E5	7654	M Green	52	D2

DEPARTMENT

DEPT_NO	NAME	MANAGER
D1	Accounts	E1
D2	Stores	E2
D3	Sales	null

EMPLOYEE_TELEPHONE

EMP_NO	OFFICE	EXTENSION
E1	R101	811
E1	R102	813
E2	R10	111
E3	R35	123
E5	R35	123

Figure 3.1 *Example relational database*

3.13.6 Retrieve the NI of employees called J Smith who do not work in department D2 and also the number of employees who are not called J Smith and do work in department D2.

3.13.7 Retrieve details of employees who are over 50 years old.

3.13.8 Retrieve details of employees who are between 20 and 40 years old.

3.13.9 Retrieve details of employees over 21 years old and whose names start with the letters Sm.

3.13.10 Retrieve details of departments whose name starts with S and where the third letter is r.

3.13.11 Retrieve details of departments whose names do not include the three-letter sequence /*%.

3.13.12 Retrieve details of departments without a manager.

3.13.13 Retrieve details of departments with a manager.

3.13.14 Retrieve for each employee their names and the number of years that have elapsed since they were 21 years old.

3.13.15 Retrieve the average employee age, the age of the youngest employee, and the age of the oldest.

3.13.16 Retrieve for each department, the average employee age, the age of the youngest employee, and the age of the oldest.

3.13.17 As for 3.13.16, but in ascending average age sequence.

3.13.18 As for 3.13.1, but in descending age sequence within ascending department number sequence.

Retrieval from two relations

3.13.19 Retrieve the names of employees and the names of the departments within which they work.

3.13.20 Write the SQL to perform a natural join of EMPLOYEE and DEPARTMENT. Why does it not make sense to perform this natural join?

3.13.21 Retrieve details of employees who share the telephone extension 123.

3.13.22 Retrieve details of employees who are the same age as employee E1.

More complex retrieval problems

3.13.23 Retrieve details of employees who are older than employee E1 but younger than employee E5.

3.13.24 How would you perform the outer equi-join, ojoin EMPLOYEE and DEPARTMENT where EMPLOYEE.DEPT_NO = DEPARTMENT.DEPT_NO, using ORACLE SQL and what would the result be?

3.13.25 How would you execute the outer join in 3.13.24 using an SQL which does not directly support outer join?

3.13.26 Retrieve a telephone directory containing employee names, room numbers, department numbers, and telephone extensions, which is ordered in alphabetical employee name sequence, within department number sequence.

3.13.27 a) Retrieve the employee numbers of employees on telephone extension 123.
b) Use the SQL in a) as a nested SELECT in a statement to retrieve the department numbers of the employees on extension 123.

c) Use the SQL in b) as nested SELECTs in a statement to retrieve the names of the departments of the employees on extension 123.

3.13.28 Retrieve the names of employees who are older than the oldest employee in department D1.

3.13.29 Retrieve the names of employees who are older than at least one employee in department D1.

3.13.30 Retrieve (using a nested SELECT) the names of employees who have the same age as employ E1.

3.13.31 a) Retrieve the names of employees who are managers of departments.
b) Retrieve the names of employees who do not share a telephone extension.
c) Use the UNION operator to retrieve the names of employees who are either managers of departments or who have a telephone extension to themselves.

Database update problems

3.13.32 Update the EMPLOYEE relation such that each employee's age is incremented by 1.

3.13.33 Change the name of employee E1 from J Smith to J Smyth.

3.13.34 Change the department number for all employees who are currently in department D1 to department D2.

3.13.35 Insert details of a new employee, E9, B Eagles, age 41, not yet assigned to a department.

3.13.36 Create a new relation, OLD_EMPLOYEES (EMP_NO NAME), and insert into it details of employees over 50 years old.

3.13.37 Delete details of all employees over 60 years old.

3.13.38 Delete details of the employee who is manager of department D1.

Views, integrity constraints and transactions problems

3.13.39 Define a view which includes employee numbers, their names, and the names of their departments. Is this view updatable?

3.13.40 Use the view in 3.13.39 to retrieve the names of employees in the same department as E1.

3.13.41 Define a view which includes all distinct names and department numbers of employees. Is this view updatable?

3.13.42 Define a view which includes the employees number and department numbers of managers. Is this updatable?

3.13.43 Define a view which contains the employee number and name of employees in department D1. Is this updatable?

3.13.44 Use INGRES SQL to specify that an age must be in the range 21 to 65.

3.13.45 How would you delete the integrity constraint created in 3.13.44?

3.13.46 What is a transaction?

3.13.47 Give three examples of transactions.

3.15 QUEL

SQL is now the standard query language. However, there are many other relational database languages. Given the standardisation on SQL, these are now mainly of academic and historical interest and so the coverage of QUEL, the most important of these, given below, is very brief. However QUEL is important because it is widely used in database research and it is supported by the INGRES RDBMS system.

QUEL is considered by many researchers to be a superior language to SQL. This is because it is closer to the manipulative part of the relational model and is therefore a more predictable and consistent language for the user, and a better tool for research work. QUEL is supported by the two versions of INGRES RDBMS: University INGRES which is widely available in higher education establishments and is a vehicle for much on-going research; and Commercial INGRES which is a much more extensive RDBMS (also supporting SQL and a range of 4GLs). Commercial INGRES was originally developed from University INGRES by Ingres (formerly Relational Technology Inc. (RTI) who market it as a commercial product.

3.16 Relational calculus

Like SQL, QUEL is relationally complete. That is to say, it has the expressive power of the manipulative part of the relational model. QUEL statements are very much like expressions in relational calculus, which is a form of mathematics with the same expressive power as relational algebra.

Relational algebra and relational calculus differ in the way in which they define relations: relational algebra defines a relation in terms of the operators that are applied to other relations in order to construct it; relational calculus defines a relation in terms of the conditions that must be true for each of its tuples.

The general form of relational calculus is

       Target__list : Predicate

The target__list specifies the attributes of the relation that is defined by the expression, and the predicate is the condition that must be true for each tuple in the new relation.

The predicate may include:

       the standard comparison operators: $<$, $>$, $=$, $=<$, $=>$, $!=$
       the standard logical operators: AND, OR, NOT
       the existential quantifier: $\exists$, which means 'there exists'
       the universal quantifier: $\forall$, which means 'for all'.

The use of the existential and universal quantifiers should become clear from the examples given later in this chapter.

3.17 The basic QUEL retrieval instruction

The basic retrieval instruction of QUEL (the equivalent of SELECT in SQL) has the form:

```
RETRIEVE [UNIQUE] (target__list)
WHERE       predicate
SORT BY     columns
```

This form is very close to the form of expressions in the calculus:

       target__list : predicate

SQL, on the other hand, is a mixture of calculus-like and algebra-like features.

3.18 Tutorial QUEL/relational calculus examples

Relational algebra (see Section 2.3) and SQL (see earlier in this chapter) have been explained at length. Below are a few examples of relational calculus and the corresponding QUEL commands, to give a flavour of this alternative way of expressing database operations.

The following examples are all executed against the example relational database illustrated in Fig. 3.2.

PRODUCT

PRODUCT_NO	NAME	COLOUR
P1	Pantaloons	blue
P2	Pantaloons	khaki
P3	Socks	white
P4	Socks	harebell
P7	Socks	blue

STOCK

WAREHOUSE_NO	BIN_NO	PRODUCT_NO	QTY
WH1	1	P1	100
WH1	2	P2	50
WH2	1	P2	50

Figure 3.2   *Example relational database*

Example 3.1

The following relational calculus expression represents the query 'Retrieve details of all red products'.

```
PRODUCT : PRODUCT.COLOUR = 'blue'
```

Note that the target list is PRODUCT, so the defined relation is defined on all the attributes of the PRODUCT relation.

The predicate is PRODUCT.COLOUR = 'blue'. Therefore the defined relation will include only those tuples of PRODUCT for which the COLOUR attribute has the value 'blue'. The corresponding QUEL instruction is

```
RETRIEVE UNIQUE (PRODUCT.ALL)
    WHERE PRODUCT.COLOUR = 'blue'
```

Note how similar relational calculus and QUEL are. They both basically comprise the same target list and predicate. ALL is the QUEL equivalent of * in SQL. PRODUCT.ALL means 'all the attributes of the PRODUCT relation'.

The equivalent SQL is

```
SELECT DISTINCT *
FROM PRODUCT
WHERE COLOUR = 'blue';
```

The result of executing the above QUEL is the following table (which is a representation of the relation defined by the above relational calculus),

PRODUCT_NO	NAME	COLOUR
P1	Pantaloons	blue
P7	Socks	blue

Example 3.2

This second example expresses the query, 'Find the product numbers of all products stored in warehouse WH1.'

```
PRODUCT.PRODUCT_NO : ∃ STOCK (STOCK.PRODUCT_NO = PRODUCT.PRODUCT_NO
            AND STOCK.WAREHOUSE_NO = 'WH1')
```

Note that the target list specifies that the result relation is made up of values taken from the PRODUCT_NO attribute of the PRODUCT relation.

The existential quantifier, ∃ (there exists), is used to specify that for each tuple of the result relation, there must exist a STOCK tuple such that specified conditions hold. The predicate may be put into words as follows,

∃ STOCK (	'there exists a tuple in the STOCK relation, such that,
STOCK.PRODUCT_NO = PRODUCT.PRODUCT_NO	the PRODUCT_NO has the same value as PRODUCT_NO in a tuple of the PRODUCT relation,
AND	and also
STOCK.WAREHOUSE_NO = 'WH1')	the WAREHOUSE_NO in the STOCK relation tuple has the value WH1'.

The equivalent QUEL command is

```
RETRIEVE (PRODUCT.PRODUCT_NO)
WHERE STOCK.PRODUCT_NO = PRODUCT.PRODUCT_NO AND
   STOCK.WAREHOUSE_NO = 'WH1'
```

Note that it is not necessary to include the existential quantifier, ∃, as it is implicit in the WHERE clause. STOCK appears in the condition but not in the target list, and so THERE EXISTS is assumed.

The equivalent SQL is

```
SELECT PRODUCT.PRODUCT_NO
FROM STOCK, PRODUCT
WHERE STOCK.PRODUCT_NO = PRODUCT.PRODUCT_NO AND
   STOCK.WAREHOUSE_NO = 'WH1';
```

The result of executing the above QUEL or SQL is as follows.

PRODUCT_NO
P1
P2

Example 3.3

This example of relational calculus expresses the query 'What is the number and quantity of products stored in warehouse WH1?'

```
PRODUCT.PRODUCT_NO, STOCK.QTY : ∀ PRODUCT ∃ STOCK (
    PRODUCT.PRODUCT_NO = STOCK.PRODUCT_NO AND
    STOCK.WAREHOUSE_NO = 'WH1')
```

Note that the target list specifies that the relation defined has two attributes, one of values taken from the PRODUCT_NO attribute of the PRODUCT relation, and the other of values of the QUANTITY attribute of the STOCK relation.

The universal and existential quantifiers have both been used.

```
∀ PRODUCT ∃ STOCK ...
```

reads, 'Where, for all tuples of PRODUCT, there exists a tuple of STOCK such that'. The predicate may be put into words as follows,

∀ PRODUCT	'where for all PRODUCT tuples
∃ STOCK	there exists a STOCK tuple
(	such that
PRODUCT.PRODUCT_NO = STOCK.PRODUCT_NO	the product numbers are equal
AND	and also
STOCK.WAREHOUSE_NO = 'WH1'	the warehouse number is WH1.'
)	

The equivalent QUEL instruction is as follows.

```
RETRIEVE (PRODUCT.PRODUCT_NO, STOCK.QTY)
WHERE PRODUCT.PRODUCT_NO = STOCK.PRODUCT_NO AND
  STOCK.WAREHOUSE_NO = 'WH1'
SORT BY PRODUCT.PRODUCT_NO
```

Note once again the quantifiers, ∀ and ∃ are implicit in the WHERE condition. The WHERE condition must be true for all product numbers in the defined relation, and for each of these, there must exist a STOCK tuple such that the warehouse number is equal to WH1.

The 'SORT BY fields' is added for pragmatic reasons. Though a relation has no sequence (it is a set of tuples), the user will often wish to view and process tuples in sequence, and so the SORT BY clause is included to enable him to specify the sequence of the tuples in the retrieved table. It is equivalent to the ORDER BY clause in SQL.

The equivalent SQL is

```
SELECT PRODUCT.PRODUCT_NO, STOCK.QUANTITY
FROM PRODUCT, STOCK
WHERE PRODUCT.PRODUCT_NO = STOCK.PRODUCT_NO AND
STOCK.WAREHOUSE_NO = 'WH1'
ORDER BY PRODUCT.PRODUCT_NO;
```

The result of executing the above QUEL or SQL is as follows.

PRODUCT_NO	QTY
P1	100
P2	50

Example 3.4

This example expresses 'Retrieve the product numbers of products for which there are no stocks in the warehouses', which may be expressed in relational calculus as follows.

```
PRODUCT.PRODUCT_NO : ∀ PRODUCT
  NOT ∃ STOCK (STOCK.PRODUCT_NO = PRODUCT.PRODUCT_NO)
```

The target list specifies that the relation has a single attribute of values taken from the PRODUCT_NO attribute of the PRODUCT relation.

The universal and existential quantifiers have been used.

```
∀ PRODUCT NOT ∃ STOCK ...
```

reads 'For all tuples of PRODUCT, such that there does not exist a tuple of STOCK for which the following condition is true'. The predicate may be put into words as follows.

∀ PRODUCT	'for all product tuples
NOT ∃ STOCK	there does not exist a stock tuple
(	such that
STOCK.PRODUCT_NO =	it has the same product number as
PRODUCT.PRODUCT_NO)	the product tuple'

The corresponding QUEL is as follows

```
RETRIEVE (PRODUCT.PRODUCT_NO)
WHERE ANY (STOCK.PRODUCT_NO = PRODUCT.PRODUCT_NO) = 0
```

Here the use of ANY needs some explanation. ANY returns a value of 0 if the condition in its brackets returns an empty set of tuples. Otherwise it returns a 1. ANY (. . .) = 0 is therefore like NOT EXISTS in SQL (see Section 3.10.6.3).

The equivalent SQL is

```
SELECT P.PRODUCT_NO
FROM   PRODUCT P
WHERE    NOT EXISTS
   (SELECT * FROM STOCK S
     WHERE S.PRODUCT_NO = P.PRODUCT_NO);
```

The result of the above QUEL and SQL is as follows.

PRODUCT_NO
P3
P4
P7

3.19 Other facilities

The above examples illustrate the style of database access commands in QUEL, but are not intended to provide a comprehensive overview of QUEL. Note that the facilities provided are very similar to those provided by the SQL SELECT. The difference is in the manner in which the set of tuples to be accessed is defined. QUEL more or less sticks to the form of relational calculus, and does not include any explicit use of the set operators of relational algebra, such as UNION.

The other facilities offered by QUEL are also similar to those of SQL. The retrieval facilities include aggregate functions such as COUNT and SUM. There is an equivalent of the GROUP BY facility of SQL. QUEL also includes instructions for updating, deleting and inserting tuples in relations; the instructions are REPLACE, DELETE and APPEND, respectively.

QUEL's schema definition instructions are: CREATE which is similar to CREATE TABLE in SQL; INDEX which is similar to CREATE INDEX in SQL; DEFINE VIEW which is similar to CREATE VIEW in SQL; and DESTROY which is similar to DROP in SQL.

Also INGRES QUEL includes a MODIFY instruction by which the storage structure with which a relation is physically represented may be changed. This MODIFY instruction is the same as the one supported within INGRES SQL (see Section 3.11.1).

3.20 Summary

★ QUEL, like SQL (see earlier in this chapter) is a relationally complete relational database language, i.e. it has the expressive power of the manipulative part of the relational model (see Section 2.3).

★ Though SQL is the standard, QUEL is still an important relational database language because it is favoured by many researchers and is supported by INGRES, a leading RDBMS product. Researchers favour QUEL because it is purer, in that it is very similar to relational calculus. Relational calculus is an alternative to relational algebra as a definition of the manipulative part of the relational model.

★ Expressions in relational calculus define relations by specifying the condition that must be true for member tuples. This contrasts with expressions in relational algebra where operations upon relations must be defined.

★ The general form of a QUEL retrieval statement is:

```
RETRIEVE [UNIQUE] (target_list)
WHERE      predicate
SORT BY    columns
```

This is very close to the form of expression in relational calculus:

```
target_list : predicate
```

★ QUEL is a comprehensive relational database language, and includes schema definition and data manipulation facilities similar to those of SQL (described earlier in this chapter).

Exercises

3.14 What is meant when it is said that QUEL is relationally complete?

3.15 For what reasons is QUEL sometimes preferred to SQL?

3.16 Write relational calculus and also QUEL statements corresponding to the following queries on the database in Figure 3.3.

3.16.1 Retrieve employee number, NI number, employee name, age and department number for all employees.

3.16.2 Retrieve the names of all employees.

3.16.3 Retrieve the name and NI numbers for all employees.

3.16.4 Retrieve a list of all the distinct employee names.

3.16.5 Retrieve NI numbers of all employees called J Smith.

3.16.6 Retrieve the NI number of employees called J Smith who do not work in department D2 and also of employees who are not called J Smith and do work in department D2.

3.16.7 Retrieve details of employees who are over 50 years old.

3.16.8 Retrieve the names of employees and the names of the departments within which they work.

3.16.9 Retrieve details of employees who share the telephone extension 123.

EMPLOYEE

EMP_NO	NI_NO	NAME	AGE	DEPT_NO
E1	123	J Smith	21	D1
E2	159	J Smith	31	D1
E3	5432	R Brown	65	D2
E5	7654	M Green	52	D2

DEPARTMENT

DEPT_NO	NAME	MANAGER
D1	Accounts	E1
D2	Stores	E2
D3	Sales	null

EMPLOYEE_TELEPHONE

EMP_NO	OFFICE	EXTENSION
E1	R101	811
E1	R102	813
E2	R10	111
E3	R35	123
E5	R35	123

Figure 3.3   *Example relational database*

3.21 Embedded SQL

An RDBMS will usually provide facilities for including the instructions of one or more of the database languages that it supports within programs written in a third generation language such as COBOL, FORTRAN, PL/1, Pascal, C. For example, INGRES allows both SQL and QUEL to be included in C programs. In this chapter typical facilities for including SQL within 3GL programs are described.

3.22 The mechanism for embedding SQL

The mechanism for embedding SQL within 3GL programs is typically as depicted in Figure 3.4.

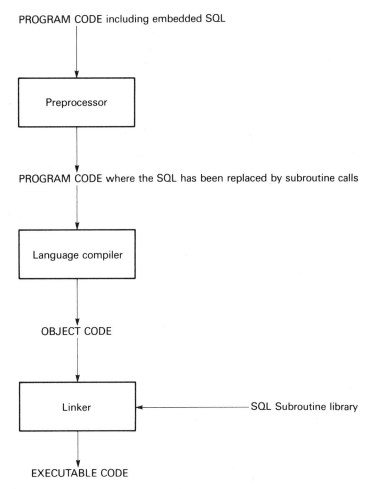

Figure 3.4   *Mechanism for including SQL in a 3GL program*

The language preprocessor changes the SQL instructions in a program into appropriate subroutine calls in the 3GL programming language. The SQL instructions are made easy for the preprocessor to identify by prefixing them with a special string of characters, SQL EXEC. The preprocessed program may then be compiled in the usual way and linked with the subroutines that are called from within the program.

The embedded SQL instructions are such that retrieved values may be transferred to the 3GL program variables. These are called host variables, because they are declared in the host programming language. The main features of embedded SQL are illustrated in the following section with the aid of an example program.

3.23 Example program

The example program listed in Figure 3.5 is written in PL/1 with embedded SQL. The problem solved by the program is 'Optionally change the area for customers in the Leeds area to the Bingley area'. The choice of programming language, PL/1, in the example program is arbitrary, since the features of embedded SQL are much the same for any third generation language. Also, the program is contrived to illustrate features within a few instructions rather than to represent a realistic application.

The main features of embedded SQL are illustrated by the example, as follows.

★ All embedded SQL statements are prefixed with a special string of characters, i.e.

        EXEC SQL . . .

★ The SQL must be able to communicate with statements in the host programming language, PL/1 in the example. This is done by the inclusion of variables, declared in the host language, within SQL instructions. In the above example C_NO, and C_NAME are PL/1 variables, and these are used in SQL statements (see line 25). All host language variables that are used in SQL must be declared within a DECLARE SECTION (lines 5–8). Host language variables are distinguished within SQL statements by prefixing them with a colon (see line 25).

★ Third generation programming languages, such as PL/1, are designed to process records one at a time, but SQL is designed to process a relation at a time. It is therefore necessary to have a facility for passing the relation output by an SQL instruction to the host programming language statements one tuple at a time. This facility is provided with the use of CURSORs.

   a) Cursors are declared for SQL retrieval statements that are to be executed within the program (see lines 12–16).
   b) An SQL retrieval statement is executed when its cursor is OPENed (line 18).
   c) Subsequently, attribute values of tuples of the retrieved relation are transferred to host language variables using a FETCH instruction (line 24). Each time FETCH is executed, it retrieves values of the next tuple in the relation retrieved by the associated SQL statement.

```
 1    EMBEDSQLEX: PROC OPTIONS (MAIN);
 2
 3      DCL ANSWER   CHAR (3);
 4
 5      EXEC SQL BEGIN DECLARE SECTION
 6         DCL C_NO   CHAR (5);
 7         DCL C_NAME       CHAR (30);
 8      EXEC SQL END DECLARE SECTION
 9
10      EXEC SQL INCLUDE SQLCA;
11
12      EXEC SQL DECLARE Z CURSOR FOR
13         SELECT CUSTOMER_NO, NAME
14         FROM CUSTOMER
15         WHERE AREA = 'Leeds'
16      FOR UPDATE OF AREA;
17
18      EXEC SQL OPEN Z
19      IF SQLCODE NOT = 0 THEN
20         GO TO QUIT;
21
22      DO WHILE (SQLCODE = 0)
23
24         EXEC SQL FETCH Z
25           INTO :C_NO, :C_NAME;
26
27         IF SQLCODE = 0 THEN DO;
28             PUT SKIP LIST ('CUSTOMER_NO=', C_NO,
29                 'NAME =', C_NAME);
30           . GET LIST (ANSWER);
31             IF ANSWER = 'YES' THEN DO;
32                 EXEC SQL UPDATE CUSTOMER
33                    SET AREA = 'Pudsey'
34                    WHERE CURRENT OF Z;
35                 IF SQLCODE NOT = 0 THEN
36                     PUT SKIP LIST ('UPDATE ERROR');
37             END;
38         END;
39
40         IF SQLCODE NOT = 100 THEN
41             PUT SKIP LIST ('SQLCODE=', SQLCODE);
42         ELSE
43         DO;
44             EXEC SQL CLOSE Z;
45             EXEC SQL COMMIT;
46         END;
47      END;
48   QUIT: RETURN;
49   END;
```

Figure 3.5   *Example PL/1 program with embedded SQL*

d) The most recently FETCHed tuple is said to be CURRENT OF the cursor. That tuple may then be manipulated by including 'CURRENT OF cursor' in the WHERE clause of the appropriate SQL statement (lines 32–34).
e) When all required processing of tuples retrieved by a specific SQL retrieval statement has taken place, the cursor is CLOSEd (line 44).
f) SELECT is an alternative SQL instruction for transferring an attribute value to a host language variable. For example,

```
SELECT C_NAME
INTO :C_NAME
FROM CUSTOMER
WHERE CUSTOMER_NO = 'C1';
```

will set the host variable, C_NAME, to the attribute value of the CUSTOMER tuple for which the attribute CUSTOMER_NO is equal to C1.

★ It is also necessary for the RDBMS to communicate to the program, for example, in order to provide information about the success or otherwise of SQL operations. This communication is done through a set of special variables in a communications area. These variables are declared for use in the program by the INCLUDE SQLCA statement (line 10).

Amongst the communications area variables is a variable called SQLCODE. Every time an SQL instruction is executed the RDBMS places a value within this variable to indicate the success or otherwise of the execution, and this variable, like other communications area variables, may be accessed by the host language instructions (lines 19, 27, 35, 40).

On successful completion of an SQL statement, SQLCODE is set to 0. A negative-valued SQLCODE indicates that an error has occurred. A positive value indicates that, though the execution was successful, some exceptional condition has occurred. SQLCODE will be set to 100 if any of the following have taken place:

a) the SQL statement was a FETCH for which a next tuple does not exist
b) the SQL was a SELECT, UPDATE, DELETE or INSERT but there were no tuples for which the WHERE condition was true.

3.24 SQL modules

Standard SQL supports an alternative method of including SQL within a third generation language program. The SQL to be used by a program may be written as a MODULE. Within this module the programmer may define a number of procedures each of which executes a single SQL statement, and these procedures may be called from the host language.

For example, consider the case where a program must execute an SQL statement to update the STOCK relation by adding to the QUANTITY attribute value for some specific tuple. The SQL to perform this operation is coded as a procedure as follows:

```
PROCEDURE UPDATE STOCK
   WH_NO    CHAR (3)
   P_NO     CHAR (3)
   B_NO     CHAR (3)
   EXTRA_STOCK    NUMERIC (5)

   UPDATE STOCK
     SET QUANTITY = QUANTITY + EXTRA_STOCK
     WHERE WAREHOUSE_NO = WH_NO AND
      PRODUCT_NO = P_NO AND
      BIN_NO = B_NO;
```

Note that the procedure definition includes:

a) a procedure name, UPDATE_STOCK;
b) a set of parameters, WH_NO, P_NO, B_NO and EXTRA_STOCK, values of which may be passed between the program that uses the procedure and the procedure itself;
c) a single SQL statement.

The program may then execute the above procedure in the same way that it would execute any other procedure written in its own language. For example, a COBOL program would execute the above procedure with the instruction,

```
CALL 'UPDATE_STOCK' USING WH, PROD, BIN, EXTRA.
```

where WH, PROD, BIN and EXTRA are COBOL variables.

All the procedures used by a particular program are declared within a single MODULE. A module is headed by a name, the name of the host language and authorisation information. For example, the above procedure may be included within a MODULE headed,

```
MODULE STOCK_CONTROL
LANGUAGE COBOL
AUTHORISATION FAIR_CHILDS
```

At the time of writing this book most RDBMSs support the first method of embedding SQL (see Section 3.2.3), but not the second (see Section 3.24).

3.25 Error handling in embedded SQL

When SQL is embedded within a third generation language, one way of detecting errors is for the program to inspect the SQLCODE variable in the communications area (see Section 3.23), but an alternative way of specifying how a program responds to errors is provided by the WHENEVER instruction. For example,

```
EXEC SQL WHENEVER SQLERROR GOTO 100
END-EXEC
```

will cause the program to branch to instructions labelled 100 when any SQL failure is detected.

3.26 Summary

★ SQL statements may be embedded within programs written in conventional third generation programming languages. This is necessary when SQL on its own provides insufficient facilities to implement the required application.

★ A preprocessor is used to convert the embedded instructions into procedure calls of the host language.

★ Alternatively, a MODULE of single-instruction SQL procedures may be created and executed from a program written in a 3GL using the 3GL facility for calling subroutines.

Exercises

3.17 What does it mean to embed SQL instructions?

3.18 Under what circumstances is it necessary to use embedded SQL, rather than stand-alone SQL?

3.19 How does the preprocessor of an embedded SQL system identify the SQL statements, and what does it do with them?

3.20 Explain how SQL MODULUEs provide an alternative to embedding SQL within the code of a 3GL program.

3.21 What are the respective purposes of SQLCODE and the WHENEVER statements?

3.27 The 4GL environment

4GLs are not exclusive to database systems, but they are usually built around a database system, normally relational. This provides the flexibility and ease of access to data that is necessary if the 4GL is to be capable of a wide variety of applications.

An important facility for the support of a 4GL environment is a data dictionary (see Sections 2.7 and 2.8) of some sort, in which details of applications may be stored, and from which the 4GL may retrieve information about the data accessed by the applications.

Typically a 4GL assumes that the database is updated by direct transaction inputs (rather than batched input). The 4GL enforces this method by imposing a fixed processing cycle: the update logic is standardised and included in a precoded procedure. This procedure then takes care of the input–update dialogue, while the user defines the screens for input and data display.

Furthermore, the 4GL will typically anticipate that applications will involve certain common tasks, such as forms definition and manipulation, database manipulation, production of reports, production of graphs, and spreadsheet manipulations.

Accordingly, the 4GL may include ready-made applications for some or all of these tasks which may be built into new applications, and special languages for specifying applications of these types. The 4GL will often make it possible to embed these special languages within programs written in conventional languages, in the same way as has been described for SQL (see Sections 3.21 to 3.26).

There are no standards for 4GL environments, and so in this chapter we first describe, as an example, the INGRES (Version 5) 4GL environment for developing database applications, and then identify some features which are general to 4GLs. This description is to give the flavour of using a 4GL environment, and is not provided as an alternative to an INGRES 4GL manual. Accordingly, the reader is advised not to labour over the detail of the examples but instead to concentrate on the concepts. The examples and explanations do not cover all the INGRES facilities.

INGRES (Version 5) is used here because that is what was available at the time of writing this book. However, it has now been superseded by later versions. Many current 4GL environments, though working in a similar manner to the example, will operate on work stations rather than terminals and these display multiple windows allowing much of the user input to be done using a pointing device such as a mouse.

3.28 The INGRES 4GL environment

The INGRES RDBMS supports two database languages, QUEL and SQL described earlier in this chapter, both of which may be used either interactively or within third generation programming languages. In addition it supports a very high-level programming language called Operations Specification Language (OSL), and a set of software tools and associated languages for rapid and relatively simple generation of applications for database manipulation, for the production of reports, for the production of graphs, and for the definition and manipulation of forms displayed on a terminal screen. OSL along with the other tools for generating data applications make up the INGRES 4GL environment which sits on top of the INGRES RDBMS as shown below.

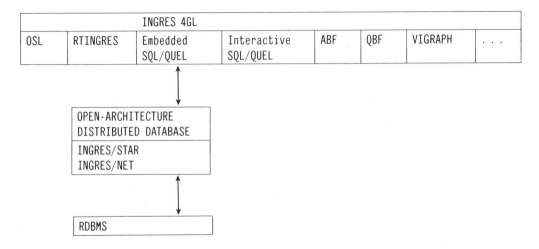

Note that the database system is split into a front end which includes the 4GL environment, and a back end RDBMS which executes SQL. The standardisation on SQL has made it possible for database system vendors to uncouple the front end products from specific RDBMSs and market them separately to sit on top of any SQL RDBMS.

The above diagram also includes the open-architecture distributed database, sandwiched between the RDBMS and the 4GL environment. The purpose of this layer is discussed in some detail in Chapter 6. The general purpose of the open-architecture distributed database is to provide a standard interface to the databases, which may be stored on a number of computers connected by a communications network.

The tools in the 4GL environment include the following.

a) QBF (Query-by-forms) is used to develop and test forms (to be displayed on a terminal screen) for specifying and executing database retrievals and updates. QBF enables the user to perform the operations that are available through QUEL or SQL, but life is made simpler for the user because by using QBF these operations are specified by filling in forms and selecting operations and parameters from menus.
b) RBF (Report-by-forms) is used to design or modify applications for generating reports.
c) GBF (Graph-by-forms) is used to design, modify or test applications for generating graphs.
d) ABF (Application-by-forms) takes the user through the task of creating, or modifying an application.
e) RTINGRES provides access to all of the INGRES tools.

There are also tools that support embedded and interactive use of SQL and QUEL, and various utilities, such as a 'visual forms editor' which makes it easier for the user to specify screens to be displayed and reports to be printed in the course of an application.

The 4GL languages and tools make use of the INGRES catalogues, which make up the INGRES data dictionary. Details of applications, as well as database structures, users and rules are stored in these catalogues.

3.29 The style of INGRES applications

The INGRES 4GL environment assumes that applications will be run on-line from terminals. When an application is run, the user solves problems by:

a) selecting operations from menus;
b) entering information in response to prompts displayed by the application;
c) providing data and parameters for operations by filling in forms displayed on screens.

In fact all of the above INGRES 4GL tools work in this manner and are themselves database applications. RTINGRES, for example, is an application which integrates the whole of INGRES and enables the user to access any of the INGRES tools, applications, and languages through filling in forms and selecting operations from menus. A typical screen, displayed in the course of an application, is illustrated by the following example.

Example 3.5

The example screen in Figure 3.6 is displayed during the execution of an application for processing sales orders. The screen enables a user to alter the details of sales orders stored in the database.

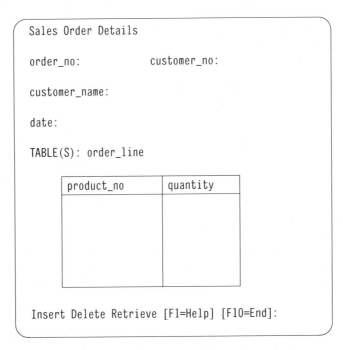

```
 Sales Order Details

 order_no:              customer_no:

 customer_name:

 date:

 TABLE(S): order_line

     ┌─────────────────┬──────────────┐
     │ product_no      │ quantity     │
     │                 │              │
     │                 │              │
     │                 │              │
     │                 │              │
     └─────────────────┴──────────────┘

 Insert Delete Retrieve [F1=Help] [F10=End]:
```

Figure 3.6   *Example application screen*

The things to note about this example screen are that there are two parts, a menu (the bottom line), and a form (the rest). The user may fill in the form in order to enter data and may select operations from the menu in order to do things with the data.

Fields in the form may be used to display retrieved or computed information, or to receive information entered by the user. For example, when the user enters a customer number, the application will retrieve the customer's name and display it. The customer_name field is for display purposes only, and may not be altered by the user. The user uses special keys (such as tab or return or the arrow keys) to move from field to field.

It is possible to move the cursor between the two parts of the screen using some special 'menu' key, e.g. function key 1. The user may move the cursor from the form to the menu and select the operation to be performed by typing the required operation name: Insert, Delete, Retrieve, End or Help. Special keys, usually function keys, are often used as an alternative to typing the name of the selected option. This reduces the number of key strokes necessary to perform operations, and therefore reduces the risk of mistyping. (In many current systems a pointing device such as a mouse may be used as an alternative to the keyboard for selecting fields and operations.)

There are two types of field that may be part of a form. These are single-value fields, such as customer_no and customer_name in the example, and table fields for sets of values, such as the fields for product_no and quantity in the example.

Screens (apart from the first in an interactive session) are displayed as a consequence of selecting options from menus, and the parameters and date values used in the selected operations are provided by entering data into fields of forms displayed on other screens. An application is usually designed as a hierarchy of screens. When an operation is selected from a menu, the screens at the level below are used to enable the user to execute that operation, and when the operation is completed, the application then returns to the screen from which the operation was selected. (Many current systems allow many forms to be displayed simultaneously as 'windows'.)

There are a number of advantages in the above form/menu style of application.

a) All applications are similar, and so the user always knows how to run an application by filling in forms and selecting from menus.
b) There is consistency within an application. All operations made available by an application are provided with data and executed in a similar way.
c) When a user is performing some operation, the current form will display all information on which the user is working. This provides the user with a context for supplying extra data values, or for understanding the significance of retrieved or computed data.
d) Forms and menus are familiar to most users, even those lacking computer skills. All users will have come across paper forms which they have had to fill in and menus from which they have had to make selections, e.g. tax forms, restaurant menus, etc.

3.30 Frames, procedures and relations

An application comprises a set of frames, procedures and relations.

3.30.1 Frames

A Frame is a form and a menu of operations (as shown above in Example 3.5).

There are four different types of frame which may occur in an application, three of which correspond to ready-written applications which are part of the INGRES system. The three ready-written application frame types are:

QBF frames	for calls to the forms based on the database manipulation application QBF (Query-by-Forms)
GBF frames	for calls to the graph writer application GBF (Graph-by-Forms)
Report frames	for calls to the report writer application.

Using the above types of frames, a user may construct an application from existing INGRES applications.

It is also possible for the implementor to define new frames for operations other than those available in QBF, GBF and the report writer. These are called user-specified frames. For each user-specified frame, the implementor must create the associated form using the visual forms editor, and must define the associated menu using the OSL.

3.30.2 Procedures

Some of the operations that may be selected from a menu may cause procedures encoded in OSL and/or other programming languages such as Pascal, COBOL, FORTRAN, or C, to be executed. A procedure will typically include embedded SQL or QUEL to access the database (see Sections 3.21 to 3.26). Procedures must be coded in the appropriate programming language and described to the application.

3.30.3 Relations

The application will access relations in the database, and for some applications it will be necessary to create new relations.

3.31 Operations Specification Language (OSL)

The OSL is used to define menus associated with frames and the associated operations. Some example OSL code is included below in the example application (see Section 3.34). This section provides a preliminary overview of the types of facility provided by OSL.

OSL code is associated with each user-specified frame in an application. This code specifies the operations that a user may select. The code is a list of specifications, each of which describes what must happen in one or more of the following circumstances:

a) initialisation, i.e. when the frame is first executed,
b) menu item, i.e. when a menu item is selected by the user,
c) field activation, i.e. when a user has entered data into a specified field,
d) key activation, i.e. when the user presses a function or control key.

The following OSL facilities may be used in defining the operations associated with the above events.

Database and form access
OSL includes facilities for directly accessing fields in the form displayed on the terminal screen and also for accessing and manipulating data in the database. In this respect it is more convenient than using a third generation language with appropriate embedded statements. In the 3GL it is necessary to embed statements from two different languages, one to access the database, and the other to access the form. In OSL it is possible to use SQL or QUEL statements which include 'forms field' variables.

Local variables and computation

OSL has facilities for computation. It is possible to declare variables for use in calculations, and to perform calculations using values taken from the database and screen.

Loops and decisions

The INGRES 4GL environment is hybrid in that it includes facilities for procedural logic, and for dropping down into conventional third generation languages when the 'ready-made' application logic built into the 4GL environment proves to be inadequate to meet the user's requirements. Accordingly, the OSL includes IF . . . THEN . . . ELSE . . . type instructions for conditional execution of operations. Also, it is possible to execute procedures written in third generation languages from OSL.

Frames

OSL includes facilities for displaying new frames and for terminating the execution of frames. This facility is used in creating a hierarchy of frames. For example, when the first frame of an application is displayed, it typically provides the user with a menu of the operations that may be performed by the applications. When the user makes a selection, the OSL associated with this first frame must cause the frame associated with the selected operation to be displayed. When the user has completed the operation, the OSL of the selected frame must be able to terminate itself and pass control back to the first frame.

3.32 Application-by-forms (ABF)

The user is guided through the process of creating the frames, procedures and relations of an application by a special application called Application-by-forms (ABF). ABF enables the user to describe the application to be programmed, mainly by filling in forms and selecting operations from menus. ABF leads the user through the following steps.

a) Create appropriate entries in the data dictionary in order to describe the application to the database system.
b) Determine the frames in the application and then define the procedures.
c) Test the application during the definition stage. In the course of determining the frames and procedures, the application may be executed in its various stages of completion. In this way the implementor may test the application as each new frame or procedure is defined, in a bottom-up or top-down manner.
d) Create an executable image of the application.
e) Run the executable image from the operating system.

ABF enables the user to perform all of the above tasks through the use of the 'standard' form/menu interface described above.

3.33 Designing an INGRES application

Traditionally, application generation should be preceded by appropriate systems analysis and design procedures, perhaps using some methodology such as SSADM. These procedures are used to analyse the information of interest, and the activities of the organisation. This analysis is then used as a basis for designing appropriate computer systems. An output from the systems analysis and design will be a set of requirements for the applications to be created. These requirements will state the services to be provided by each application and the constraints under which they will be provided.

In practice, a 4GL environment, such as ABF, makes it simpler, cheaper and faster to create new applications. A consequence is that users have a greater say in determining their own applications. When it was the case that all applications had to be developed using third generation languages, the user was very much in the hands of the computer specialists. The months that went into designing and programming or making alterations to an application made it impracticable or uneconomic for the user to oversee the development of an application and to dictate alterations to the implemented application. However, this is no longer the case where a 4GL environment is used.

The user has greatest control over the development of applications where the computing resources are devolved to the departments or users, through the use of small departmental or personal computers, perhaps connected to each other and to central computer resources through some communications network. In such cases extensive systems analysis and design procedures are often omitted, and the implementation of an application may be initiated by a 'wouldn't it be nice if we could . . .' type of request. The requested system may then be developed using the prototyping approach previously described (see Section 3.3). In such cases the computer professional will act mainly in an advisory role.

Once a particular application has been requested, the designer of an application must decide on:

a) the external appearance of the application in terms of the screens that will be displayed and the reports that will be produced,
b) what data must be accessed,
c) what operations must be performed in order to manipulate the data.

The implementor of the application has two tasks. The application structure must be specified in terms of the frames and procedures. This structure defines the 'flow' of the application, i.e. the sequence in which frames call other frames or procedures. Secondly individual frames and procedures must be designed.

It is also necessary for the implementor to decide on the privacy and security aspects that must be built into the application. A third task is therefore to decide on any restrictions on access to parts of the application. For example, it may be decided that only certain members of staff may have access to sensitive information or to activities to do with the transfer of money.

Designing the application to be created is very much simpler than designing a conventional applications program to be implemented in a third generation language. The 4GL environment makes the above design simpler on two accounts.

Firstly, the operations to be performed must be defined in terms of formulas, report and screen layouts, and database manipulation operations (expressed in the database language); but for many applications, the implementor need not define how they are to be implemented in terms of loops, decisions and sequences. The task is more like specifying what a program is to do, rather than deciding how the program is to work. The implementor therefore does not necessarily require programming skills.

Much of the application design is done by 'painting' images of the required screens using a terminal, rather than by writing sequences of instructions in a programming language. Also, much of the information required to implement the application is solicited from the designer by the 4GL tools, either in a question and answer style, or a 'please, fill in the form' style.

Secondly, the implementor may use ready-made ('default') frames for standard operations, and, for near-standard operations, the implementor may tailor ready-made frames.

3.34 Example application

3.34.1 Requirements

The design and generation of an application using ABF is illustrated by the narrative given below, which describes some of the steps necessary to create a simplified 'sales dispatch' application.

The application requirement is 'for an application which will enable sales orders to be recorded and dispatch documents and corresponding picking lists to be produced. A picking list is to enable the warehouse workers to select the ordered products from the stores and put them together into loads to be dispatched to the customers'.

3.34.2 Application structure

The following hierarchical structure is decided on.

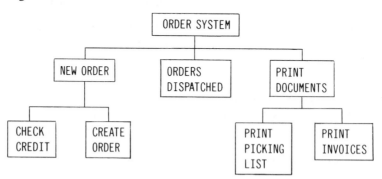

The boxes represent frames and procedures of the application and the lines represent where a frame activates another frame or procedure. The frame or procedure represented by the box above activates the one represented by the box below. Note that the system has a typical hierarchical structure. The user selects to perform a particular operation at the first level and then drops down to the level below to use the frames and procedures in order to perform that operation. On completion, the user returns to level 1 to select some other operation.

3.34.3 Screen design

The design of the individual screens associated with the frames and the manner in which they are used is illustrated below by a typical sequence of screens.

Screen 1

On entering the ORDER system the following screen is displayed.

```
    FAIR-CHILDS ORDER SYSTEM
1 New Order Entry
2 Orders Dispatched
3 Print Documents
Your Choice: 1


New_Order Dispatch Documents End(F9)
```

This is the main menu which enables the user to select one of the three operations available, or to terminate the application. On completion of each operation the system returns to this screen.

This screen has been designed to illustrate a number of different ways of selecting operations.

a) The user may enter a value into a field of the form, e.g. enter 1, 2 or 3 into the Your Choice field.
b) The user may select operations from the menu. To do this the user must press the special 'menu' key, and then type sufficient of the name of the operation to uniquely identify it, e.g. Di would select Dispatch.
c) The user may press specified keys in order to select operations. For example, the function key F9 will select End.

In the example execution, the user selects New Order Entry by entering a '1' in the Your Choice field, so as to display the screens which enable him to enter details of a new sales order.

Screen 2

```
    FAIR-CHILDS ORDER SYSTEM
Customer Number: C1
Customer Name: Nippers Ltd
Balance: 200.00
Credit Limit: 500.00

Accept Reject End(F9)
```

The user enters the Customer Number and the system retrieves and displays details of the customer, i.e. Customer Name, Balance, and Credit Limit. This information is necessary for the user to decide whether to accept or reject the customer's sales order.

In this example, the user then selects Accept from the menu.

Screen 3

```
┌─────────────────────────────────────────────────────────┐
│                                                           │
│         FAIR-CHILDS ORDER SYSTEM                          │
│    Customer Order Number: 1234X                           │
│    Fair-Childs Order Number: 089                          │
│                                                           │
│                                                           │
│    ┌───────────────────┬──────────────┬──────────────┐   │
│    │ Product Number    │ Product Name │ Order Quantity│  │
│    │ P1                │ Pantaloons   ·│ 100          │   │
│    │ P3                │ Socks        │ 200          │   │
│    │                   │              │              │   │
│    │                   │              │              │   │
│    │                   │              │              │   │
│    └───────────────────┴──────────────┴──────────────┘   │
│    Accept Forget End(F9)                                  │
│                                                           │
└─────────────────────────────────────────────────────────┘
```

The Customer Order Number and Fair-Childs Order Number are displayed as information fields, and may not be altered by the user. The user must enter the Product Numbers and Quantity. When a product number is entered the product name is automatically retrieved from the database and displayed, and may not be altered by the user.

Note that this form includes two types of field, simple fields and table fields. The simple fields, Customer Order Number, and Fair-Childs Order Number, are for single values, and the rest of the form is a table field for a table of order line details.

On completion of the above order entry, the user selected the Accept operation from the menu. The order details are added to the database, and the application returns to the first screen, the main menu. If the user had selected the Forget operation the order information would have been forgotten and no changes made to the database.

Screen 4

```
┌───────────────────────────────────────────┐
│                                           │
│       FAIR-CHILDS ORDER SYSTEM            │
│    1 New Order Entry                       │
│    2 Orders Dispatched                     │
│    3 Print Documents                       │
│    Your Choice:                            │
│                                           │
│    New_Order Dispatch Documents End(F9)    │
│                                           │
└───────────────────────────────────────────┘
```

The example user next selects Orders Dispatched.

Screen 5

```
┌──────────────────────────────────────────────────────────────┐
│                                                                │
│        FAIR-CHILDS ORDER SYSTEM                                │
│          Orders Dispatched                                     │
│   Fair-Childs Order Number: 089                                │
│   Customer Number:          C1                                 │
│   Date of Order:            12/12/89                           │
│                                                                │
│                                                                │
│    ┌─────────────────┬────────────────┬─────────────────┐     │
│    │ Product Number  │ Product Name   │ Order Quantity   │     │
│    │ P1              │ Pantaloons     │ 100              │     │
│    │ P3              │ Socks          │ 200              │     │
│    │                 │                │                  │     │
│    │                 │                │                  │     │
│    │                 │                │                  │     │
│    └─────────────────┴────────────────┴─────────────────┘     │
│                                                                │
│   Accept Reject End(F9)                                        │
│                                                                │
└──────────────────────────────────────────────────────────────┘
```

The user enters the order number, and the system retrieves and displays details of the order lines. These details may then be altered by the user, e.g. if there is insufficient of a product in stock to meet the order a smaller quantity may be dispatched.

The user selects Accept and details of the dispatch are written to the database. If the user had selected Reject then no change would have been made to the database. After Accept or Reject the form is filled with blanks and the user may process another dispatch. End returns the user to the main menu.

Screen 6

```
┌──────────────────────────────────────────────────┐
│                                                    │
│        FAIR-CHILDS ORDER SYSTEM                    │
│     1 New Order Entry                              │
│     2 Orders Dispatched                            │
│     3 Print Documents                              │
│     Your Choice:                                   │
│                                                    │
│     New_Order Dispatch Documents End(F9)           │
│                                                    │
└──────────────────────────────────────────────────┘
```

This time the user has selected to print out the documents associated with the sales order.

Screen 7

```
     FAIR-CHILDS ORDER SYSTEM
 * Print Picking List
 * Print Invoices

 Picking Invoices End(F9)
```

In this example, the user selects to print the picking list.

Screen 8

```
     FAIR-CHILDS ORDER SYSTEM
 Produce Picking List

 Confirm Cancel End(F9)
```

The user select the Confirm option from the menu, and the system then produces the required documents. On completion, the application returns to the level above to enable the user to print other documents.

Screen 9

```
     FAIR-CHILDS ORDER SYSTEM
 * Print Picking List
 * Print Invoices

 Picking Invoices End(F9)
```

This time the user selects Print Invoices.

Screen 10

```
     FAIR-CHILDS ORDER SYSTEM
 Produce Invoices

 Confirm Cancel End(F9)
```

The user selects Confirm and the system produces the required documents. On completion the application returns to the print menu.

Screen 11

```
    FAIR-CHILDS ORDER SYSTEM
* Print Picking List
* Print Invoices

Picking Invoices End(F9)
```

This time the special 'End' key is pressed, and the system returns to the main menu.

Screen 12

```
    FAIR-CHILDS ORDER SYSTEM
1 New Order Entry
2 Orders Dispatched
3 Print Documents
Your Choice:

New_Order Dispatch Documents End(F9)
```

Finally, the user once again presses the 'End' key, and the application terminates.

3.34.4 Frame definition

The following narrative details how some of the frames of the above example application are defined using ABF.

3.34.4.1 Creating the main menu frame

A description of the FAIR-CHILDS ORDER SYSTEM main menu frame is created and stored by the following screen dialogue with the ABF application.

Step 1: Specifying the type of frame
The main ABF screen menu includes a DEFINE operation. If this is selected, ABF then prompts for the following information about the 'object' to be defined.

a) Type of object to be defined, (frame, relation or procedure)? We are defining a frame.
b) Name of the frame? We shall call it 'mainmenu'.
c) Type of frame? USER (rather than QBF, REPORT or GRAPH).
d) Database language to be used? We shall use SQL (rather than QUEL).

Step 2: Defining the form
ABF now displays the 'user-specified frame definition' screen. The next task is to define the screen layout. This is done using the visual forms editor which may be selected from the menu of the current screen.

ABF now displays the visual forms editor screen. A new frame is being created, and so the CREATE option is selected from the menu. The editor now enables us to select a standard form, based on the attributes of relations in the database, or a blank form. We choose to start with a blank form. The visual forms editor allows the user to compose a form from fields, trim and blank lines.

Fields. A field is an area of the screen where values may be displayed, and/or into which the user may enter values. Each field has a field title and the data area, which has a type, e.g. character, numeric, date or money. Various attributes may also be associated with each field. For example, we may associate validation checks, we may make it 'display only' so as to protect it from being altered by the user, we may make it mandatory for the user to enter data into the field. Fields may be for single values, or for tables of values. For example, there is an example of a table field in the new sales order screen of the above FAIR-CHILDS ORDER SYSTEM. There is only one single-value field in the main menu, i.e. the part of the screen into which the user enters the selected option number.

Trim. Trim is the name given to the characters on the screen which are there to make it more intelligible. The title line and the three lines explaining the three choices of the main menu are trim.

Blank lines. A screen may include blank lines to space out the trim and fields.

Fields, trims or blank lines are added to the form under construction by positioning the cursor at the position of the screen where the object is to be added, and selecting the CREATE option from the menu. When an object is CREATEd, ABF then presents appropriate forms, prompts and menus so that the designer may specify the details of the object. Objects may be deleted in a similar way, i.e. by moving the cursor to the object on the screen and selecting the DELETE option. In this way the screen is 'painted'.

The only field of the main menu is defined as having a type of CHARACTER(1), and its attributes are:

a) it is a mandatory field, which means that the user *must* enter a value in this field,
b) the internal name of the field is the default name 'yourchoice',
c) the validation check on values entered into this field is

   'yourchoice > 0 and yourchoice < 4'

d) the error message that is displayed when an invalid value is entered is

   'Choice must be in range 1 to 3'.

When the screen has been defined its definition is saved and added to the application by selecting the SAVE option from the menu. This returns ABF up a level to the 'user-specified frame definition' screen.

Step 3: Defining the menu

The next task in defining a frame is to create the associated OSL code. To do this the EDIT option is selected from the menu. This causes ABF to enter a text editor (the text editor to be used is specified when INGRES is installed). The OSL code for the main menu is as follows.

```
    field yourchoice = {              /* The following is executed
                                      when the user places a
                                      value in the 'your choice'
                                      field. */
      if yourchoice = 1 then
         callframe neworders;        /* The 'callframe' instruction */
      elseif yourchoice = 2 then     /* is used to execute other */
         callframe ordsdisp;         /* frames. Here the next frame */
      elseif yourchoice = 3 then     /* is selected on the basis of */
         callframe printmenu;        /* the value of 'your choice'. */
    }
    'New_Order' {                    /* The following is executed
                                      when 'New_Order' is selected
                                      from the menu. */

      callframe neworders;
    }
    'Dispatch' {                     /* The following is executed
                                      when 'Dispatch' is selected
                                      from the menu. */

      callframe ordsdisp;
    }
    'Documents' {                    /* The following is executed
                                      when 'Documents' is selected
                                      from the menu. */

      callframe printmenu;
    }
    'End(F9)', Key frskey9 = {       /* The following is executed
                                      when 'End' is selected
                                      from the menu, or when the
                                      key designated 'frskey9'
                                      has been pressed. */
      return;                        /* 'return' terminates
                                      execution of this frame. */

    }
```

The above OSL illustrates the following points. Comments have been included in the above OSL so as to make it self-explanatory. (Comments are bounded by /* and */.) Note that this OSL is mainly non-procedural in that it does not specify the sequence in which things are done and does not specify loops. It is a list of specifications each of which is associated with a field of the form, or with a menu option, or with a special key. The order of this list is not important. The above OSL illustrates how one frame can be activated by another. The 'callframe' instruction causes the named frame to be executed.

Once the OSL code has been input the designer will exit from the editor, causing ABF to return to the 'user-specified frame definition' screen. The OSL may then be checked for syntax errors by selecting the COMPILE option from the menu. Once the screen has been defined (using the visual forms editor), and the OSL has been created, we have a complete frame definition. ABF returns to the 'application definition' menu when the user selects the END option from the menu, or when the special 'End' key is pressed.

Step 4: Testing the application
The above steps have created part of the SALES ORDER application. ABF enables the designer to execute frames and procedures of an incomplete application. To execute the main menu frame, the designer selects the GO option from the menu. The implementor may then test for errors by looking at the displayed screens to make sure that everything is correctly displayed and by entering values in the displayed forms or making selections from the menus and checking that the application responds correctly. The frame specification created in Steps 1 to 3 can, if necessary, be edited to remove any errors.

3.34.4.2 Creating other frames

Other user frames are specified in the manner described above, i.e. using the visual forms editor to 'paint' the screens and the system editor to create the associated OSL code. The OSL code for the first 'new order' frame is given below to illustrate some other features of the OSL.

```
initialize (rcount = integer4) = {     /* 'initialize' is executed
                                        when the frame is first displayed.
                                        This type of specification is
                                        usually used to declare
                                        and initialize variables. */
    rcount = 0;
}
field 'customernumb' = {               /* The following is executed
                                        when a value is entered into
                                        the 'customer number' field. */
  neworders :=                         /* First, customer details are */
    select customername = cust_name,
                                        /* retrieved from the database */
       balance = balance,              /* and displayed in the form. */
       creditlimit = credit_limit
       from customer
       where cust_no = :customernumb;
  inquire_ingres (rcount = rowcount);
                                        /* rcount is set to the number
                                        of customer tuples retrieved
                                        by the previous instruction */
  if rcount < 1 then                   /* If no customer tuple were found
                                        then a message is displayed. */
    message 'Customer does not exist';
    sleep 2;                           /* 'sleep 2' suspends the application
                                        for 2 seconds, to give the
                                        user a chance to read the message.
                                        The user can then enter other form
                                        data, or make another menu selection */
    endif;
}
```

```
'Accept' = {                              /* The 'callframe' statement
                                          passes the customer number to
                                          the called frame */
    callframe new2(new2.cust_no := customernumb);
}
'End(F9)', Key frskey 9 = {
    return;
}
```

The above OSL is a list of specifications associated with fields and special keys, but it illustrates some additional facilities. Note that the above OSL includes an `initialize` section which is executed when the frame is first displayed, and is usually used to declare variables and assign initial values to them. The OSL also includes SQL for retrieving values from the database into fields in the form. The full range of SQL instructions may be included in the OSL code.

The `inquire_ingres` statement retrieves from the RDBMS the number of rows retrieved by the SQL into the OSL variable, `rcount`. The `message` instruction causes the specified message to be displayed on the screen, and `sleep` causes the application to wait for a specified period of time, to give the user a chance to read the message. Note also that the `callframe` instruction passes values to the specified frame. OSL includes facilities for passing values to and from frames and procedures.

3.34.4.3 Creating the picking lists report frames

The RBF (Report-by-forms) application may be entered from ABF and used to create report frames, i.e. frames which create printed reports. The example application includes two report frames, i.e. for printing the picking list and for printing the invoice documents.

An RBF screen enables the designer to specify the report name, type and style. When a report name corresponds to the name of a relation or view, then a default report specification is created which may be further tailored to the designer's requirements if desired.

In the case of the picking list, the information to be listed is contained in the view created by the SQL instruction,

```
CREATE VIEW pickview (prod_no, prod_name, ord_no, ord_qty)
AS SELECT P.PRODUCT_NO, NAME, OL.ORDER_NO, QUANTITY
   FROM   PRODUCT P, ORDER_LINE OL
   WHERE  P.PRODUCT_NO = OL.PRODUCT_NO;
```

The report frame is named 'pickview' and the 'default' style of report is specified. RBF automatically creates a report specification similar to the following.

```
┌─────────────────────────────────────────────────────────────────┐
│  ─────────────────Title──────────────────Title──────────────     │
│                                                                   │
│      report on Table: pickview                                    │
│                                                                   │
│  ───────────Column-Headings───────────Column-Headings────────     │
│                                                                   │
│  Prod_no           Prod_name        Ord_no          Ord_qty       │
│                                                                   │
│  ───────────Detail-Lines───────────────Detail-Lines──────────     │
│                                                                   │
│  c____            c_____      i_____        i_____         │
│                                                                   │
│  ─────────────End-of-Detail─────────────End-of-Detail────────     │
│  ───────────────────────────────────────────────────────────     │
└─────────────────────────────────────────────────────────────────┘
```

Note that the report specification defines the report and column headings, and the types for the values to be printed below the headings.

The visual forms editor may be used to modify the above specification. For the example application it is necessary only to modify the title and column headings. Thus the report specification becomes

```
┌─────────────────────────────────────────────────────────────────┐
│  ─────────────────Title──────────────────Title──────────────     │
│                                                                   │
│      Fair-Childs Picking List                                     │
│                                                                   │
│  ───────────Column-Headings───────────Column-Headings────────     │
│                                                                   │
│  Product Number   Product Name    Order Number   Order Quantity   │
│                                                                   │
│  ───────────Detail-Lines───────────────Detail-Lines──────────     │
│                                                                   │
│  c____            c_____      i_____        i_____         │
│                                                                   │
│  ─────────────End-of-Detail─────────────End-of-Detail────────     │
│  ───────────────────────────────────────────────────────────     │
└─────────────────────────────────────────────────────────────────┘
```

On returning to RBF, it is possible to specify the order of the rows in the report by selecting the ORDER option from the menu. This enables the designer to specify the fields that are to be used as sort keys, ascending or descending, and whether there is to be a break in the report when a value changes. In the case of the picking lists report the designer specified the following order information,

Column Name	Sequence	Direction	Break?
prod_no	1	a	y
prod_name	0		
ord_no	2	a	n
ord_qty	0		

meaning that the report is to be sorted by order number, within product number, both in ascending order, and that there will be a gap in the report before each new product number. On completion the report definition may be saved and added to the applications frames.

3.34.4.4 The complete application

Other frames are created in ways similar to those described above. When the complete application has been assembled and tested, an operation in the ABF menu enables the user to compile it so that it may be run from the operating system level.

3.35 General comments about application generation

The above description of application generation using the INGRES 4GL environment illustrates many of the features common to 4GL environments.

Style of application. The applications generated are on-line. The user runs the application by selecting operations from menus and filling in forms. The software for generating the application can display forms and menus and enables the user to use them, and so all the user must do is describe the format of the forms and the operations associated with fields and menu items.

Hybrid 4GL. The INGRES 4GL environment is an example of a hybrid 4GL. Though many applications may be specified by specifying what the application must do, rather than how they do it, it is not possible to solve all problems in this way. For this reason, the 4GL provides access to conventional third generation languages with embedded database language statements, and the very high-level language, OSL, includes some procedural facilities for specifying loops, sequences and decisions. A pure 4GL would not have these procedural facilities and would therefore lack the flexibility to generate non-standard applications.

Special languages. A 4GL environment will often include support for a number of special languages, e.g. for defining reports, graphs and forms. There may also be easy-to-use ways of generating code in these languages. For example, the user may specify reports and graphs by filling in forms, or by painting images of them on a screen, or by modifying default forms.

Complexity. A 4GL environment will usually make it very easy to create many straightforward applications but there is no way of avoiding some complexity when the application deviates from the type of applications assumed in the 4GL software.

3.36 Summary

★ A pure 4GL environment makes possible the generation of applications from a specification of what the application must do, rather than how it must do it. This is possible because the knowledge of how to implement certain standard types of application is built into the 4GL environment.

★ A hybrid 4GL environment will also include facilities for procedural programming, which allows creation of non-standard applications. The INGRES 4GL has been described as an example of such a language.

★ 4GLs typically include ready-made applications for standard tasks such as spreadsheet and database manipulation, and generation of graphics and reports. These may be incorporated into new applications.

★ Applications generated using 4GLs are typically operated on-line by filling in forms and selecting from menus. These are displayed either as windows or as a succession of screens, and the user uses the keyboard and/or some pointing device such as a mouse to enter data and make selections.

Exercises

3.22 What is a 4GL and under what circumstances is it used?

3.23 What are the limitations of a pure 4GL and how are these overcome using a hybrid 4GL?

3.24 In what manner does an application generated using a 4GL typically operate?

3.25 What are the components of an application generated using the INGRES 4GL, and what is the purpose of each?

3.26 Identify four ready-made applications typically included in a 4GL environment.

3.27 Write a report for the manager of a computer services department justifying a change from file to relational database technology in terms of programmer productivity.

3.28 If you have access to an RDBMS fourth generation environment, analyse its capabilities and write a report on the environment's limitations, identifying cases where a 3GL with embedded SQL would provide better solutions.

4 Relational database design

4.1 Introduction

This chapter discusses how relational databases are designed. The two phases of the design process are: logical database design, in which the designer decides on the logical structures, i.e. the relations, of the database; and physical database design, in which the designer decides how the relations are to be physically represented, e.g. using files, indexes, etc. The two main approaches to logical database design are entity attribute relationship analysis and data aggregation. These methods are described in Sections 4.3 to 4.9. Sections 4.10 to 4.15 explain normalisation, which is the process of improving a logical database design by modifying it so that it satisfies various constraints which avoid unnecessary duplication of data. Finally, Section 4.16 onwards discusses physical database design and describes widely used methods for physically representing relations.

4.2 Logical database design

Logical database design is the process of designing a database such that the structure of the database is the same as the structure of the part of the real world about which the data represents information. A well-designed database should be a model of the part of the world that is of interest to the organisation that it serves. In the following sections we discuss some basic ideas and general approaches to logical database design.

4.3 Types and occurrences

When discussing logical database design it is necessary to distinguish between types and occurrences. A logical database design will describe the types of thing that are of interest, rather than the actual occurrences of those things. The occurrences will be described by the data that is stored in the database.

Example 4.1

Fair-Childs wish to represent information about customers, i.e. things of type 'customer'. Super-Brat Ltd is an actual customer, and is an occurrence of a thing of type 'customer'.

4.4 Entities, attributes and relationships

The structure of the information that is to be represented in a database is thought of in terms of three types of component:

165

entities, i.e. the things about which the data represents facts,
attributes, i.e. facts about entities,
relationships, i.e. connections that may exist between entities.

Sometimes we shall want to represent facts about a relationship, in which case the relationship is another entity, an association entity.

Example 4.2

The Fair-Childs children's clothing business must represent entities, attributes and relationships within their database, e.g.

a) Derek and Sue Fairchild are interested in products, customers, suppliers, and sales orders. These are entities.
b) Fair-Childs must record certain facts about each of these entities, such as customer name and address. A customer name and address are attributes of customer entities.
c) There are various relationships between entities that must also be recorded. For example, there is a relationship between a customer and the sales orders placed by that customer.
d) A sales order may be thought of as a relationship between a customer and the products that the customer wishes to purchase. However, there are facts about the sales order itself, such as order date, and quantities ordered, and so a sales order is an association entity, with order date and quantity ordered being attributes.
e) There may be many actual sales orders current and these are the occurrences of the sales order entity. Similarly each employee is an occurrence of the employee entity type. However, it is possible to have an entity for which there are no occurrences. For instance, a new manufacturing organisation may not yet have any occurrences of the customer entity.

An entity is anything about which we wish to represent facts. It may be an object, an event or an activity. Sometimes we may be interested in facts about a relationship between other entities, in which case that relationship is also an entity (an association entity). However, it is not always obvious which of these a particular entity is, or whether a particular value represents an attribute or an entity. For example, is marriage a relationship, an event, an activity, an object or an attribute? In fact marriage may be viewed as any or all of these. Analysis of the world is subjective and different individuals may produce different, but equally valid, analyses. Database designers take a very selective view of the world and categorise the things that they observe within the context of the intended database applications.

The following definitions of entity, attribute and relationship reflect the fact that an entity is very much in the eye of the beholder. The important thing is that what designers identify as an entity does correspond to something in the real world about which they are interested, and which exists independently of whether or not facts are known about it. For example, customers may be thought of as entities, because they do not cease to exist if we do not know their names and addresses.

★ *Entity.* An entity is a thing which has independent existence in the real world, and for which there exist facts that are of interest to us.

★ *Attribute*. Facts about an entity are to do with some quality, feature or characteristic of the entity. We call a particular type of fact an attribute.
★ *Entity identity*. Each occurrence of an entity must be uniquely identifiable. That is to say, it must have attributes that provide a unique name or key for it.
★ *Relationships*. Facts about an entity may identify other entities, e.g. a fact about a customer may be that he deals through a particular sales office. These cross-references between entities represent relationships or associations between entities.

4.5 Information gathering

Logical database design is based upon information about the organisation that the database is to serve. This information may be gathered in the following ways:

a) by observing the organisation working,
b) by talking to the individuals and particularly those who are experts within different areas of operation within the organisation,
c) by inspecting documents within the organisation and, in particular, those used to record data,
d) by surveying experts within the areas of operation using questionnaires,
e) by using other information already known by the individuals carrying out the design exercise.

This information-gathering exercise will result in a documented description of the organisation, possibly in the form of a set of descriptions, each describing the organisation from the viewpoint of a different area of operation. These descriptions are gathered as a preliminary to logical database design, during which they are analysed in order to deduce the existence of types of entity, attribute and relationship.

4.6 Data analysis and design

There are two major stages to logical database design: data analysis and data design. Data analysis produces from the organisation's description, a model of the organisation, and data design implements that model using the structures of the data model of the DBMS (see Figure 4.1).

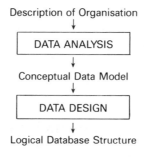

Figure 4.1   *Logical database design*

4.6.1 Data analysis

Data analysis is the first stage of the logical database design process, and its objective is to determine the natural structure of the data. Data analysis, or data modelling as it is sometimes called, takes as input a description of the organisation (see Section 4.5), and produces a model of the part of the world about which the database is to represent information. This model describes the world in terms of the things about which the data is to represent information, and relationships between them, and is called a conceptual data model.

The conceptual data model is not usually expressed in terms of the relational model. The reason for this is that the relational model is not a very good vehicle for expressing the meaning of data. The relational model does not include any way of explicitly expressing how relations and their attributes correspond to real world objects.

The building blocks from which a conceptual data model is constructed include symbols for representing types of entities, attributes and relationships. Entities and relationships are usually represented in diagrammatical form, where boxes represent entity types and connecting lines represent the relationships.

Example 4.3

Customer, sales order and product type entities and the relationships between them may be depicted by the following data structure diagram.

The above diagram depicts three entity types CUSTOMER, SALES ORDER and PRODUCT and two relationship types represented by the connecting lines. 'Crow's-feet' on the ends of the lines indicate where many entities may be connected by a relationship. The relationships are that an occurrence of CUSTOMER may be related to zero, one, two or more occurrences of SALES ORDER, but that each occurrence of SALES ORDER is related to only one CUSTOMER, and that an occurrence of PRODUCT may be related to zero, one, two or more occurrences of SALES ORDER, and that each occurrence of SALES ORDER may be related to many occurrences of PRODUCT.

4.6.2 Top-down and bottom-up analysis

There is no consensus on what is the best method of data analysis. However, data analysis methods do generally fall into one of two categories, top-down and bottom-up, though some methods include a bit of each. Top-down is working from a general analysis of things to the detail, and bottom-up is the opposite.

4.6.3 Bottom-up data analysis

The bottom-up approach to data analysis is to work from the attributes upwards towards the entities and relationships that are to be represented in the database. This method is sometimes called data aggregation or synthesis. This approach can be likened to viewing the world as comprising a lot of free-floating facts, and then analysing how they interrelate in order to make some sense of them.

Bottom-up data analysis works on the basis that entities are implicit in the data values. By analysing all of the attributes referred to in descriptions of the organisation, it is possible to identify the relationships between them and hence the existence of entities. The entities are implied by those data items which determine other data items. Data items which determine others are the natural keys.

Example 4.4

As employee number is related to just one employee name, and so the employee number attribute is said to determine the employee name attribute. We therefore deduce the existence of an entity, occurrences of which are identified by the values of the employee number attribute. Employee number is the natural key of this entity.

The bottom-up database design process is as follows.

Step 1: Identify data items
Data items are identified in descriptions of the organisation to be served by the database. They may be identified from, for example, the fields on some data recording forms, and the contents of the organisation's files and records.

Example 4.5

An example organisation maintains a file containing details of employees. By inspecting the record form used in this file we may identify a number of data items, including the following:

        EMPLOYEE__NUMBER
        NATIONAL__INSURANCE__NUMBER
        DEPARTMENT__NAME
        TELEPHONE__EXTENSION
        EMPLOYEE__NAME
        HOME__ADDRESS

Step 2: Identify relationships between data items
The designer must identify which attributes are related to other attributes, and the type of relationship, i.e. one-to-many, one-to-one, many-to-many, or zero-or-one-to-many. In order to determine the type of relationship it is necessary to consider it in both directions. If things of type X and Y are related we must consider how X is related to Y, and also how Y is related to X.

A relationship between X and Y is one-to-one if each occurrence of X is related to no more than one occurrence of Y, and each occurrence of Y is related to no more than one occurrence of X. For example,

        Department ——— Manager   a department has only
                                  one manager and a manager
                                  manages only one department.

        Husband ——— Wife   a husband has only one wife, and
                                  a wife has only one husband.

A relationship between X and Y is one-to-many if each occurrence of X may be related to many occurrences of Y, but each occurrence of Y is related to only one occurrence of X.

Customer ———< Sales Order   a customer may place many sales orders, but each sales order is placed by only one customer.

Father ———< Son   a father may have many sons, but a son has only one father.

A relationship between attributes X and Y is many-to-many if each occurrence of X may be related to many occurrences of Y, and each occurrence of Y may be related to many occurrences of X. For example,

Parent >———< Child   a child will have two parents and a parent may have many children.

Supplier >———< Part   a supplier may supply many parts, and a part may be available from many suppliers.

A relationship between attributes X and Y is zero-or-one-to-many if each occurrence of X may be related to many occurrences of Y, but occurrences of Y are related either to one occurrence of X, or none. For example,

School ***———< Child   a school is related to the many children who attend it and a child may attend only one school, but some children do not attend any school.

Example 4.6

Continuing with the analysis of the attributes identified in Step 1:

        EMPLOYEE_NUMBER,
        NATIONAL_INSURANCE_NUMBER,
        DEPARTMENT_NAME,
        TELEPHONE_EXTENSION,
        EMPLOYEE_NAME,
        HOME_ADDRESS.

There are many ways in which values of these attributes may be related, but the designer must identify just those relationships which he or she thinks are relevant to the structure and activities of the organisation. Different designers may come to different but equally valid conclusions as to what the relevant relationships are.

In this example, the designer identifies the existence of the following relationships.

a) DEPARTMENT_NAME is related to the EMPLOYEE_NUMBERs of the department's employees and the department manager.
b) EMPLOYEE_NUMBER is related to the TELEPHONE_EXTENSIONs by which he or she may be contacted, NATIONAL_INSURANCE_NUMBER, EMPLOYEE_NAME, and HOME_ADDRESS.

c) EMPLOYEE_NUMBER is related to the EMPLOYEE_NUMBER of the employee to whom he or she is responsible.

These relationships between attributes are depicted in the diagram below. Initially all the relationships are represented as one-to-one, but the diagram will be modified later to indicate the actual relationship types as they become apparent.

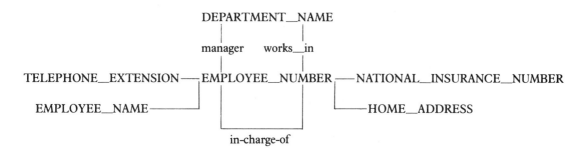

Note that there are two types of relationship between EMPLOYEE_NUMBER and DEPARTMENT_NAME. The 'manager' relationship is between an occurrence of DEPARTMENT_NAME and the occurrence of EMPLOYEE_NUMBER for the employee who is the department's manager. The 'works-in' relationship is between an occurrence of DEPARTMENT_NAME and the occurrences of EMPLOYEE_NUMBER for the employees who work within the department.

We next have to determine the types of the relationships. Each employee will work either within a single department or may not be attached to any particular department, but a department may have many employees, and so the 'works_in' relationship between DEPARTMENT_NAME and EMPLOYEE_NUMBER is zero-or-one-to-many.

$$\text{DEPARTMENT\_NAME} \quad \overset{\text{works\_in}}{\text{***}\!-\!\!\!<} \quad \text{EMPLOYEE\_NUMBER}$$

Each department will have only one manager and an employee may manage only one department, and so the 'manager' relationship between DEPARTMENT_NAME and EMPLOYEE_NUMBER is one-to-one.

$$\text{DEPARTMENT\_NAME} \quad \overset{\text{manager}}{-\!\!\!-\!\!\!-} \quad \text{EMPLOYEE\_NUMBER}$$

Each employee has a unique National Insurance number, and so relationship between EMPLOYEE_NUMBER and NATIONAL_INSURANCE_NUMBER is one-to-one.

$$\text{EMPLOYEE\_NUMBER} \quad -\!\!\!-\!\!\!- \quad \text{NATIONAL\_INSURANCE\_NUMBER}$$

Employees may share an office in which there are a number of telephone extensions, each of which may be used to contact any of them, and so the relationship between EMPLOYEE_NUMBER and TELEPHONE_EXTENSION is many-to-many.

$$\text{EMPLOYEE\_NUMBER} \quad >\!\!\!-\!\!\!< \quad \text{TELEPHONE\_EXTENSION}$$

Many employees may have the same name and may share the same address (e.g. two John Smiths may share the same flat), and so the relationships between

EMPLOYEE_NUMBER and EMPLOYEE_NAME and HOME_ADDRESS are many-to-one.

EMPLOYEE_NUMBER >———— EMPLOYEE_NAME

EMPLOYEE_NUMBER >———— HOME_ADDRESS

An employee will be responsible to some named person, i.e. a manager (for example, Mr Smith is Mr Brown's boss). However, there are employees at the top of the command hierarchy who do not have a manager. There is therefore a zero-or-one-to-many relationship between employees and other employees whom they manage.

in-charge-of

EMPLOYEE_NUMBER *****————————< EMPLOYEE_NUMBER

Thus, we end up with the following relationships

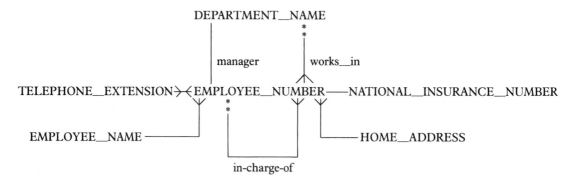

Step 3: Identify entities
Entities are derived from the attributes and relationships identified in Steps 1 and 2 above. An entity is deemed to exist where there appear to be attributes that name it and others which represent facts about it. The existence of an entity is implied by the following relationships.

In an occurrence of a many-to-one relationship values of the 'many' attributes determine a value of the 'one' attribute, and so we assume the values of the 'many' attributes are the names of entities and the 'one' values represent facts about these entities.

Example 4.7

There is a many-to-one relationship between EMPLOYEE_NO and EMPLOYEE_NAME and HOME_ADDRESS, i.e.

EMPLOYEE_NO >————EMPLOYEE_NAME

————————HOME_ADDRESS

This is because for any one occurrence of EMPLOYEE_NUMBER there is only one value of EMPLOYEE_NAME and of HOME_ADDRESS. The converse is not true, as, for example, there may be more than one John Smith, or there may be two employees living at 25 High Street, Leeds. We therefore have a situation where the value of EMPLOYEE__NUMBER determines the value of EMPLOYEE__NAME and the value of HOME__ADDRESS, and so we deduce that there exists an entity type, occurrences of which are named by a value of EMPLOYEE__NO, and facts about which are represented by the values of EMPLOYEE__NAME and HOME__ADDRESS. We therefore add the following entity to the data structure diagram.

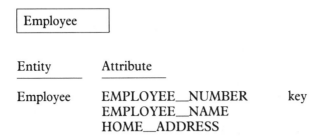

Entity	Attribute	
Employee	EMPLOYEE__NUMBER	key
	EMPLOYEE__NAME	
	HOME__ADDRESS	

In general where there is a many-to-one relationship, the 'many' attribute is assumed to provide the name of an entity, and the 'one' is an attribute of the entity.

In zero-or-one-to-many relationships a value of the 'many' attribute determines a value of the 'zero-or-one' attribute, though some values of the 'many' attribute may be unrelated to any of the 'zero-or-one' attribute values. We therefore assume that the values of the 'many' attribute are the names of entities, and the values of the 'zero-or-one' attributes are the names of other entities which are sometimes related to them.

Example 4.8

There is a zero-or-one-to-many relationship between DEPARTMENT__NAME and EMPLOYEE__NO.

> DEPARTMENT__NAME ********** ————< EMPLOYEE__NO

We therefore deduce the existence of two entities, one identified by values of DEPARTMENT__NAME, and the other identified by values of EMPLOYEE__NO (already deduced in Example 4.7). Similarly, the zero-or-one-to-many relationship,

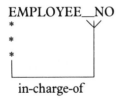

in-charge-of

also implies the existence of the employee entity.

The data structure diagram becomes

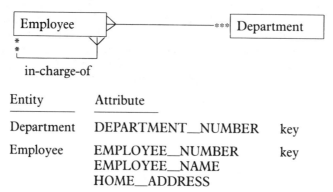

Entity	Attribute	
Department	DEPARTMENT__NUMBER	key
Employee	EMPLOYEE__NUMBER	key
	EMPLOYEE__NAME	
	HOME__ADDRESS	

In general, where two attributes are related in a zero-or-one-to-many relationship, two entities named, respectively, by the 'zero-or-one' and the 'many' attribute values are implied.

Many-to-many relationships identify three entities. The values of the two sets of 'many' attributes in the relationship each identify an entity, and the relationship itself is considered to be an association entity.

Example 4.9

There is a many-to-many relationship between EMPLOYEE__NUMBER and TELEPHONE__EXTENSION because employees share extensions with other employees. There may be many extensions in a particular office, each shared by the employees of that office.

EMPLOYEE__NUMBER >————< TELEPHONE__EXTENSION

We therefore deduce the following set of entities.

a) The employee entity, which is identified by EMPLOYEE__NUMBER.
b) The telephone entity, which is identified by TELEPHONE__EXTENSION.
c) The entity, occurrences of which represent the fact that a particular employee uses a particular telephone extension. This third entity may be thought of as an entry in a telephone directory.

The data structure diagram therefore becomes

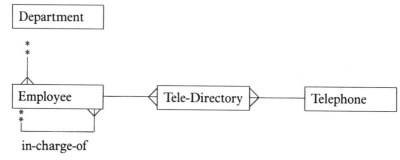

Entity	Attribute	
Department	DEPARTMENT_NUMBER	key
Employee	EMPLOYEE_NUMBER EMPLOYEE_NAME HOME_ADDRESS	key
Telephone	TELEPHONE_EXTENSION	key
Tele-Directory	EMPLOYEE_NUMBER } TELEPHONE_EXTENSION }	key

Note that the many-to-many is replaced by two one-to-manys. All many-to-many relationships may be broken down in this way.

One-to-one relationships may imply one or two entities. The two attributes in the relationship may simply be alternative identifiers for a single entity, or they may identify two distinct entities.

Example 4.10

There is a one-to-one relationship between EMPLOYEE_NUMBER of department manager and DEPARTMENT_NAME, so we identify two entity types,

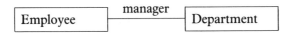

There is also a one-to-one relationship between EMPLOYEE_NUMBER and NATIONAL_INSURANCE_NUMBER, but in this case just one entity is identified

Employee

where EMPLOYEE_NUMBER and NATIONAL_INSURANCE_NUMBER are alternative identifiers. A National Insurance number may be thought of as a fact about, or an attribute value of, an employee, rather than an entity in its own right.

At the end of this bottom-up data analysis we have identified a list of entities and their attributes, and have also identified the relationships between these entities. The entities and relationships are as in the following diagram.

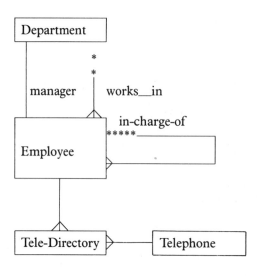

Entity	Attribute	
Department	DEPARTMENT_NAME	key
Employee	EMPLOYEE_NUMBER	key
	NATIONAL_INSURANCE_NUMBER,	
	EMPLOYEE_NAME, HOME_ADDRESS	
Telephone	TELEPHONE_EXTENSION	key
Tele-Directory	EMPLOYEE_NUMBER }	key
	TELEPHONE_EXTENSION }	
Department	DEPARTMENT_NAME	key

Step 4: Combine the data models

The above analysis may be performed for a number of descriptions of the organisation, each from the perspective of different activities. The set of data models so produced must then be combined to form a single conceptual data model, which will be the basis from which the database itself is designed. Models may be merged where they include the same entity types, in which case the lists of entity attributes for common entities must be merged. This combining may be iterative and may involve some re-analysis and redefinition or renaming of entities, attributes and relationships.

4.6.4 Top-down data analysis

Top-down or entity-attribute-relationship data analysis works from the real world, to the things or objects that are of interest within the real world, to the relationships between those objects and to the properties of those objects. The following sequence of analyses are applied and the result is a conceptual data model of the organisation.

Step 1: Identify entities

An entity is a thing that has independent existence and about which we wish to represent information (see Section 4.4). We can deduce the existence of entities by reasoning about the organisation and in particular about the activities that take place and the data that is recorded within it. The grammar of a written description of the operation of the organisation (see Section 4.5) provides clues which help identify the entities. An entity is usually referenced in text by a noun or a noun phrase.

It is not always easy to distinguish between entities and attributes. An attribute may also be referenced by a noun or a noun phrase. We distinguish between an entity and a property or attribute as follows: an entity has an existence of its own, whereas an attribute exists only as a property of an entity. For example, employee is an entity type because employees exist whether or not we know details of their names and National Insurance numbers, etc. The last two are attributes of an employee because they exist only if the employee exists.

This distinction may be somewhat blurred and there may be cases where the designer could legitimately choose to treat a referenced object as either an entity or an attribute. For example, an employee's address exists whether or not we know of its attributes, but it may be of interest only as an attribute of an employee.

A property of an entity is that *each occurrence is uniquely identifiable*. That is to say, it must have attributes or groups of attributes, which uniquely identify it; these form its keys in relational terminology. We will work through an example similar to that used in the discussion on bottom-up data analysis, to illustrate top-down design.

Example 4.11

Consider the following partial description of the workings of the organisation, as provided by the personnel officer. 'A new employee is allocated an employee number and is assigned to a department. We record details of the new employee, including the number and name of the employee's department, the employee's name, National Insurance number, home address, and the telephone extension numbers by which they may be contacted, and also the number of the employee who has been put in charge of the new employee, and the manager of the department.'

Through analysis of the nouns and noun phrases of the above text, we identify the following which may be entities.

> employee
> department
> telephone extension
> employee's manager
> department name
> department number
> manager of the department
> employee's name
> employee's number
> National Insurance number
> home address

However, the last four of the above are attributes rather than entities; employee's manager and manager of department are employee entities; and department name and number are attributes. Thus, we deduce the existence of the following entities.

employee	department	telephone extension

Step 2: Identification of relationships between entities

Having identified a set of entities, the next step is to determine if and how pairs of entities are related. These relationships represent the types of connections that can exist between the real world objects represented by the entities. There are many ways in which objects may be connected. Some examples are given below.

Once again, the grammar of the organisation description provides clues which assist the identification of relationships. A relationship is implied by phrases of the type: 'has . . .' or 'requires a number of . . .' or 'is a part of . . .'. This type of phrase references one entity in describing another.

An objective of this analysis is to identify only those relationships which are direct links between entities. For example, a department may be related to an employee who is related to a spouse who works in a different department, but we are not interested in directly modelling this indirect relationship between departments.

In some cases a relationship may already have been identified as an entity. This will be the case when that relationship is given a name, e.g. 'Marriage is the union between this man and this woman'. Here, marriage will have been identified as an entity, which is in fact a relationship between two other entities, man and woman.

Example 4.12

Continuing with the analysis of the example fragment of a description of Fair-Childs, in Example 4.11, by inspection we identify the following relationships:

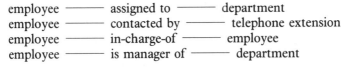

```
employee ——— assigned to ——— department
employee ——— contacted by ——— telephone extension
employee ——— in-charge-of ——— employee
employee ——— is manager of ——— department
```

Thus, the data structure diagram becomes,

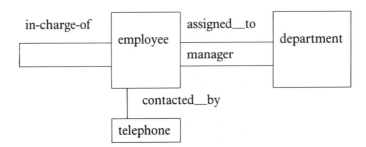

Note that the one-to-one relationships in the above diagram will be replaced by the actual types of relationship as they are identified.

The type of the relationships must be determined. This is done through a similar sort of reasoning as was used in bottom-up data analysis (see Section 4.6.3). However, whereas in bottom-up design we reasoned about values, here we must reason in terms of the real world entities themselves.

Example 4.13

Considering the relationship

> employee ———— in-charge-of ———— employee

we must ask how many employees may there be under any particular manager, and how many managers may an employee work under.

The answer depends on the management structure of the organisation. In our case study, each employee is directly responsible to one manager. However, managers at the top of the command hierarchy are not subordinate to any other employee. This is therefore a zero-or-one-to-many relationship.

> employee *****———— in-charge-of ————< employee

If we consider the relationship

> employee ———— assigned_to ———— department

and ask a similar question to that asked above, it can be seen that this is also a zero-or-one-to-many relationship. This is because each employee is assigned to just one department or may not be attached to any department, and a department may have many employees.

> employee >———— assigned_to ————*** department

Consider

> employee ———— manager ———— department

A department has only one department manager, and an employee may not manage more than one department, and so this is a one-to-one relationship. Consider

> employee ———————— telephone

An employee may be contacted via any of the telephone extensions in his or her office, but the office may be shared by other employees, and so this is a many-to-many relationship.

> employee >————————< telephone

The data structure diagram therefore becomes

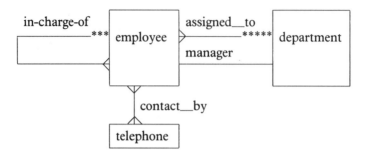

Step 3: Identify entity attributes

The third stage is to identify the types of fact about the entities that must be represented in the database. Again, the grammar of the organisation description gives clues which aid this task. Attributes are implied by nouns and noun phrases, as are the entities themselves. The attributes are implied where the noun or noun phrases identify something that is a property, quality or characteristic of some entity.

Example 4.14

Returning to the example descriptive text in Example 4.11, the following attributes may be deduced

entity	attribute
employee	employee number
	name
	National Insurance number
	home address
department	department name
	department number
telephone	telephone extension number

Step 4: Combine any separate models

This is the same process as for bottom-up design. A number of descriptions may have been analysed and the different conceptual data models must be merged.

4.7 Functional analysis

Functional analysis is the analysis of the part of the real world that the database is to serve in terms of the things that happen, i.e. activities, and in terms of the information used in and generated by those activities.

Some entities, relationships and attributes may not become apparent during data analysis.

This can be because of omissions, or imprecision and ambiguity of natural language in descriptions of an organisation, or oversights by the designer. Missing relationships can result in what are called connection traps. These occur when a user wants to know how some entity is related to another entity in some specific way but either no such connection exists in the database or the connection between the two entities is of a more general nature.

The likelihood of such omissions may be reduced by analysing both the meaning of the data (data analysis) and also the ways in which data is, or will be, used (functional analysis). For this reason, many database design methods include functional analysis in order to compliment and validate data analysis.

Functional analysis is also a preliminary to the identification and design of database applications programs, as it focuses on the processing requirements of the database applications.

The functional model produced by functional analysis models the world in terms of the activities that take place within it, and the information that flows between these functions.

Functional analysis is by its nature application-dependent. However, care should be taken to identify only the intrinsic nature of those activities and not to be unduly influenced by the current methods by which those operations are carried out. For example, some entities may exist only because of the method currently used.

It is sometimes the practice for two separate teams to carry out data analysis and functional analysis. In this way the results of functional analysis can provide an important validation of the results of the data analysis. The two results can be brought together to check for the following.

a) *The validity of the data model.* Are the objects identified in data analysis those which are utilised in current applications? The database must serve these applications as well as future ones.
b) *The completeness of the data analysis.* Do the applications use any data that has not been included in the data model?
c) *Redundancy.* Does the data model include the same object more than once under different classifications?

The natural structure of the data, i.e. the objective of data analysis, is not biased by current applications. So it follows that functional analysis must not be the main tool for designing a database. It should be used only as a means of supplying additional information with which to validate the results of data analysis and with which to make more appropriate judgements where the classifications of data objects are unclear. A full description of functional analysis is therefore outside the scope of this book.

4.8 Data design

This second phase of logical database design is to represent the natural structure recorded in the conceptual data model as a database structure. The designer will seek to use the structures supported by the DBMS to represent the entities, attributes and relationships of the conceptual data model. In an RDBMS these must all be represented using relations. The designer must find a way of representing the entities, attributes and relationships as relations, without loss of information or unnecessary duplication of data values.

Example 4.15

To illustrate this process we shall implement the following conceptual data model.

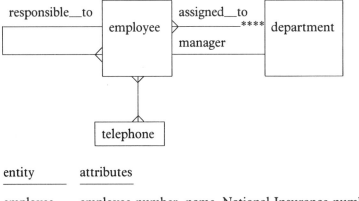

entity	attributes
employee	employee number, name, National Insurance number home address
department	department name, department number
telephone	telephone extension number

Note that this is the conceptual model derived in the top-down design examples, but the 'in-charge-of' relationship has been changed to a many-to-one relationship so as to illustrate all types of relationship.

A conceptual data model is transformed into a relational database by applying the following rules:

Rule 1: Entities
Each entity in the diagram becomes a relation. Each property becomes an attribute in the relation. A primary key is selected.

Example 4.16

By applying Rule 1 we produce three relations as follows.

EMPLOYEE (<u>EMPLOYEE NO</u>, NAME, NI_NO, HOME_ADDRESS)
DEPARTMENT (<u>DEPARTMENT NO</u>, DEPARTMENT_NAME)
TELEPHONE (<u>TELEPHONE NUMBER</u>)

Note that primary keys are underlined.

Rule 2: One-to-many relationships
The primary key of the one (parent or owner) relation migrates to the many (child or member) relation. Thus each tuple in the many relation may cross-reference a tuple in the one relation. These 'migrated' primary keys become foreign keys.

Example 4.17

The one-to-many relationship is the 'responsible_to' relationship between employee and employee. We therefore add (manager) employee number to the employee relation so that an employee tuple cross-references the tuple of the employees to whom he is responsible.

>   EMPLOYEE (EMPLOYEE NO, NAME, NI_NO, HOME_ADDRESS,
>   MANAGER_EMPLOYEE_NO)
>   DEPARTMENT (DEPARTMENT NO, DEPARTMENT_NAME)
>   TELEPHONE (TELEPHONE NUMBER)

Note that foreign keys are underlined with dots.

Rule 3: Many-to-many relationships
Many-to-many relationships may be resolved as two one-to-many relationships. Rules 1 and 2 above then apply.

Example 4.18

There is a many-to-many relationship between employee and telephone,

Any many-to-many relationship may be replaced by two one-to-many relationships. This is done by introducing an entity which respresents a link or association between two of the participating entities. In the example we will introduce a link entity for each pair of employee and telephone, giving:

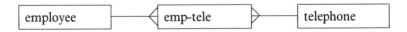

We now have two one-to-many relationships and Rules 1 and 2 may be applied, giving

>   EMPLOYEE (EMPLOYEE NO, NAME, NI_NO, HOME_ADDRESS,
>   MANAGER_EMPLOYEE_NO)
>   DEPARTMENT (DEPARTMENT NO, DEPARTMENT_NAME)
>   TELEPHONE (TELEPHONE NUMBER)
>   EMP_TELE (EMPLOYEE NO, TELEPHONE NO)

Rule 4: Zero-or-one-to-many relationships
These are relationships which hold only for some of a particular type of entity. For instance, we may have ownership as a relation between a person and their house, but many people do not own, but rent, their home. These relationships may be represented by a separate relation, in the same way that many-to-many relationships are.

Example 4.19

The 'assigned_to' relationship between employee and department is a zero-or-one-to-many relationship, and so it is represented by a separate relation defined on the primary keys of DEPARTMENT and EMPLOYEE relations. Thus, our database design becomes as follows.

EMPLOYEE (EMPLOYEE NO, NAME, NI_NO, HOME_ADDRESS,
    MANAGER_EMPLOYEE_NO)
DEPARTMENT (DEPARTMENT NO, DEPARTMENT_NAME)
DEPT_EMP (DEPARTMENT_NO, EMPLOYEE NO)
TELEPHONE (TELEPHONE NO)
EMP_TELE (EMPLOYEE NO, TELEPHONE NO)

The above is an implementation of the example conceptual data model. However, further adjustments may still be made to this design, for example to remove any unnecessary duplication of information that may still exist within the design, or to make the database design more suitable for the requirements of time-critical or high-priority applications. Removal of unnecessary duplication of information is accomplished by means of normalisation (see Section 4.10), and adjustment for the convenience of critical applications is part of physical database design (see Section 4.16).

4.9 Summary

★ Logical database design is the process of determining a natural structure for a database.

★ Having collected information about the organisation that the database is to serve, the logical database designer must identify the types of entities, attributes and relationships that are to be represented in the database, and design appropriate database structures to represent them.

★ Identifying the natural structure is called data analysis, and this produces a conceptual data model.

★ Data analysis may be conducted in a top-down or bottom-up manner. Top-down data analysis involve identifying entities, then relationships between them, and finally their attributes. Bottom-up data analysis is the reverse process.

★ Functional analysis is the analysis of the activities of an organisation and the information that each activity uses and produces. Functional analysis should be secondary to data analysis in determining the logical design of a database, but is sometimes used to validate the results of data analysis.

★ Designing the logical database structure is called data design.

Exercises

4.1 What are the objectives of logical database design?

4.2 Consider the following statement, 'Customer number C99 John Smith has placed order number 925 for seven pairs of pink socks, product number P22, at £2.99 each. The order was placed through Jane Sharp, salesperson S11 through the Leeds sales office, on 1/5/91. Each order may only be for a single product type, and the price is negotiable on an order-by-order basis. A salesperson may be assigned to a specific sales office, but not to specific customers. Also, some salespersons work independently and deal directly with head office, rather than through a sales office.

Identify the following:

a) entity types and occurrences,
b) attribute types and occurrences,
c) relationship types and occurrences.

4.3 List four ways in which information relevant to designing a database may be gathered.

4.4 What is data analysis?

4.5 Describe the steps of bottom-up and top-down data analysis, and identify the differences in the two approaches.

4.6 Perform a top-down data analysis and also a bottom-up data analysis, working from the statement in 4.2.

4.7 Perform the data design to represent the conceptual data model produced in 4.6 as relational database(s).

4.10 Normalisation

The theory of relational databases includes some wisdom about what is and what is not a good database design. These notions are expressed in terms of sets of restrictions, each of which excludes certain undesirable properties from database designs. These sets of restrictions are called normal forms, and normalisation is the name given to the process of creating a database design that does not violate them.

Database design methods invariably include normalisation at some stage. Typically, a method will prescribe that bottom-up or top-down data analysis (see Sections 4.6.3 and 4.6.4) is followed by data design (see Section 4.8) to produce a gross database design, and then normalisation is applied to improve it.

Normalisation achieves a good database design by reducing the amount of data duplication. This data redundancy, as it is called, is undesirable for three reasons.

a) It is a consequence of an unnatural representation of information. Attribute values represent facts about entities and relationships between entities. Since a particular instance of an entity or relationship occurs only once within the real world, it should be represented just once in the database. An unnatural representation of information may make it impossible for certain types of information to be represented, and this will make the database inappropriate for certain applications.
b) It causes problems when the database is updated. Updating a data item will cause inconsistency unless all other copies of that data item are also updated.
c) It causes the database to take up more storage space than is necessary.

Normalisation therefore makes the database design a closer model of the organisation that it serves, i.e. it is a more natural representation of information as data, it removes many database update problems and it makes the database smaller. Researchers have defined many normal forms, but there are six that are well established in the theory of databases.

★ *First Normal Form (1NF)* which is concerned with simplifying the structures in a database so as to ensure that each attribute has only single values.
★ *Second Normal Form (2NF)*, *Third Normal Form (3NF)* and *Boyce–Codd Normal Form (BCNF)* which are all concerned with eliminating the duplication of data that represents single-valued facts. The restrictions imposed by these normal forms are defined in terms of the relation keys (see Section 2.3.5) and functional dependencies (FDs) (explained below in Section 4.12.2).
★ *Fourth Normal Form (4NF)* and *Fifth Normal Form (5NF)* which are concerned with eliminating the duplication of data that represents multi-valued facts. 4NF deals only with cases where multi-valued facts are independent of each other, and is defined in terms of keys and multi-valued dependencies (MVDs) (explained below in Section 4.13.1). 5NF or Project/Join Normal Form deals with the cases where multi-valued facts are not independent of each other, and is defined in terms of keys and join dependencies (JDs) (explained later in Section 4.13.3).

4.11 First normal form (1NF)

1NF imposes the restrictions that tuples of a relation may only contain attribute values that cannot be split into smaller component values. In this way 1NF ensures that each attribute value represents a single fact. More complex structures such as attributes which contain subattributes and repeating groups of attributes are not permitted. The 1NF restriction is built into the relational model itself; the relational model requires attributes to be defined on atomic domains (see Section 2.3.1).

The advantages of 1NF are simplicity and uniform access to all facts represented in the database. No relationships or entities may be hidden within complex structures.

Example 4.20

Consider the 0NF__CUSTOMER__ORDER relation shown below.

ONF_CUSTOMER_ORDER

			CUSTOMER		ORDER_LINES		
					PRODUCT		
ORDER_NO	AREA	SOFF	C_NO	CNAME	P_NO	PNAME	QTY
01	W Yorks	Leeds	C1	Nippers Ltd	P1 P2	Pantaloons Pantaloons	100 50
02	Middl	Oxf'd	C2	Tots-Gear	P1 P5	Pantaloons Pinafore	100 200
03	Middl	Oxf'd	C2	Tots-Gear	P3	Socks	50
04	Middl	Oxf'd	C9	Kid-Naps	P3	Socks	50

The above relation represents information about sales orders placed by Fair-Childs' customers. The attributes and their meaning are as follows:

Attribute	Meaning
ORDER_NO	A unique number which identifies the order.
AREA	The sales area within which the customer resides.
SOFF	The sales office with which the customer deals – a sales office may cover a number of areas.
CUSTOMER	Details of the customer who placed the order.
C_NO	A unique number which identifies the customer.
CNAME	The name of the customer.
ORDER_LINES	Details of the products ordered.
PRODUCT	Details of a product ordered.
P_NO	A unique number which identifies a product.
PNAME	The name of the product.
QTY	The quantity of a product that has been ordered.

ONF_CUSTOMER_ORDER is *not* in 1NF. This is because it includes attributes that are combinations of other attributes, i.e. ORDER_LINES, CUSTOMER and PRODUCT. ORDER_LINES is an example of a repeating group: an occurrence of ORDER_LINES is made up of many occurrences of PRODUCT and QTY.

The relation may be normalised to 1NF by a 'flattening out' process whereby the non-atomic attributes are replaced by corresponding combinations of atomic attributes. This conversion procedure is as follows.

Step 1

Attributes which are combinations of other attributes, for example CUSTOMER and PRODUCT in ONF_CUSTOMER_ORDER, are removed. Only the lowest level component attributes are included in the 1NF relation.

Step 2

Repeating groups, such as ORDER_LINES in ONF_CUSTOMER_ORDER, are removed by including the repeating attributes, e.g. (P_NO, PNAME, QTY) in ONF_CUSTOMER_ORDER, just once.

A separate tuple is created for each occurrence of the repeated attributes. For example, the tuple

$$\langle 01, \text{ W Yorks, Leeds, C1, Nippers Ltd, } \langle \text{P1, Pantaloons, 100} \rangle,$$
$$\langle \text{P2, Pantaloons, 50} \rangle \rangle$$

is translated into two tuples,

$$\langle 01, \text{ W Yorks, Leeds, C1, Nippers Ltd, P1, Pantaloons, 100} \rangle$$
$$\langle 01, \text{ W Yorks, Leeds, C1, Nippers Ltd, P2, Pantaloons, 50} \rangle$$

Example 4.21

The above conversion procedure applied to ONF_CUSTOMER_ORDER produces the 1NF_CUSTOMER_ORDER relation shown below.

1NF_CUSTOMER_ORDER

ORDER_NO	AREA	SOFF	C_NO	CNAME	P_NO	PNAME	QTY
01	W Yorks	Leeds	C1	Nippers Ltd	P1	Pantaloons	100
01	W Yorks	Leeds	C1	Nippers Ltd	P2	Pantaloons	50
02	Middl	Oxf'd	C2	Tots-Gear	P1	Pantaloons	100
02	Middl	Oxf'd	C2	Tots-Gear	P5	Pinafore	200
03	Middl	Oxf'd	C2	Tots-Gear	P3	Socks	50
04	Middl	Oxf'd	C9	Kid-Naps	P3	Socks	50

The 1NF_CUSTOMER_ORDER relation in the above example now includes some duplicate data. It contains the name of a customer in every tuple that describes an order placed by that customer, the name of a product in every tuple that describes an order for a quantity of that product, and the name of an area's sales office for each order placed by a customer in that area. This unnecessary duplication of data is called data redundancy and should not occur in a well-designed database. However, it is shown in the remainder of this chapter how normalisation removes this redundancy.

4.12 Second normal form (2NF), third normal form (3NF) and Boyce–Codd normal form (BCNF)

2NF, 3NF and BCNF exclude unnecessary duplication of attribute values that represent single-valued facts. CNAME in 1NF_CUSTOMER_ORDER is an example of this type of attribute. Its values represent facts concerning the names of customers, and these are single-valued facts because there is only one name for each customer.

Unnecessary duplication of single-valued facts occurs when a relation represents information about more than one type of object. For example, if each tuple of a relation represents facts about both a department and also an employee, then department information must be duplicated for each employee in the same department. However, normalising the database to BCNF will split the relation up, so that facts about employees and departments are represented in separate relations. In a BCNF database, each tuple will represent single-valued facts about just one object.

2NF, 3NF and BCNF are all defined in terms of relation keys and functional dependencies (FDs). Keys have already been explained in Section 2.3.5, but a short revision is given below, followed by an explanation of FD.

4.12.1 Keys

A relation key is one or more attributes, the values of which will always uniquely identify tuples within the relation, and where all of those attributes are necessary for this identifying purpose. Key values can therefore be used as names for the objects about which the tuples represent information. A relation may have many keys, called candidate keys, but one of them will be designated as the primary key, which will be used for tuple identification purposes. The primary key must never have a null value, and may be used elsewhere as a foreign key to cross-reference tuples so as to represent relationships between objects.

4.12.2 Functional dependency (FD)

The relationship between attributes whose values identify objects, and attributes whose values represent single-valued facts about those objects is modelled by an FD. The concept of an FD is explained below with the aid of an example.

Example 4.22

Consider the following EMPLOYEE relation.

EMPLOYEE

EMPLOYEE_NO	NAME	HOME_ADDRESS
123	J Bloggs	25 High Street, Leeds
314	D Brown	5 Low Street, Leeds
127	R Bloggs	25 High Street, Leeds
500	J Smith	19 Grand Way, Leeds
512	J Smith	20 Parsons View, Leeds

The object identifying attributes and those which represent single-valued facts about the objects are as follows:

a) *Identifying attributes.* An employee is uniquely identified by their EMPLOYEE_NO.
b) *Attributes that represent single-valued facts.* Values of NAME and HOME_ADDRESS represent single-valued facts about employees.

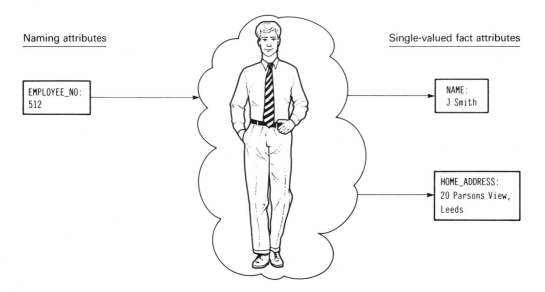

Figure 4.2   *Naming attributes and single-valued fact attributes of EMPLOYEE*

Note that NAME and HOME_ADDRESS are both inappropriate as identifying attributes since, for example, there is more than one employee called John Smith and there are two employees who share the same home address. The above relationships between attributes (see Figure 4.2) are modelled by FDs as follows. Since NAME is a single-valued fact about the object identified by EMPLOYEE_NO, we say that NAME is *functionally dependent* on EMPLOYEE_NO, or alternatively, EMPLOYEE_NO *functionally determines* NAME. This FD is written,

    EMPLOYEE_NO ⟶ NAME

It is also the case that,

    EMPLOYEE_NO ⟶ HOME_ADDRESS
    EMPLOYEE_NO ⟶ (NAME, HOME_ADDRESS)

The above FDs mean that for any specific employee number there can be only one name and only one home address, e.g. employee number 123 is J. Bloggs of 25 High Street, Leeds, and nobody else. However, it is incorrect to write:

    HOME_ADDRESS ⟶ EMPLOYEE_NO

because there may be more than one employee number associated with a particular address, e.g. J. Bloggs (123) lives with his brother R. Bloggs (127).

The left-hand side of an FD is called the determinant, and the right hand side, the determined attributes.

FD is formally defined as follows. A database relation satisfies an FD $X \to Y$ if X and Y are sets of attributes of the relation, and for any two tuples, t_1 and t_2 say, where $t_1(X) = t_2(X)$, it is true that $t_1(Y) = t_2(Y)$. In other words, if $X \to Y$, then wherever a particular value of X occurs with a Y value, it must always occur with the same value of Y.

The meaning of a functional dependency $X \to Y$ is that 'the value of Y represents a single-valued fact about the entity or relationship identified by the value of X'.

4.12.3 Second normal form (2NF)

2NF prohibits the situation where each tuple of a relation represents single-valued facts about more than one object, and where the identifiers of those objects are contained in key values. This situation is outlawed by requiring that relations are in 1NF and that there are no *partial* FDs on a relation's key. A partial FD on a key is an FD where the determinant is part of a key. 2NF is explained in the following example, by further considering the 1NF_CUSTOMER_ORDER relation in Example 4.14.

Example 4.23

Each tuple of 1NF_CUSTOMER_ORDER describes a line of a sales order, and so the key must be (ORDER_NO, P_NO); each value of (ORDER_NO, P_NO) will uniquely identify an order line because no sales order may include two order lines for the same product.

The FDs that hold for 1NF_CUSTOMER_ORDER are:

FD	Meaning
(ORDER_NO, P_NO) → QTY	QTY represents single-valued facts about objects identified by (ORDER_NO, P_NO), i.e. orders lines.
ORDER_NO → C_NO, CNAME, AREA, SOFF	C_NO, CNAME, AREA and SOFF represent single-valued facts about objects identified by ORDER_NO, i.e. sales orders.
P_NO → PNAME	PNAME represents single-valued facts about objects identified by P_NO, i.e. products.
C_NO → CNAME, AREA, SOFF	CNAME, AREA and SOFF represent single-valued facts about objects identified by C_NO, i.e. customers.
AREA → SOFF	SOFF represent single-valued facts about objects identified by AREA, i.e. sales areas.

Note that if the FD $X \to Y$ holds, it does not follow that $Y \to X$. For example, AREA → SOFF because there is only one sales office for each sales area, but SOFF → AREA does not hold, because a sales office may serve a number of sales areas.

There are two partial FDs on the key in the above list. These are:

```
P_NO  —→  PNAME
ORDER_NO  —→  C_NO, CNAME, AREA, SOFF
```

These are partial FDs on the key because the values of PNAME, C_NO, CNAME, AREA and SOFF are each determined by only parts of the key, (ORDER_NO P_NO).

A partial FD on a key occurs when the key includes the identifier of more than one object, and the relation also includes single-valued facts about more than one of those identified objects. In the example, a key value identifies an order line, but also includes the identification of the whole sales order and of a product. A value of PNAME represents a fact about a product, and values of CNAME, AREA and SOFF represent facts about a sales order. QTY represents facts about an order line (see Figure 4.3).

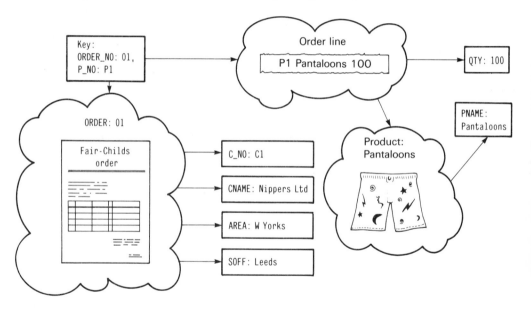

Figure 4.3   *Objects represented by 1NF__CUSTOMER__ORDER*

Partial FDs on a key should be avoided because they result in data redundancy. In the example it can be seen that for each order of product P1, the name Pantaloons has to be duplicated. Similarly, for each order placed by customer C2, the customer name Tots-Gear must be duplicated. Data redundancy of the above type has three undesirable consequences.

a) It is not possible to represent certain types of information. For example, if there are no current orders for product P1 then there will be no record of its name. Similarly, it is impossible to record within 1NF_CUSTOMER_ORDER the name of a customer who has not placed an order; to do so requires a tuple with null valued ORDER_NO and P_NO attributes, but since they form the key they may not be null. It is therefore possible, by deleting the tuple for the last order placed by a particular customer, which is also the only order for a particular product, to inadvertently lose all record of the names of that customer and product.

b) Update anomalies may occur when individual tuples are inserted or amended. For example, if the tuple ⟨O1, C2, Tiny-tots, P1, socks, 100⟩ is amended to become ⟨O1, C2, Tiny-socks, P1, socks, 100⟩, then other tuples which describe orders placed by customer C2 must also be amended to record the customer's change of name.

c) Redundancy obviously causes more store to be used than is necessary.

A relation is normalised to 2NF by splitting it up using the project operator of relational algebra (see Section 2.4.7). This splitting up of the original relation is done strategically so as to remove the partial FDs on the keys, but without any loss of information. The process is as follows.

Step 1

Where there is an FD on part of a key, $X \rightarrow Y$ say, form a new relation within which X is a key, and in which the attributes determined by X are also included. This new relation is formed by projecting the original relation on (X, Y).

Step 2

Form a new relation which is defined on the attributes of the keys of the original relation, and in which are also to be found every attribute which is not functionally determined by just part of the key.

Example 4.24

1NF_CUSTOMER_ORDER is put into 2NF using the above process as follows.

Step 1

There are two FDs on part of the key, (ORDER_NO, P_NO), i.e.:

> P_NO ⟶ PNAME
> ORDER_NO ⟶ C_NO, CNAME, AREA, SOFF

We therefore create two new relations, (P_NO, PNAME) and (ORDER_NO, C_NO, CNAME, AREA, SOFF) in which P_NO and ORDER_NO are the respective keys.

Step 2

The key of the original relation, (ORDER_NO, P_NO) and the remaining attribute, QTY, form a new relation. In this way the relation 1NF_CUSTOMER_ORDER becomes the set of relations given below.

2NF_PRODUCT

P_NO	PNAME
P1	Pantaloons
P2	Pantaloons
P3	Socks
P5	Pinafore

2NF_CUSTOMER_ORDER

ORDER_NO	C_NO	NAME	AREA	SOFF
01	C1	Nippers Ltd	W Yorks	Leeds
02	C2	Tots-Gear	Middl	Oxf'd
03	C2	Tots-Gear	Middl	Oxf'd
04	C9	Kid-Naps	Middl	Oxf'd

2NF_ORDER_LINE

ORDER_NO	P_NO	QTY
01	P1	100
01	P2	50
02	P1	100
02	P5	200
03	P3	50
04	P3	50

Note, that all of the FDs still hold for the new database and there has been no loss of information, but the database is now in 2NF because there are no longer any partial FDs on the keys in any of the three new relations.

4.12.4 Third normal form (3NF)

3NF prohibits the situation where each tuple of a relation represents single-valued facts about more than one object, and where the identifiers of those objects are contained in key values and also in non-key attributes values. 3NF does this by imposing the same restrictions as does 2NF, but also prohibits *transitive* FDs of non-key attributes on keys.

A transitive FD of a non-key attribute on a key occurs where a non-key attribute is functionaly determined by another non-key attribute which is also functionally determined by a key. For example, if attribute X is a key, and attributes Y and Z are not included in keys, then there is a transitive FD of Z on X if $X \rightarrow Y$ and $Y \rightarrow Z$.

3NF is explained in the following example, through further examination of the 2NF_CUSTOMER_ORDER relation in Example 4.24.

Example 4.25

The key of 2NF_CUSTOMER_ORDER is ORDER_NO, as its values uniquely identify each tuple. FDs which hold for this relation are:

```
ORDER_NO  →  C_NO, AREA, SOFF
C_NO  →  AREA, SOFF
```

because each order is placed by only one customer, and each customer resides in a single sales area and deals through a single sales office.

SOFF and AREA are both said to be transitively functionally dependent on ORDER_NO because ORDER_NO functionally determines C_NO which functionally determines AREA and SOFF, i.e. ORDER_NO → C_NO → AREA, SOFF.

Transitive FDs on a key occur when each tuple in a relation describes more than one object, one of the objects being named by the keys, but other objects being named by non-key attributes. In the example a tuple contains facts about both a sales order (identified by the key value, ORDER_NO) and also about a customer (identified by C_NO) (see Figure 4.4).

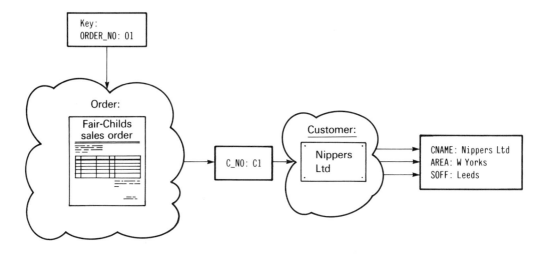

Figure 4.4   *Objects represented by 2NF__CUSTOMER__ORDER*

Data redundancy may occur where there are transitive FDs on the key. For example details of customer C2 are repeated because they have placed two sales orders. This redundancy may cause the same inability to represent certain types of information, and update anomalies that were a consequence of partial dependencies on the key and which were removed by 2NF normalisation.

Information about an object of the type identified by a non-key attribute cannot be represented if there are no associated objects identified by the keys. For example, 2NF_CUSTOMER_ORDER cannot represent information about customer C7, because they have not placed any sales orders.

Update anomalies may occur when a tuple is altered, or a new tuple is inserted. For example, if the tuple ⟨02, C2, Tots-Gear, Middl, Oxf'd⟩ is amended to ⟨02, C2, Tots-Gear, Reading, Oxford⟩, it will also be necessary to alter ⟨03, C2, Tots-Gear, Middl, Oxf'd⟩ to ⟨03, C2, Tots-Gear, Reading, Oxford⟩.

The following procedure transforms a 2NF relation into 3NF relations.

Step 1
Where there is a transitive FD on a key, $X \to Y \to Z$, say, form a new relation within which Y is a key and which contains attributes determined by Y. This new relation is formed by projecting the original relation on (Y, Z).

Step 2
Form a new relation which is defined on the attributes of the keys of the original relation and every attribute which is not transitively functionally determined by a key.

Example 4.26

The above process is applied to 2NF_CUSTOMER_ORDER as follows.

Step 1

The transitive FD on the key is

$$\text{ORDER\_NO} \longrightarrow \text{C\_NO} \longrightarrow \text{AREA, SOFF}$$

and so a relation is formed by projecting on (C_NO, AREA, SOFF).

Step 2

The original key is ORDER_NO, and the attribute that is not transitively dependent on the key is C_NO, and so a second relation is formed by projecting 2NF_CUSTOMER_ORDER on (ORDER_NO, C_NO).

In this way 2NF_CUSTOMER_ORDER becomes:

3NF_ORDER

ORDER_NO	C_NO
01	C1
02	C2
03	C2
04	C9

2NF_CUSTOMER

C_NO	NAME	AREA	SOFF
C1	Nippers Ltd	W Yorks	Leeds
C2	Tots-Gear	Middl	Oxf'd
C9	Kid-Naps	Middl	Oxf'd

In fact, the 2NF_CUSTOMER relation is still not in 3NF, because further analysis of the information that it represents reveals another transitive FD on its key, C_NO.

Example 4.27

Each sales area is represented by a single sales office, though that sales office may also handle other areas, and it follows that AREA functionally determines SOFF, i.e. AREA $\longrightarrow$ SOFF. The FDs that hold for 2NF_CUSTOMER are therefore,

$$\text{C\_NO} \longrightarrow \text{AREA, SOFF}$$
$$\text{AREA} \longrightarrow \text{SOFF}$$

and SOFF is therefore transitively functionally dependent on the key, C_NO, since C_NO $\longrightarrow$ AREA $\longrightarrow$ SOFF.

2NF_CUSTOMER includes some data redundancy, e.g. the sales office, Oxf'd, must be repeated for each customer in the Middl area. This redundancy causes information representation problems, e.g. we cannot represent the fact that Ware is the sales office for the Herts area, since there are as yet no customers in Herts. It also causes update anomalies, e.g. if it is decided to move the Oxf'd sales office to Reading, then tuples for all customers served by that sales office must be altered. The redundancy is a consequence of the fact that each tuple describes two objects, i.e. a customer and a sales area.

Following the above 2NF to 3NF conversion procedure, 2NF_CUSTOMER can be normalised to 3NF giving the following two relations.

3NF_CUSTOMER

C_NO	NAME	AREA
C1	Nippers Ltd	W Yorks
C2	Tots-Gear	Middl
C9	Kid-Naps	Middl

3NF_AREA

AREA	SOFF
W Yorks	Leeds
Middl	Oxf'd

Note that after normalisation to 3NF, all unnecessary duplications of single-valued facts in the example relations has been removed. For example, the information that Middl is served by the Oxf'd sales office is represented only once, whereas in 2NF_CUSTOMER it was stated for each customer in that area.

4.12.5 Summary definition of 1NF, 2NF and 3NF

An easily remembered summary definition of 1NF, 2NF and 3NF is as follows. Each non-key attribute is dependent on the key (1NF), the whole key (2NF) and nothing but the key (3NF).

4.12.6 Boyce–Codd normal form (BCNF) or strong 3NF

BCNF ensures that each tuple of a relation represents single-valued facts about only one object, by requiring that every group of attributes that functionally determines single-valued facts is also a candidate key. So, for instance, consider a relation which includes two attributes, employee numbers (employee_number), and the age of the employees (employee_age). Since employee_number $\rightarrow$ employee_age it follows that the relation is in BCNF only if employee_number is a candidate key for that relation.

BCNF is defined as follows. A relation is in BCNF if every determinant (i.e. left-hand side, X say, of a functional dependency, $X \rightarrow Y$) is a candidate key. BCNF is stronger than 3NF, since a relation in 3NF is not necessarily in BCNF, but a BCNF relation will always be in 3NF. The distinction between 3NF and BCNF is explained below with the aid of an example.

Example 4.28

Consider the relation 3NF_STOCK given below.

3NF_STOCK

P_NO	Ware_House	Bin_NO	Quantity
P1	WH1	B1	100
P1	WH1	B3	200
P2	WH3	B2	3000
P5	WH4	B9	50
P5	WH4	B10	50
P5	WH4	B11	50

Each tuple records the type of product and its quantity stored within a specific bin in a specific warehouse. The only candidate key is (Ware_House, Bin_NO) and this determines both P_NO and Quantity. The FD that hold for this relation is therefore:

(Ware_House, Bin_NO) → P_NO, Quantity

There are no partial or transitive FDs and so the relation is in 3NF, and since all determinants are keys the relation is also in BCNF.

Consider now a different situation where each type of product is stored only at one site; for example, P1 is stored only in warehouse WH1, and P2 is stored only at warehouse WH3. Given this new situation different FDs hold. The product number now functionally determines the warehouse number, and consequentially, Quantity is functionally determined by (P_NO, Bin_NO), and also by (Ware_House, Bin_NO). The FDs that hold, given the new situation, are therefore,

(P_NO, Bin_NO) → Quantity
(Ware_House, Bin_NO) → P_NO, Quantity
P_NO → Ware_House

There are now two candidate keys, (Ware_House, Bin_NO) and (P_NO, Bin_NO). The relation is still in 3NF (check this to be true for yourself) but it is not in BCNF because P_NO is a determinant but not a candidate key.

A relation that does not satisfy BCNF may have some data redundancy within it. For example, 3NF_STOCK records that product P5 is stored in WH4 three times, because it is stored in bins B9, B10 and B11, but P5 is always stored in WH4. This redundancy occurs because each of the tuples represents two different relationships, the relationship between a product and the warehouse in which it is always stored, and the relationship between a bin and its contents. To get rid of this data redundancy it is therefore necessary to represent these relationships in separate relations.

The above type of data redundancy is arguably undesirable because a consequence is the inability to represent some information and the problem of anomalies when updates take place.

It is not possible to represent certain types of information. For example, if stock of P1 runs out there will be no record that P1 is always stored in WH1. It is therefore possible that information may be inadvertently lost when a tuple is deleted. Update anomalies may occur when tuples are inserted or amended. If for example it is decided to re-house P1 in some other warehouse then tuples for all bins containing P1 must be updated.

The above data redundancy and associated problems are removed if the 3NF relation is decomposed into BCNF. This can be done by repeatedly applying the following process. Given a relation, $R(X, Y, Z)$ say, for which the FD $X → Y$ holds, and where the determinant, X, is not a key, form a new relation including both X and Y. This is done by projecting on (X, Y). Also, remove the determined attribute, Y, from the original relation. This is done by projecting on (X, Z).

Example 4.29

3NF_STOCK can be decomposed into BCNF relations by projecting out (P_NO, Bin_NO, Quantity) and (P_NO, Warehouse), forming the two following relations.

BCNF_STOCK

P_NO	Bin_NO	Quantity
P1	B1	100
P1	B3	200
P2	B2	3000
P5	B9	50
P5	B10	50
P5	B11	50

BCNF_PART_WH

P_NO	Warehouse
P1	WH1
P2	WH3
P5	WH4

Note that BCNF_STOCK is now in BCNF because the only FD that holds for this relation is (P_NO, Bin_NO) → Quantity, and (P_NO, Bin_NO) is its only candidate key. Similarly, BCNF_PART_WH is in BCNF because its FD is P_NO → Warehouse, and P_NO is its only candidate key. A consequence is that data redundancy has been removed. For example, the database now represents the fact that P5 is stored in WH4 just once.

A word of caution about BCNF

It is not always desirable to normalise to BCNF, since the cost may be that the BCNF database no longer directly represents all of the fundamental relationships. For instance, BCNF_STOCK and BCNF_PART_WH above no longer represent the FD,

(Ware_House, Bin_NO) → P_NO, Quantity

There is no longer a single relation within which all four of the attributes, Bin_No, Warehouse, P_NO and Quantity are included. Consequently the database becomes less understandable and it becomes more costly to retrieve certain related data.

In the above example BCNF database, it is not obvious in which warehouse a particular product is stored, and to find this out it is necessary to perform a join between BCNF_PART and BCNF_STOCK. The designer may therefore often choose to normalise to 3NF only.

4.13 Fourth normal form (4NF) and fifth normal form (5NF)

Sometimes attribute values are used to represent multi-valued facts about objects, and then 4NF and 5NF are necessary to remove unnecessary duplication of data. A multi-valued fact is a type of fact, many occurrences of which may be about a single object. Examples of multi-valued facts are:

a) product colour, where each product may come in a range of colours,
b) customer address, when a customer may have a number of addresses,
c) name of a person's child or person's hobby, since a person may have many children and many hobbies.

4NF and 5NF restrict a database design so as to remove unnecessary duplication of data that represents multi-valued facts. 4NF is defined in terms of multi-valued dependencies (MVDs) (explained below in Section 4.13.1) which model the relationship between attribute values that identify an object and those which represent independent multi-valued facts about the object. 5NF is defined in terms of join dependencies (JDs) (explained below in Section 4.13.3) which model the relationship between attribute values that represent interdependent multi-valued facts about objects.

4.13.1 Multi-valued dependencies (MVDs)

MVDs are explained below with the aid of an example.

Example 4.30

Let us consider the problem of representing information about parents, their children and hobbies. If we assume that a parent is uniquely identifiable by his or her name, we may then represent this information as in the following relation.

NOT_4NF_PARENT

NAME	CHILD	HOBBY
Barry	David	Horn playing
Barry	Michael	Horn playing
Barry	David	Painting
Barry	Michael	Painting
John	Nicky	Motorcycling
John	David	Motorcycling
John	Nicky	Painting
John	David	Painting

Here we represent the information that Barry has two children, David and Michael, and has two hobbies, Horn playing and Painting (see Figure 4.5). John has two children called Nicky and David, and two hobbies, Motorcycling and Painting.

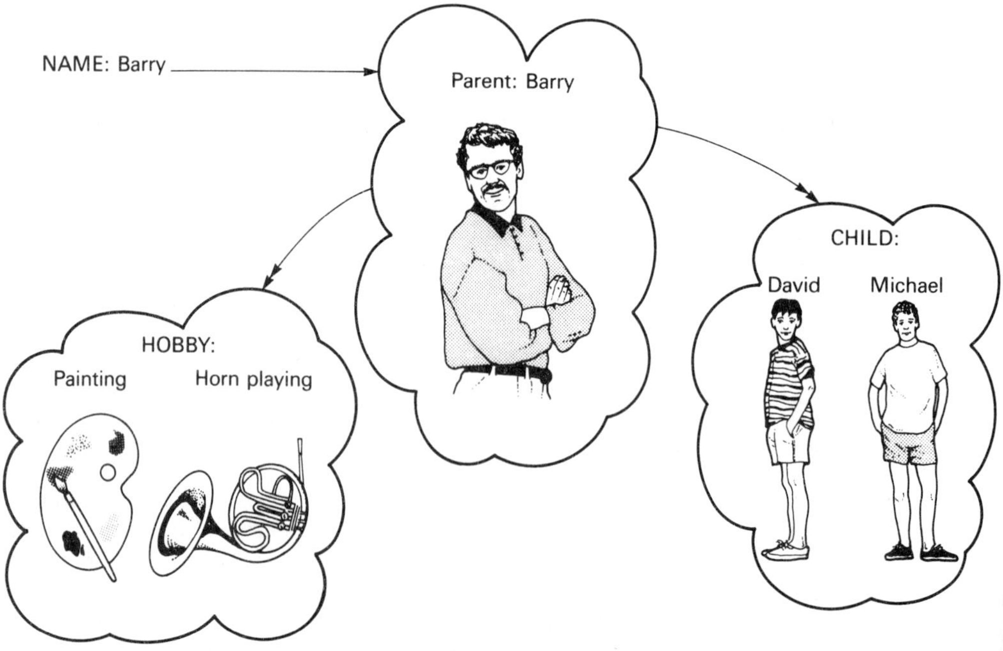

Figure 4.5   *Objects represented by NOT__4NF__PARENT*

NOT_4NF_PARENT is in BCNF because the only key is (NAME, CHILD, HOBBY), i.e. the whole relation, and so there cannot be any partial or transitive FDs on the key. In fact there are no FDs at all, and so there cannot be any determinants which are not keys.

HOBBY and CHILD are types of independent multi-valued facts because there may be many values of HOBBY and of CHILD associated with any one parent, and there is no general relationship between the name of a child and a hobby of a parent. The relationship between identifying attributes and those that represent multi-valued facts is modelled by an MVD. For example, in NOT_4NF_PARENT the relationship between NAME and CHILD is modelled by the MVD,

> NAME $\twoheadrightarrow$ CHILD   i.e., NAME multi-valued determines CHILD.

Similarly, the relationship between NAME and HOBBY is modelled by the MVD,

> NAME $\twoheadrightarrow$ HOBBY

The above two MVDs may be written together in the form,

> NAME $\twoheadrightarrow$ CHILD | HOBBY

An alternative way of viewing multi-valued facts is as implied repeating groups. A 'conventional' record devised to represent information about a parent would have a field of child names and a field of hobby names, as shown below, i.e. the implied record structure includes two repeating groups.

NAME	CHILD	HOBBY
Barry	David, Michael	Horn playing, Painting
John	Nicky, David	Motorcycling, Painting

In general, the relationship between a type of multi-valued fact about an entity, represented by attribute Y, say, and the type of fact that names the entity, represented by attribute X, say, is modelled by the MVD, $X \twoheadrightarrow Y$.

The definition of an MVD is fairly complicated, but its meaning should be easy to grasp with the aid of an intuitive explanation and a few examples. First, we state the definition. An MVD $X \twoheadrightarrow Y$ holds for a relation $R(X, Y, Z)$ if, where there exists two tuples, t_1 and t_2 say, where $t_1(X) = t_2(X)$, there must exist a tuple, t_3 say, where $t_3(X) = t_1(X)$, $t_3(Y) = t_1(Y)$, and $t_3(Z) = t_2(Z)$.

The above definition simply states that in a relation that represents multi-valued facts, Y, and other facts, Z, about objects, X, then each distinct combination of X and Z values must occur with *all* the associated values of Y.

Example 4.31

The instance of NOT_4NF_PARENT given above does satisfy the MVD,

> NAME $\twoheadrightarrow$ CHILD,

because all values of CHILD associated with Barry the horn player are represented, and all values of CHILD associated with Barry the painter are represented, etc.

Now consider an instance of NOT_4NF_PARENT for which NAME $\twoheadrightarrow$ CHILD does not hold. This is the case if we remove any of the tuples in the above NOT_4NF_PARENT relation. For example, we may remove the first of the tuples, giving,

NOT_4NF_PARENT

NAME	CHILD	HOBBY
Barry	Michael	Horn playing
Barry	David	Painting
Barry	Michael	Painting
John	Nicky	Motorcycling
John	David	Motorcycling
John	Nicky	Painting
John	David	Painting

The above relation now lacks the information that Barry the horn player has a son called David, and so the MVD, NAME $\twoheadrightarrow$ CHILD no longer holds. We establish this by applying the above definition of MVD. The relation included two tuples, ⟨Barry, David, Painting⟩ which we can call t_1, and ⟨Barry, Michael, Horn playing⟩ which we can call t_2. t_1(NAME) $= t_2$(NAME), i.e. the values of NAME are equal, but the definition states that there must then be a tuple, t_3, where $t_3(X) = t_1(X)$, i.e. NAME = 'Barry', t_3(CHILD) $= t_1$(CHILD), i.e. CHILD = 'David', and t_3(HOBBY) $= t_2$(HOBBY), i.e. HOBBY = 'Horn playing', but this third tuple is the one that has been removed.

The above definition reveals a difference between FDs and MVDs. FDs are equality-generating dependencies, and MVDs are tuple-generating dependencies. This is because enforcing an FD ensures that wherever a particular fact occurs it always has the same value. Enforcing an MVD on the other hand ensures that all facts are present. Example 4.31 demonstrated how enforcing an MVD may cause tuples to be added.

MVDs always occur in pairs. If we have a relation with attributes (X, Y, Z) and $X \twoheadrightarrow Y$, then it must also be true that $X \twoheadrightarrow Z$. The values of Y and Z will represent multi-valued facts about the things identified by the values of X, and which are independent of each other. (One of the MVDs may in fact be an FD, as FD is a special case of MVD where the multi-valued fact always has only one value per object.)

When a pair of independent multi-valued facts is represented within the same relation, unnecessary duplication of data occurs. This is because when the facts are independent it is necessary to store all combinations. For example, in the example NOT_4NF_PARENT relation, each child must occur with every one of the parent's hobbies.

There are two problems associated with this type of data redundancy.

a) Certain information cannot be represented. It is impossible to represent details of an object where there are no occurrences of one or other of the independent facts. For example in NOT_4NF_PARENT we cannot represent details of childless people, or any parents who do not have hobbies.

b) Update anomalies may occur. When the set of values for one type of multi-valued fact changes, then many tuples have to be altered or inserted. For example, if Barry's wife has a daughter, Amanda, then it is necessary to insert both ⟨Barry, Amanda, Horn playing⟩ and ⟨Barry, Amanda, Painting⟩. Also, multiple deletions are often necessary to maintain consistency. For example, if Barry gives up the horn, then it is necessary to delete ⟨Barry, David, Horn playing⟩ and also ⟨Barry, Michael, Horn playing⟩.

4.13.2 Fourth normal form (4NF)

4NF addresses the problems associated with representing independent multi-valued facts by prohibiting their coexistence within the same relation. 4NF only allows MVDs that are also FDs. In this way the type of data redundancy described above is removed and with it the problems of information representation and update anomalies.

4NF is defined as follows. A relation is in 4NF if the relation is in BCNF, and all MVDs that hold for the relation are in fact FDs.

An alternative definition is as follows. A relation is in 4NF if it is in BCNF and does not contain an implied repeating group that is independent of other attributes of the relation.

A relation that contains more than one type of multi-valued fact is decomposed into 4NF by splitting it up so as to separate the multi-valued facts into different relations. The MVDs then either disappear or become FDs. This process is as follows. A relation with attributes (X, Y, Z) for which the MVDs, $X \twoheadrightarrow Y|Z$, hold is split into two relations by projecting on (X, Y) and (X, Z), respectively.

Example 4.32

Following the above process we may convert NOT_4NF_PARENT to two 4NF relations as follows. The MVDs which hold for NOT_4NF_PARENT are:

NAME $\twoheadrightarrow$ CHILD | HOBBY

and so we separate the independent multi-valued facts, by creating two relations which are projections on (NAME, CHILD) and (NAME, HOBBY), giving:

4NF_CHILD

NAME	CHILD
Barry	David
Barry	Michael
John	Nicky
John	David

4NF_HOBBY

NAME	HOBBY
Barry	Horn playing
Barry	Painting
John	Motorcycling
John	Painting

The decomposition of NOT_4NF_PARENT into 4NF_CHILD and 4NF_HOBBY has produced a superior design by separating the independent multi-valued facts. In this way the unnecessary duplication of data and the associated problems of information representation and update anomalies have been removed. For example if John gives up all of his hobbies, it is still possible to record details of his children. The addition, alteration or deletion of a tuple no longer requires other updates. For example, if John takes up hang gliding then this requires the insertion of a single tuple ⟨John, Hang gliding⟩ into 4NF_HOBBY, whereas previously it would have required the insertion of both ⟨John, Nicky, Hang gliding⟩ and ⟨John, David, Hang gliding⟩ into NOT_4NF_PARENT.

4.13.3 Fifth normal form (5NF) or project/join normal form

A situation that can cause data redundancy and consequential information representation problems and update anomalies is when there are interdependent multi-valued facts. This problem may occur in relations which satisfy 4NF, because 4NF only ensures that independent multi-valued facts are not duplicated, but cannot occur in 5NF relations. Interdependent multi-valued facts and associated problems are illustrated in the following example.

Example 4.33

A set of committees is established to represent specific special interest groups (SIGs). People who are members of these committees will represent the relevant SIGs to which they belong. We then have the situation that, associated with each committee is a set of SIGs, and also a set of people who sit on that committee. However, persons on a committee will represent only those SIGs to which they belong. This set of relationships is shown in Figure 4.6 and may be represented as in the NOT_5NF_COMMITTEE relation, given below.

NOT_5NF_COMMITTEE

COMMITTEE	MEMBER	GROUP
C1	Barry	Keep Music Live
C1	Barry	Horn Society
C1	John	Bob Dylan Fan Club
C2	Barry	Arts Soc
C2	John	Arts Soc
C2	John	Bob Dylan Fan Club
C2	Ruth	Pig Breeders Soc

A tuple in the above relation represents the information that a particular person is a member of a particular committee, on which he or she represents a particular SIG. For instance, ⟨C1, Barry, Keep Music Live⟩ represents 'Barry is a member of committee C1 on which he represents the Keep Music Live SIG'.

The key of the NOT_5NF_COMMITTEE relation is (COMMITTEE, MEMBER, GROUP). The relation is in BCNF, because there are no FDs. Also, the relation is in 4NF, because there are no MVDs which hold; though committee, member and SIG are all multi-valued facts, they are not independent.

The problems with a relation such as NOT_5NF_COMMITTEE are not immediately obvious. However, on close inspection it can be seen that there is data redundancy and there are associated problems of information representation and update anomalies. In the example relation the following data redundancy exists.

a) The fact that John is a member of the Bob Dylan Fan Club has been represented twice.

b) The fact that Barry is on committe C1 is represented twice.
c) The fact that committee C2 represents the Arts Soc. is represented twice.

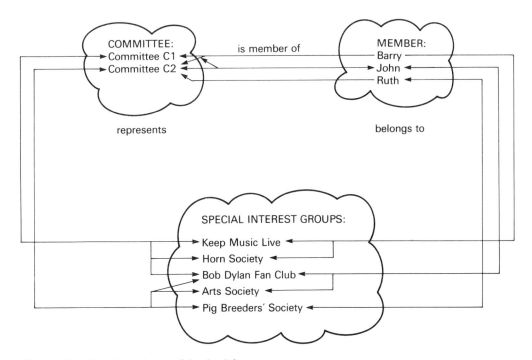

Figure 4.6   *Interdependent multi-valued facts*

There are two problems that result from this type of duplication.

a) Certain types of information may not be represented. For instance, in the example
relation it is not possible to represent the following:
   i)   that a committee's terms of reference include representing a particular SIG, but
       the committee does not currently have a member who is also a member of that
       SIG,
   ii) that a person who is not a member of a committee is a member of some SIG,
   iii) that a SIG with no members on committees exists.
   Information may therefore be inadvertently lost when tuples are deleted. For example,
   if an entire committee resigns, then all record of the existence of that committee is lost
   from the relation.
b) Update anomalies may occur. For example, if the constitution of a committee changes,
   e.g. if it is decided that it should represent some new SIG, then this necessitates
   adding an additional tuple for every member of the committee who also belong to that
   SIG.

The above type of duplication data can be removed by splitting the relation up using
PROJECT but it is not as straightforward as for previous normal forms. For example, if
NOT_5NF_COMMITTEE is projected on (COMMITTEE, MEMBER) and on (COMMITTEE, GROUP) so as to
separate the two multi-valued facts about committees, the result is as follows.

CM

COMMITTEE	MEMBER
C1	Barry
C1	John
C2	Barry
C2	John
C2	Ruth

CG

COMMITTEE	GROUP
C1	Keep Music Live
C1	Horn Society
C1	Bob Dylan Fan Club
C2	Arts Soc
C2	Bob Dylan Fan Club
C2	Pig Breeders Soc

The above would, at first glance, appear to be an improvement on NOT_5NF_COMITTEE because we now state only once facts about who is on each committee and about which SIG a committee represents. However, the weakness of this design is revealed if we try to recreate NOT_5NF_COMITTEE by joining CM and CG. This join gives the following relation.

REMADE_CMG

COMMITTEE	MEMBER	GROUP
C1	Barry	Keep Music Live
C1	Barry	Horn Society
C1	Barry	Bob Dylan Fan Club
C1	John	Keep Music Live
C1	John	Horn Society
C1	John	Bob Dylan Fan Club
C2	Barry	Arts Soc
C2	Barry	Bob Dylan Fan Club
C2	Barry	Pig Breeders Soc
C2	John	Arts Soc
C2	John	Bob Dylan Fan Club
C2	John	Pig Breeders Soc
C2	Ruth	Arts Soc
C2	Ruth	Bob Dylan Fan Club
C2	Ruth	Pig Breeders Soc

The reconstituted relation, REMADE_CMG, includes many more tuples than did the original, and therefore represents spurious and incorrect information. For this reason this type of join is called a lossy join. The additional tuples are generated because not all information represented in NOT_5NF_COMMITTEE is represented in the two projected relations, CM and CG. The information about which SIG a member belongs to is lost. In order to preserve this information a third relation with attributes (MEMBER, GROUP), must also be projected out of NOT_5NF_COMMITTEE, giving the relation below:

MG

MEMBER	GROUP
Barry	Keep Music Live
Barry	Horn Society
Barry	Arts Soc
John	Arts Soc
John	Bob Dylan Fan Club
Ruth	Pig Breeders Soc

All information represented in NOT_5NF_COMMITTEE is preserved in the three relations, CM, CG, and MG, and joining these three relations will always recreate the original NOT_5NF_COMMITTEE relation. For this reason this decomposition is called a lossless or information preserving decomposition.

A join dependency (JD) models the above situation, i.e. where there are interdependent multi-valued facts, by defining all of the groups of attributes which represent some meaningful information about the objects described. For example, the JD that holds for NOT_5NF_COMMITTEE defines the attribute groups (COMMITTEE, MEMBER), (COMMITTEE, GROUP) and (MEMBER, GROUP), and is written as follows:

JD ((COMMITTEE, MEMBER), (COMMITTEE, GROUP), (MEMBER, GROUP))

Since a JD defines all meaningful groups of attributes, it follows that the relation for which the JD holds may be split up by projecting on each of those groups without any loss of information. Consequently, the join of those relations will always recreate the original relation for which the JD holds.

JD is defined as follows. If a relation R can be losslessly decomposed into relations R_1, $R_2, \ldots, R_n$, then R obeys the join dependency, $JD(R_1, R_2, \ldots, R_n)$. By losslessly decomposed, we mean projected from a relation such that the relation may be recreated by joining the projected relations.

JD is a generalisation of MVD, which in turn is a generalisation of FD. For example, consider the following relation and its FDs.

3NF_CUSTOMER

C_NO	NAME	AREA
C1	Nippers Ltd	W Yorks
C2	Tots-Gear	Middl
C9	Kid-Naps	Middl

C_NO ⟶ NAME
C_NO ⟶ AREA

The above FDs can also be expressed as MVDs, because NAME and AREA represent what may be thought of as multi-valued facts, even though in this case each multi-valued fact has just one value. Therefore, the following MVDs also hold for 3NF_CUSTOMER,

C_NO ⟶⟶ NAME | AREA

The above FDs, and the corresponding MVDs, may also be expressed as a JD. The meaningful groups of attributes are: (C_NO, NAME), i.e. the value of NAME represents the name of the customer identified by the value of C_NO; and (C_NO, AREA), i.e. the value of AREA represents the area in which the customer identified by the value of C_NO resides. Therefore, the following JD holds for 3NF_CUSTOMER,

JD ((C_NO, NAME), (C_NO, AREA))

In fact the above JD is an example of a trivial JD. A trivial JD is one in which a candidate key is contained in each of the attribute groups. Trivial JDs hold for relations where each tuple represents just single-valued facts about an object, and so are not a problem. Trivial JDs do not cause data redundancy, and can therefore be ignored.

Consider now the following relation and its MVDs,

NOT_4NF_PARENT

NAME	CHILD	HOBBY
Barry	David	Horn playing
Barry	Michael	Horn playing
Barry	David	Painting
Barry	Michael	Painting
John	Nicky	Motorcycling
John	David	Motorcycling
John	Nicky	Painting
John	David	Painting

NAME →→ CHILD | HOBBY

In NOT_4NF_PARENT, the meaningful groups of attributes are: (NAME, CHILD), i.e. the value of CHILD is the name of one of the children of the parent identified by the value of NAME; and (NAME, HOBBY), i.e. the value of HOBBY identifies a hobby of the parent identified by the value of NAME. Therefore, the following JD also holds,

JD ((NAME, CHILD), (NAME, HOBBY))

This is not a trivial JD since the key (NAME, CHILD, HOBBY) is not contained in each of the attribute groups. Non-trivial JDs are undesirable because they cause data redundancy, a consequence of which is the inability to represent certain types of information, and problems of update anomalies. However problems associated with JDs which are also MVDs (as in the above example) are removed by decomposing the relation into 4NF.

Consider now the JD that holds for NOT_5NF_COMMITTEE, i.e.

JD ((COMMITTEE, MEMBER), (COMMITTEE, GROUP), (MEMBER, GROUP))

This JD is non-trivial because the key is (COMMITTEE, MEMBER, GROUP) which is not contained in any of the attribute groups. The undesirable consequences of this non-trivial JD, i.e. the inability to represent information, and update anomalies, have been identified in the above discussion. Furthermore, the JD is not also an MVD because the multi-valued facts represented by the attributes are not independent. (The relation is already in 4NF.) 5NF, however, prohibits non-trivial JDs of this type and in that way removes the associated data redundancy and its problems. 5NF is defined as follows. *A relation is in 5NF if it is in 4NF and it does not obey any non-trivial JDs.*

Conversion of a relation into 5NF is accomplished by the following process. If a relation obeys the non-trivial JD, $JD(R_1, R_2, \ldots, R_n)$, then form new relations by projecting on $R_1, R_2, \ldots, R_n$, respectively.

Example 4.34

The above NOT_5NF_COMMITTEE relation obeys the JD,

JD ((COMMITTEE, MEMBER), (COMMITTEE, GROUP), (MEMBER, GROUP))

Accordingly, the NOT_5NF_COMMITTEE relation may be decomposed into 5NF by projecting on each of the three attribute groups. This process produces the following set of relations.

CM

COMMITTEE	MEMBER
C1	Barry
C1	John
C2	Barry
C2	John
C2	Ruth

CG

COMMITTEE	GROUP
C1	Keep Music Live
C1	Horn Society
C1	Bob Dylan Fan Club
C2	Arts Soc
C2	Bob Dylan Fan Club
C2	Pig Breeders Soc

MG

MEMBER	GROUP
Barry	Keep Music Live
Barry	Horn Society
Barry	Arts Soc
John	Arts Soc
John	Bob Dylan Fan Club
Ruth	Pig Breeders Soc

The consequence of normalising to 5NF is that each meaningful group of attributes is stored in a separate relation. In this way relations are made to correspond to the basic entities and relationships of the real world about which the database is to represent information.

5NF is believed to be the ultimate normal form when projection alone is used for decomposition, though there are higher normal forms when other operators are used. Also, there are constraints which are more general than FDs, MVDs and JDs, and which are the basis for other higher normal forms. However, the six normal forms described above are those which have proved to be of most practical use. In particular, most database design methods include normalisation up to 3NF.

4.13.4 Database complexity versus database size

A result of normalisation is that the structure of the database is made more complex. This is because normalisation causes single relations to be split into two or more relations. A casual glance at the more complex normalised database may give the false impression that greater redundancy has been introduced. For instance, whereas in NOT_4NF_PARENT in Example 4.30 there was only a single attribute called NAME, in the 4NF version there are two NAME attributes. In fact there is no such increase in data redundancy. For example, consider the case where there are five parents, each with three children and four hobbies. This results in $5 \times 3 \times 4 = 60$ tuples in NOT_4NF_PARENT, each of which are three attributes in size. In the 4NF version there would be $5 \times 3 = 15$ tuples, each two attributes in size in 4NF_CHILD, and $5 \times 4 = 20$ tuples two attributes long in 4NF_HOBBY. The 4NF database then has a total of 35 short tuples, as opposed to 60 longer tuples in NOT_4NF_PARENT.

The cost of normalisation is that the increased number of relations causes extra work for application programs. For example, consider a relation which describes both departments and employees. Normalisation will split this relation so as to store employee and department data in separate relations, but an application which processes data about both entity types will execute faster by accessing the unnormalised relation. In some cases this penalty may outweigh the advantages of normalisation (see denormalisation, later in this chapter).

4.14 Pitfalls of automating normalisation

The above discussion described how 5NF can be achieved by repeatedly splitting up a relation. This process is called normalisation through decomposition. An alternative approach is normalisation through synthesis, whereby we start with individual attribute names and dependencies, and then, through analysis, piece together the normalised relations. In fact, there are automatic synthesis procedures that will generate a 3NF design from a set of attributes and FDs, and the best known is called Bernstein's synthesis algorithm. However, these procedures are not widely used, and those who do use them should be wary. 3NF relational database designs which are generated automatically may contain unrealistic or incorrect combinations of attributes, and so the resulting designs must be scrutinised and adjusted as necessary. The poor results of automatic synthesis procedures have four causes.

a) Automatic normalisation from attributes and FDs uses rules for deducing the existence of FD from other FDs, but these rules can produce meaningless and sometimes incorrect results. For example, consider the following situation: A scientist (identified by EMPLOYEE_NO) has an office (identified by OFFICE_NO) and a laboratory (identified by LAB_NO). There is a telephone extension (identified by EXTENSION_NO) in the office and another in the laboratory. We therefore have the FDs,

```
EMPLOYEE_NO  →  OFFICE_NO
EMPLOYEE_NO  →  LAB_NO
OFFICE_NO    →  EXTENSION_NO
LAB_NO       →  EXTENSION_NO
```

Using the theory of FDs which is the basis of 3NF synthesis, it is possible to deduce that since EMPLOYEE_NO → OFFICE_NO and OFFICE_NO → EXTENSION_NO, then it must be true that EMPLOYEE_NO → EXTENSION_NO. But this deduced FD is obviously untrue. For it to be true the scientist must have only one telephone extension, but she has two!

b) FDs are a rather blunt tool for deducing real world entities and relationships. For example, automatic normalisation will not distinguish between entities, where there is a one-to-one relationship between them. Automatic normalisation algorithms will treat husband and wife as a single entity, and their names are alternative keys.

c) There are often many possible groupings of attributes which satisfy the 3NF constraints, and it is a matter of human judgement as to which one most closely models the world. Therefore, automatic normalisation may produce a theoretically correct database design which does not correspond well to the natural structure of the data.

d) Meaningful relation names cannot be generated automatically.

In summary, though the normal forms do provide a useful basis for analysing the goodness of a database design and for improving it, they should not be used without the application of common sense. The database designer should be the ultimate arbiter of the quality of a database design and its correspondence with the real world, not the theory.

4.15 Summary

★ Normal forms are restrictions on database designs that exclude various undesirable design characteristics which cause unnecessary repetition of data. Consequences of this data redundancy are: the inability to represent information, update anomalies, and excessive database size.

★ Normalisation is the process of applying the constraints of the normal forms.

★ Normal forms are defined in terms of FDs, MVDs and JDs.
An FD, $X \to Y$, models the relationship between the attributes X which identify objects, and the attributes Y which represent single-valued facts about them. A particular value of X will always occur with the same values of Y.
An MVD, $X \twoheadrightarrow Y$, models the relationship between the attributes X which identify objects, and attributes Y which represent multi-valued facts about them. A particular value of X will always occur with all of the associated values of Y.
A JD, JD $((X, Y), (X, Z), (Y, Z))$, say, models general relationships between attributes of a relation, $R(X, Y, Z)$. It models the situation where, given any tuple of R, the values of any one of the groups of attributes, (X, Y), (X, Z) or (Y, Z), will convey meaningful information; and there are no other meaningful combinations of attribute values. If the relation, R, is decomposed, then it must be projected on all of the JD groups if the information content of R is to be preserved.

★ The six well-established normal forms are:
a) 1NF which requires each value of a database to be atomic; this simplifies the database and provides uniform access to all data;
b) 2NF which also outlaws partial FDs on keys; each attribute must be determined by the whole key;
c) 3NF also outlaws transitive FDs on the key; each attribute must be determined by nothing but the key;
d) BCNF also requires each determinant (i.e. left-hand side, X, say, of an FD, $X \to Y$) to be a candidate key;
2NF, 3NF and BCNF are defined to remove unnecessary duplication of data that represents single-valued facts.
e) 4NF also require that all MVDs are FDs; this stops unnecessary duplication of data that represents independent multi-valued facts;
f) 5NF also require all JDs to be trivial; this stops the unnecessary duplication of data that represents related multi-valued facts.

★ A database design may be put into 5NF by repeatedly splitting it up using the PROJECT operator. This is called normalisation by decomposition.

★ Alternatively, there are automatic procedures for analysing a set of attributes, and the FDs which hold, and piecing together a 3NF database design. This is called normalisation through synthesis. Automatic normalisation procedures do not always provide reliable designs.

Exercises

4.8 What is a normal form and what is normalisation?

4.9 Define 1NF and translate the following relation into its 1NF equivalent. What advantages are gained by this translation?

PARENT_CHILD

PARENT		CHILDREN	
IDENTITY NO	NAME	NAME	AGE
P1	Barry	David	12
		Michael	11
P2	John	Nicky	14
		Kim	11

4.10 Define functional dependency. What does an FD model?

4.11 EMPLOYEE_NO → EMPLOYEE_NAME, but it is not true that EMPLOYEE_NAME → EMPLOYEE_NO. Explain why this is so.

4.12 Identify the functional dependencies which hold for the relation shown in Figure 4.7.

PRODUCT

BRAND NAME	SIZE	PRICE	MANUFACTURER
Bonzo	Large	2.99	Fat-Dog
Bonzo	Economy	1.99	Fat-Dog
Woffles	Large	3.00	Fat-Dog
Woffles	Small	1.00	Fat-Dog
Dog Drops	Standard	3.50	Pet Treats
Dog Drops	Large	5.50	Pet Treats

Figure 4.7   *Example database*

4.13 Define 2NF, explain why the PRODUCT relation in 4.12 does not satisfy 2NF, and decompose PRODUCT into a set of relations which do satisfy 2NF. What advantages are gained by this decomposition?

4.14 Identify the FDs which hold for following relation shown in Figure 4.8.

EMPLOYEE

EMP_NO	NAME	ADDRESS	DEPARTMENTS	DEPARTMENT_MANAGER
E1	Smith	Chez Nous	D1	E1
E2	Brown	Mon Repose	D1	E1
E3	Smith	Mon Repose	D1	E1
E4	Jones	Sea View	D2	E9
E9	Bloggs	The Nook	D2	E9

Figure 4.8   *Example database*

4.15 Define 3NF, explain why the EMPLOYEE relation in 4.14 does not satisfy 3NF, and decompose EMPLOYEE into relations which do satisfy 3NF. What advantages are gained by this decomposition?

4.16 Identify the FDs which hold for the following relation.

MAKE_STORE

P_NO	FACTORY	WAREHOUSE
P1	F1	WH1
P1	F2	WH1
P2	F2	WH1
P3	F2	WH2
P4	F2	WH2

The above MAKE_STORE relation indicates where each product is made, and where it is stored. Each product may be produced at a number of different factories, but may only be stored at one warehouse.

4.17 Define BCNF, explain why the MAKE_STORE relation in 4.16 does not satisfy BCNF, and decompose MAKE_STORE into a set of relations which do satisfy BCNF. What advantages are gained by this decomposition?

4.18 Define MVD and explain what an MVD models.

4.19 Which MVDs hold for the following relation?

PCS

P_NO	COLOUR	SIZE
P1	Red	Large
P1	Green	Large
P1	Red	Medium
P1	Green	Medium
P1	Red	Small
P1	Green	Small
P2	Black	Large
P2	Black	Small

Each product comes in a range of colours and sizes.

4.20 Define 4NF, explain why the PCS relation in 4.19 does not satisfy 4NF, and decompose PCS into a set of relations which do satisfy 4NF. What advantages are gained by this decomposition?

4.21 What MVDs hold for PCS if only certain products of certain sizes come in a reduced range of colours? Does PCS then satisfy 4NF?

4.22 Define JD and explain what a JD models.

4.23 Which JDs hold for the following relation?

PCH

PARENT	CHILD	HOBBY
Barry	David	Horn Playing
Barry	David	Concert Going
Barry	Michael	Sailing
John	Nicky	Sailing
John	Kim	Sailing
John	Kim	Golf

A parent has a number of children and hobbies, but only engages in certain of the hobbies with certain of the children, e.g. Barry goes to concerts with David, but not Michael. Assume that parents and children are uniquely identified by their names.

4.24 Define 5NF, explain why the PCH relation in 4.23 does not satisfy 5NF, and decompose PCH into a set of relations which do satisfy 5NF. What advantages are gained by this decomposition?

4.16 Physical database design

Physical database design is the last phase in the design process, wherein the designer decides how the database is to be stored. RDBMSs usually support a number of alternative physical representations of relations and the designer must select the most appropriate. It is therefore essential that the designer understands the advantages and penalties associated with each alternative.

The following sections describe the physical database design process and gives an overview of the more widely used techniques for storing relations. The examples given are small scale, but readers should keep in mind that real databases may include millions of data values. Skilful physical database design is therefore often essential for a database system to perform satisfactorily.

4.17 Physical database design objectives

The designer's objectives are to select physical representations for each relation such that the database has the following properties:

a) data may be accessed with acceptable speed,
b) the database does not use up too much of the computer's store,
c) the database is reasonably resilient to catastrophes; it should always be possible to recover a damaged database system, and if only part of the system fails it should still be possible for the remainder to 'limp' along.

The above three objectives are such that the designer will often achieve one at the expense of the others. For example, making the database efficient for one application may slow down other applications and make the database larger. The designer must therefore come to some compromise design.

4.18 The design process

Physical design decisions should be based on knowledge of the following.

The logical database design. The designer must know which relations are to be included in the database. In fact it may be decided that the logical design should be changed so as to favour certain applications.

Quantities and volatility of data. The designer should know the numbers of tuples that are likely to occur in each relation, the frequency with which each relation will be altered, and the rate at which each relation will grow.

The ways in which the data is to be used. Ideally, the designer should know for each database application:

a) the frequency with which the application will be run,
b) its ranking compared with other applications to indicate importance relative to other applications,
c) the longest acceptable time for the application to execute.

Also, for each transaction which can occur during an application, the designer should know:

a) the number of times the transaction is generated each time the application is run,
b) the relations and attributes accessed by the transaction, and the type of access, i.e. retrieval, update, delete or insert,
c) the longest acceptable time for the transaction to execute.

Costs associated with storing and accessing data, given each of the available representations of relations. For any given file organisation the designer must be aware of how it affects the speed with which records may be accessed, inserted and deleted and also store overheads, i.e. the amount of store, in addition to the data, necessary to implement the representation.

Though in theory it is possible to use the above information to calculate costs and advantages of different designs, it is more usual to base a design on general properties of different representations. The designer will select representations that appear to make the database efficient for anticipated data manipulations, and then improve the design on the basis of its actual measured performance.

This 'implement–test–improve' method of physical database design is used because RDBMSs make it relatively easy to detect and correct inappropriate design decisions. RDBMSs support facilities that allow the database administrator to monitor the operation of a database system during its lifetime, and to tune it, i.e. alter the physical design, without disrupting the running of the system. The designer may therefore experiment with different representations of the database and iterate towards a physical database design that gives acceptable access speed, use of computer resources and reliability.

Physical database design typically proceeds as follows.

Step 1
An initial physical database design is arrived at through analysis of the database applications. The relation representations which appear most appropriate for the anticipated data manipulation are selected.

Step 2
The initial design is tested. A 'test' database is created with realistic amounts of data. If real data is unavailable then 'fake' data must be contrived. The anticipated data manipulations are then timed, or 'bench-marked'. These tests should be as realistic as possible. For example, if the database system is to be a multi-user system, then the database should be tested with simultaneous data manipulations.

Step 3
The initial design will be modified to remove the shortcomings revealed in Step 2. 'Bottle-necks' should be identified and if possible the physical design modified to remove them.

Step 4
During its operational life-time, the database system's performance should be monitored and modifications should be made so as to correct inappropriate design decisions, adjust to changing requirements and maintain the storage structures being used.

4.19 Physical representation of relations

RDBMSs typically support a number of alternative representations of relations. The requirements of any strategy for representing a relation are as follows:

a) the representation must make it possible to access all data without having to specify where tuples are stored; it must be possible to access data on the basis of the attribute values alone;

b) it must be possible to apply the relational algebra operators restrict, project, join, etc. (see Section 2.3);

c) it must be possible to display the relation as a table of values.

The above requirements are usually achieved by representing relations as computer files in which each record represents a tuple. Various direct-access techniques are then used for rapidly locating the records that represent the tuples that satisfy specified search conditions.

A file comprises fixed-size pages, each possibly containing many records. A page is the 'unit of transfer' between disk and main store. When a file is read from or written to, complete pages are transferred, not just the relevant records.

Example 4.35

Consider the following STOCK relation.

STOCK

P_NO	WareHouse	Bin_NO	Quantity
P1	WH1	B1	100
P1	WH1	B3	200
P4	WH3	B2	3000
P2	WH4	B9	50
P5	WH4	B10	50
C5	WH4	B11	50

A physical structure for representing this relation is to store it as the file depicted in the diagram below (we assume that there is sufficient space in one page for three records).

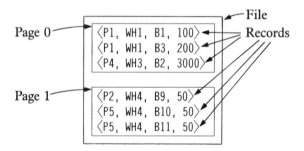

Whenever the above file is read from or written to, a whole page must be transferred between disk and main store. So if, for example, it is necessary to access the record ⟨P1, WH1, B1, 100⟩, then all of page 0 must be read.

Files are handled by the operating system, and accordingly RDBMSs usually sit on top of the operating system's file manager. The relationship between the RDBMS and file manager is shown in Figure 4.9. A user or applications program will make requests to the RDBMS using a database language such as SQL. These requests are expressed in terms of the logical database, i.e. relations and attributes. The RDBMS will then issue the corresponding requests to the file manager in terms of the files and pages that are used to represent the relations and tuples. The file manager in turn accesses the corresponding blocks of data on the computer's storage devices.

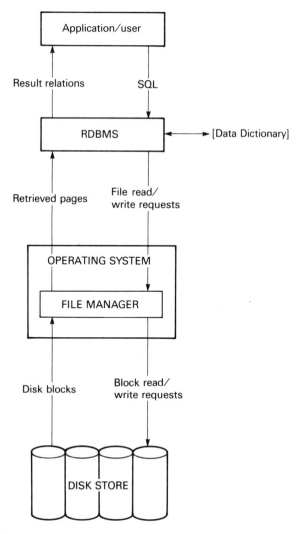

Figure 4.9 *RDBMS and the file manager*

The mapping between the objects in the logical database and objects in the physical database is defined in the storage schema (see Sections 2.7 and 2.8), which is stored in a relational database as part of the data dictionary or catalogue.

The designer of the physical database must therefore specify details of the database to both the RDBMS and the operating system. The designer must specify, to the RDBMS, the file structures that are to be used to represent each relation, and to the operating system, details of the operating system environment within which the database is to operate. In particular the designer must specify where each file is to be physically located i.e. on which storage device and in which directory.

The positioning of files is important for a large database because it affects both performance and resilience to system failure. The designer should position the files so as to achieve the following.

a) *Balanced use of the computer resources*. This is necessary to reduce the risk of bottle-necks at the channels between storage devices and the main store, such as may occur if all of the database is stored on a single disk unit. Better performance may be achieved by spreading the data over a number of storage devices. This makes available more channels and takes advantage of the fact that many storage devices can operate simultaneously.

b) *Physical partitioning of the database*. This is desirable because if all of the database is stored on one storage device, a breakdown of that device will cause all of the database system to crash with it. By strategic distribution of the database across a number of devices the designer can ensure that when one device fails, there will still be sufficient of the database available for some applications to run. This partitioning is just one of a number of ways by which database resilience can be ensured. Other techniques are discussed in Chapter 5.

4.20 File structure and tuple access techniques

Representations of relations vary from RDBMS to RDBMS. However, there are a number of basic techniques, and these are described in the following sections.

4.20.1 Heap files and serial search

The simplest file structure that may be used to represent a relation is a heap file. A heap file is constructed as a list of pages and when a new record is inserted it is simply stored in the last page of the file. If there is insufficient space left, an extra page is added.

There are two advantages of using a heap file.

a) *Fast record insertion*. Insertion is faster for a heap file than for any of the alternative file structures. With other structures it is necessary to search for the correct place in which to store the new record, to allocate space in which to store the record, and possibly to insert other information to enable that record to be rapidly located at some later time. In a heap file new records are simply added to the end of the file.

b) *Economic use of store*. It is necessary only to store the data records. There are no store overheads.

However, the disadvantage is that the only possible method of accessing records in a heap file is by serial searching. Serial searching is the process of searching a file, record by record, from beginning to end. Each record must be tested to see if it represents information that satisfies the search condition. This is the slowest of all methods of record retrieval as it involves searching through every record in the file. The search has to continue right to the last record because there may be more than one record that satisfies the search condition.

When records are deleted from a heap file it is not possible to reclaim the space. This means that the performance of a heap file will progressively deteriorate as it gets clogged up with deleted records. A heap file which is frequently updated must therefore be periodically recreated by the DBA so as to release the space occupied by deleted records.

4.20.2 When to use a heap file

Heap files are appropriate in the following situations:

a) when a batch of records is to be inserted, for example when a relation is first created and populated with tuples; however, once populated it will often be appropriate to alter the representation to a structure that supports faster retrieval;

b) when a file is only a few pages long; in that case search times will be short, even using a serial search;

c) when every record of a file is accessed (in no particular sequence) whenever the file is used;

d) as part of some other structure; for example, it may be appropriate to store a large file as a heap file, but also to have indexes (see Section 4.20.11) for fast access on specific attribute values.

Heap files should not be used when only selected tuples of a relation (not a small one) are to be accessed. The only way of locating selected tuples is by serial searching and that is the slowest of all methods.

4.20.3 Access keys

When accessing data, a search condition is used to restrict the tuples that are retrieved. For example, consider the following SQL which queries the STOCK relation in Example 4.35.

```
SELECT *
FROM STOCK
WHERE P_NO = 'P1' AND
      Quantity > 100;
```

This instruction accesses the STOCK relation on the basis of values of attributes P_NO and Quantity. The time taken to execute this query can therefore be decreased if the file used to store STOCK is organised such that the RDBMS can go directly to the records that store tuples with specified values of P_NO or Quantity. When a file is organised to provide direct access to records on the basis of values of specific attributes, then those attributes are called access keys. (A heap file of course does not support any access keys.)

All of the attributes named in a search condition (e.g. attributes in the WHERE clause of an SQL SELECT) are candidate access keys, and the designer must decide which of those candidates should actually be used.

The most appropriate access keys can be selected on the basis of how tight they are. A tight access key is one where there are relatively few tuples containing specific access key values. If there are many such tuples, the access key is said to be loose. For example P_NO would be a tighter access key than Quantity for the STOCK relation; there are few tuples with any specific value of P_NO, e.g. P_NO = 'P1', but many for each of the values of Quantity that we may wish to test for, e.g. Quantity > 100.

To illustrate extreme examples of tight and loose access keys, consider the problem of accessing an ELECTORAL_REGISTER relation which contains details of voters in a district. The attribute SEX would be an extremely loose access key because searching on a value of SEX will restrict a search to only 50% or so of the tuples. On the other hand (NAME, ADDRESS) would be an extremely tight access key because testing for specific values will restrict the search to just one tuple.

Tight access keys are desirable because they can be used to restrict a search to just a few tuples, and there is then relatively little work necessary to test the rest of the search condition. In general, the tightest candidate access key is used for each relation.

In the above examples, P_NO would be used in preference to Quantity as access key for STOCK; (NAME, ADDRESS) would be used in preference to SEX as access key for ELECTORAL_REGISTER. Sometimes it is not clear-cut which attributes should be used as access keys. The designer must then take into account other factors, such as the relative importance and frequency of the different applications.

Alternative file organisations by which access keys are implemented are discussed in the following sections and the situations where each is most appropriate are discussed.

4.20.4 Sorted files

A relation has no sequence (see Section 2.2), but this is not true of the file that represents it; there will always be a first record, a second, and so on. The speed of certain types of access may be improved by making sure that the records of a file are stored in some specific order. For example, since the records of the file in Example 4.35 are in ascending WareHouse order, it is necessary only to search the records in page 0 to retrieve details of stock in warehouse WH1. By maintaining this file in WareHouse sequence, WareHouse becomes an access key.

A further advantage of maintaining sorted files is that it is then possible to use an alternative and faster way of accessing tuples, i.e. the binary search.

Binary search is the technique of repeatedly halving a file and searching the half in which the required record resides. The process can be likened to that of searching for a clock hidden in a tree trunk, using a chain-saw and stethoscope. The tree is cut in half, and then the half in which ticking can still be heard is halved, and so on, until the ticking stops. The following example demonstrates the significant improvement binary search gives over serial searching.

Example 4.36

Consider a CUSTOMER relation for which CUSTOMER_NO is the primary key. CUSTOMER represents details of customers C1, C2, C3, C5, C7, C9, C12, C15 and C19, and the records of the file which represents this relation are sorted into CUSTOMER_NO sequence.

The binary search can be used to execute the following SQL,

```
SELECT *
FROM CUSTOMER
WHERE CUSTOMER_NO = 'C9';
```

in the manner depicted below.

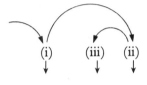

| | (i) | (iii) | (ii) |

Records:

| C1 | C2 | C3 | C5 | C7 | C9 | C12 | C15 | C19 |

The binary search proceeds as follows:

a) The middle record, (C7) is accessed; C9 is greater than the CUSTOMER_NO in this record, so the required record must be in the top half of the file;

b) The middle record of the top half of the file (C12) is accessed; C9 is less than C12 and so we conclude that the required record is in the lower half of the top half of the file;

c) The middle record of the lower half of the top half of the file, (C9), is accessed and the required record is located.

Note that the above binary search requires 3 record accesses, where a serial search would have required 6.

4.20.5 When to use sorted files

It is appropriate to use sorted files when tuples are normally accessed in some specific sequence.

A problem of sorted files is that of maintaining the sequence when new records are inserted. The position in the file of the new record must be found and then space must be allocated in which to store it. In fact, sorted files are usually used within the context of indexed file structures, described later (see Section 4.20.11). Some RDBMSs (e.g. INGRES) do allow heap files which represent relations to be sorted, but make no attempt to maintain the sequence when new records are inserted; they are simply added to the end. The sorted file therefore reverts to a heap file structure.

4.20.6 Hash files

Hashing is the process of calculating the location of a record (the page address) from the value of an access key. The computed address is called the record's home address, the access key is also called the hash key, and the calculation necessary to compute the home address is called the hashing function. Records in a hash file will appear to be randomly distributed across the available file space and for that reason hash files are sometimes called random files.

Hashing potentially provides the fastest access to a record via an access key. This is because when it works at its best, a record may be retrieved by reading just one page. However, there are the following problems in achieving this ideal.

The range of record access key values is typically too large for it to be feasible to allocate one page for every possible value. Also, a page will typically have capacity for more than one record. Hashing functions can therefore generate the same disk address for different access key values. When the same home address is computed for two records, a collision is said to have taken place. If there are too many colliding records to store at the one home address, then some of them must be stored elsewhere as overflow records. It takes longer to access an overflow record, because it is necessary to calculate the home address from the access key value, and then, having found that the record is not stored in that page, to search other pages.

The performance of hashing will deteriorate over time. This is because updating the file will cause overflow records. These overflow records will be stored in the home addresses of other records, which consequently may also become overflow records, and so on. The number of overflow records increases the more the file is updated, and data access accordingly become slower. It is therefore necessary to recreate regularly a hashed file which is updated frequently.

The basic hashing technique is diagrammatically represented in the following example.

Example 4.37

The diagram given below represents the following operations on a hash field.

Record insertion: Three records are inserted.
a) The first has access key value of k. We apply the hash function, f, to k and that returns the home page address i, i.e. $f(k) = i$. The record, record (k), is then stored at page i.
b) A second record with an access key of l is similarly inserted into page i.
c) The third record has an access key of m. The hashing function once more returns the home address of i, but there is now insufficient space in page i for this record. The record is therefore stored as an overflow record in a different page.

Record retrieval: The three records are retrieved as follows.
a) To find the record with the access key value of k, the hashing function is applied and returns the home address i; page i is read and searched and within it the required record is found.
b) The record with access key value l is found in the same way as record (k).
c) To retrieve the record with access key value m, the hashing function returns home address i; page i is read and searched, but the required record is not found; other pages are then searched until the required record is eventually found in page j.

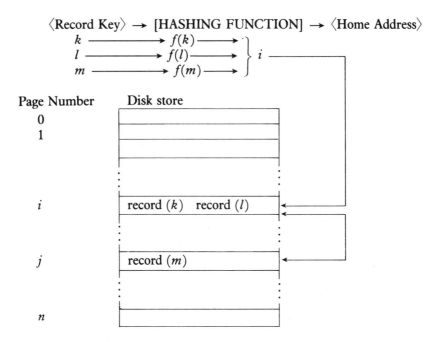

The above example gives no details about the hashing function used or the technique used for determining where to store overflow records and how to retrieve them. In fact there are many different techniques for each of these. Some of the more common ones are detailed below.

4.20.7 Hashing functions

The objective of the hashing function is to distribute records evenly over the available pages. This will minimise the number of collisions and hence minimise the number of overflow records and the consequential increase in record access time. There are many hashing functions, one of which is modulo. The modulo hashing function is widely used, and works as follows. The access key value is divided by the number of pages allocated to the file, and the home address is the remainder.

Example 4.38

Pages 0 to 28 have been allocated for storing a hash file, and modulo-29 has been selected as the hashing function because it will generate home addresses in the required range, i.e. 0 to 28.

Given a record with an access key value 1234, its home address is calculated by dividing 1234 by 29 and taking the remainder, 16, i.e.

modulo-29 (1234) = 16

Given a record access key of value 45, the remainder after division by 29 is also 16, i.e.

modulo-29 (45) = 16

Therefore, if both of the above records are stored within the file, a collision will occur. Both records will be stored in page 16, unless there is insufficient space, in which case one or both will become overflow records.

The effectiveness of modulo hashing depends upon five factors.

a) *The number of pages available.* The more pages, the less the chance of collisions. However, the price that is paid is an increase in the amount of allocated but unused disk space. In general it has been found that space allocated for a hashed file should not be allowed to become more than 70 per cent full. If it does, an excessive number of overflow records will occur, and record access times will become significantly longer.

b) *The number that divides the access keys.* Division by some numbers produces more collision than others. Good results are produced by dividing by prime numbers, but in general numbers with many factors produce poor results.

c) *The characteristics of the access keys.* An uneven spread of key values may cause an uneven distribution of the records over the available pages. Hence, many collisions may occur for some pages while other pages remain unoccupied.

d) *Record size.* The likelihood of overflow records is reduced by increasing the number of records that may be stored in a single page.

e) *Page size.* The larger the page, the smaller the range of addresses for a given file space, and accordingly the more collisions.

Where hashing is used it is necessary for the DBA to monitor its effectiveness. The RDBMS must therefore provide information about the amount of the address space allocated for the storage of a hash file that is occupied. When this space becomes more than 70 per cent full the DBA should allocate more pages and recreate the file.

The RDBMS must also provide statistics about the average number of pages that must be read in order to retrieve a record. This depends on the number of overflow records, and how they are handled. When the average number of page accesses becomes excessive, the DBA should recreate the file. When recreating the file, the number of overflow records can be reduced to a minimum. This is done by recreating the file in two phases. Firstly all records that will fit into their home address pages are stored, and only then are the overflow records inserted.

4.20.8 Overflow records

Four techniques for managing overflow records are as follows.

a) In progressive overflow, an overflow record is placed in the next available location after the home address. When the last page is reached, it is necessary to loop back to the first. When searching for a record, the record is deemed not to exist if an unused record store is located before the record is found.

b) A variation on progressive overflow is chained progressive overflow where overflow records are chained to the home address. This is done by storing the address of the first overflow page in the home address page, the address of the second in the first, and so on. This reduces the number of page reads necessary to locate an overflow record.

c) A problem with progressive overflow is that the overflow records occupy the home addresses of other records and increase the likelihood of other overflow records. A technique for avoiding this is to store overflow records in a special overflow storage area, reserved for them only.

d) Another variation is rehashing. This is the technique of applying a different hashing function to overflow records to find an alternative home address. This second home address may be in a special overflow area.

Example 4.39

Consider a hash file with the following characteristics:

a) pages 0–4 are allocated
b) each page has space for two records
c) the following are the access keys of records to be inserted: 12, 22, 17
d) the hashing function is modulo-5.

Initially the file space is occupied as shown in the following diagram.

Page No	Disk store
0	record (10)
1	
2	record (42)
3	record (3) record (8)
4	record (4)

The hash function returns a home address of 2 for all the records to be inserted, and so the insertions are as follows:

Inserting record (12). This record is stored in the home address, i.e. Page 2, giving:

Page No	Disk store
0	record (10)
1	
2	record (42) record (12)
3	record (3) record (8)
4	record (4)

Inserting record (22). There is no room in Page 2 for this record and so it becomes an overflow record. Using chained progressive overflow, we then search forward for unoccupied space, store the record there, and chain it to its home page. Thus, the file becomes

```
Page No          Disk store
   0       | record (10)                    |
   1       |                                |
   2       | record (42) record (12) 4 |----+
   3       | record (3) record (8)          | |
   4       | record (4) record (22)     |<--+
```

Inserting record (17). This is also an overflow record as its home page is full. The overflow page for Page 2 is Page 4, which is also full. Page 4 does not yet have an overflow page, and so we locate the next page with available space, i.e. Page 0 and store the record there. This produces the following.

```
Page No          Disk store
   0       | record (10) record (17) |<----+
   1       |                                |
   2       | record (42) record (12) 4 |---+
   3       | record (3) record (8)          | |
   4       | record (4) record (22) 0 |<--+
```

Retrieving record (17).

a) Apply the hashing function to 17 returns 2.
b) We read Page 2 and search it for record (17). It is not there and so we follow the chain to the overflow page, Page 4.
c) We read Page 4. The record is not there and so we follow the overflow chain and read Page 0 in which we find the required record.

Note that if the end of the overflow chain is reached without locating the required record, then we know that no such record exists. Note also that by chaining the overflow records we have reduced the number of accesses; in this case it was not necessary to read Page 3.

4.20.9 Dynamic hashing

The above hashing techniques are static in that they assume a fixed allocation of space when the file is created. When that space becomes over-full it is said to be saturated and the DBA must then allocate extra space and recreate the file. Dynamic hashing is a technique whereby saturation is avoided because additional space is automatically added to the file when pages become full, and records are then automatically redistributed.

4.20.10 When to use hash files

Hash files should be used when retrieval is always on the basis of the value of a single access key. However, hash files are inappropriate in the following situations.

a) When retrieval is on the basis of pattern matching. For example hashing could not be used to retrieve tuples from an EMPLOYEE relation for employees whose names begin with Mac, or from a PRODUCT relation for products with product numbers which begin with 99.

b) When retrieval is on the basis of a range of values. For example, hashing could not be used to retrieve details from a STOCK relation of products stored in quantities in the range 1000 to 2000.

c) When access is on the basis of values of only part of the access key. For example, if an EMPLOYEE relation is stored as a hash file with hash key (NAME, ADDRESS), then hashing could not be used to retrieve details of employees at a particular address, or with a particular name.

4.20.11 Indexes

Indexes are an alternative to hashing as a mechanism for direct access to records. An index is a table of access key values, along with the addresses of the records within which each value is stored.

By searching the list of values, the address of required records may be located. Searching for a record using an index is usually much faster than serially searching through the data records, because an index is relatively short, each index record comprising only a single access key value and an address. On the other hand, access via indexes is not as fast as access using hashing. Hashing (at its best) requires a single page access (see Section 4.20.6), but using an index it is necessary to read pages in which the index is stored as well as those in which the data record is located. However, there are a number of advantages of indexes over hashing.

a) Indexes provide access to sequences of records. For example, an EMPLOYEE relation with an index on the AGE attribute will provide direct access to tuples for employees who are some specific age, 21 say, or if required for employees who are in some age band, 31 to 40 say.

b) Indexes may be used to implement many access keys for one relation, whereas there can be only one hash key. It is possible, for example, to hash on an access key and then support secondary access keys using indexes. The cost of each additional index is the storage space it occupies and slower updates because the RDBMS must update all of a relation's indexes whenever the relation is updated.

In some RDBMSs indexes are visible as relations. An index relation has one tuple for each tuple of the relation to which it is an index. Each index relation tuple includes two values, an access key value, and the address of a tuple in the indexed relation that contains that value. The user may not directly alter an index relation; its values are changed only by the RDBMS to reflect changes to the indexed relation.

Example 4.40

An index relation on P_NO for STOCK in Example 4.35 is shown below.

P_NO_INDEX   STOCK

P_NO	ADDRESS		P_NO	WareHouse	Bin_NO	Quantity
P1	*	►P1	P1	WH1	B1	100
P1	*	►P1	P1	WH1	B3	200
P2	*	►P4	P4	WH3	B2	3000
P4	*	►P2	P2	WH4	B9	50
P5	*	►P5	P5	WH4	B10	50
P5	*	►P5	P5	WH4	B11	50
P6	*	►P6	P6	WH5	B1	20

In order execute the following SQL,

```
SELECT *
FROM STOCK
WHERE P_NO = 'P5';
```

the index relation is searched for tuples where P_NO has the value P5, and these provide the addresses of the records which store the required tuples.

Many RDBMSs make it easy for users or the DBA to experiment in order to find the most effective combination of indexes. SQL for example includes the CREATE INDEX instruction to add a new index on some specified access key and the DROP INDEX instruction to remove an index (see Sections 3.9.4 and 3.9.5).

An index relation is an example of a full index, i.e. one which addresses every single record. A B-tree, described below, is another example. A partial index is one where the data records are stored in access key sequence and the index addresses the pages, rather than individual records. ISAM files, also described below, are based on partial indexing. There can be only one partial index for a file because the data records can have only one sequence, but there may be many full indexes.

4.20.12 Physical representation of indexes

An index is not always visible as an index relation, and strictly speaking it should not be. An index is not part of the relational model, it is just an implementation device for speeding up data accesses. Whether or not an index is visible as a relation, there are a number of ways in which it may be stored. It may be stored as a heap file, but the time it takes to search an index may be decreased using the previously mentioned techniques, i.e. the index may be sorted (see Section 4.20.4), or it may be stored as a hash file (see Section 4.20.6). However, there are a number of file organisations specific to indexes, and the more widely used ones are described in the following sections.

4.20.13 Multi-level indexes

The shorter the index, the faster the search. When an index is large the search time can become significant because it then becomes necessary to store the index across many pages. A solution to this problem is to split the index up into a number of shorter indexes and to provide an index to the indexes. This creates a two-level index, as illustrated in the following example.

Example 4.41

Figure 4.10 depicts data records which represent the STOCK relation in Example 4.4, and a two-level partial index on P_NO. It is a partial index because the data records are in access key sequence, and the index addresses each page, not each record.

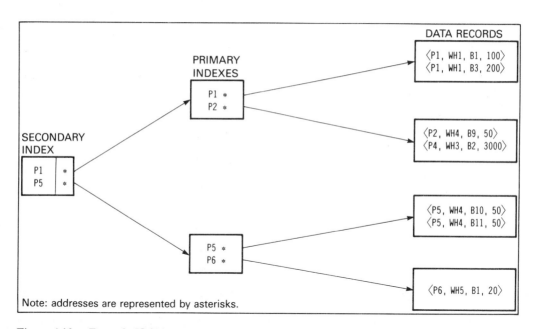

Figure 4.10   *Example ISAM structure*

The data records are stored in pages, each of which may store two. In this simplified example, there are also only two index records per page, but index records are short (they contain only a single access key value and an address) and so in an actual indexed file there would be many within a single page. It is this compression of the access key information, together with the fact that partial indexes are in access key sequence which makes fast searching possible. Each index entry includes the lowest key stored in the addressed page or index.

To locate a record that represents a tuple with a specific P_NO value, (P4 say), the secondary level index is searched for the last entry with a value that is less than or equal to the specified P_NO value P1. This entry contains the address of the primary index to be searched next. The addressed primary index is searched in the same way, and the index entry (P2) that is located contains the address of the page that contains the record with the specified P_NO number (P4).

Note that since the data records are in access key sequence it is possible to access data records in P_NO order without using the indexes. Also, if only a particular range of P_NOs is of interest, P3 to P5 say, then the first record in the range can be found using the index and subsequent records can be found by proceeding serially through the data records.

If the top-level index is still too long, it may also be split into short indexes, and another level of index introduced, giving a three-level index. As many levels may be introduced as are necessary to avoid searching long individual indexes. In general it takes less time to search a number of short indexes (each occupying a single page, say) than to search an equivalent multi-page index.

4.20.14 Indexed sequential access method

Indexed Sequential Access Method (ISAM) is based on partial indexing (see Section 4.20.11). The data records are stored in access key sequence and the index addresses the pages, each of which will contain a sequence of records rather than an individual record (as illustrated in Example 4.41).

The access time will be approximately the same for all records in an ISAM file immediately after the file has been constructed, but may lengthen for some records as a result of file updates. This is because the index is fixed for the life of the file, and therefore rigidly determines the page in which each record should be stored. However, pages will eventually fill up, and then records must be stored as overflow records in other pages, usually chained to the relevant home address page. Overflow records are stored in a separate overflow area. This deterioration in access time becomes rapid when many new records in the same key range are inserted, or when the key range is repeatedly extended. In the latter case the inserted records will all overflow from the last page of the file (see Example 14.42).

This problem of 'fixed for life' indexes is not shared by all 'ISAM' implementations. Many implementations described as ISAM do overcome the above restriction by dynamically adjusting and extending the indexes, sometimes in a way similar to that used by B-trees, described later.

Example 4.42

The diagram on page 231 shows the ISAM file in Example 4.41 after tuples ⟨P6, WH1, B4, 20⟩, ⟨P9, WH1, B5, 300⟩ and ⟨P8, WH1, B6, 250⟩ have been inserted.

Note that the index determines that all three new records should be stored in the last page, but since there is only room for one of them the others are stored as overflow records in a separate area of store. The overflow page is chained to the home page so as to provide an access path to the overflow record. This is done by storing the address of the overflow page in the home page.

Note also that the P_NO sequence of the records within a page and its overflow pages is

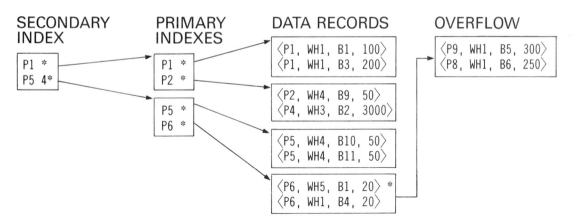

destroyed when new records are inserted, since they are simply added in the order in which they are inserted.

The DBA must monitor the performance of an ISAM file, and recreate it when overflow records cause access times to deterioriate excessively.

4.20.15 B-trees

A B-tree is a type of multi-level full index. B-trees are widely used because they are largely self-maintaining. They expand and contract automatically according to the number of data records in the file. In this way the uneven deterioration in access speeds that occurs when an ISAM file is updated is avoided. A B-tree keeps itself balanced such that it always takes approximately the same time to access any data record. (For this reason, B-trees are sometimes referred to as balanced trees.) It does this by ensuring that each component index has no less than some fixed minimum and no more than some fixed maximum number of entries. Also, being a full index, every single record is addressed from the index and there is therefore no need to store the data records in sequence; they may be stored as a heap file. There may therefore be many B-trees for a single file of data records.

The balance of a B-tree is maintained by the following mechanism. When an index becomes too full, a new index is created and the entries are distributed between the two. The parent index is adjusted to take account of the new index and the redistribution of index entries. If the parent again becomes too large, it is similarly split, and so on. A similar contraction of the B-tree occurs when deleting a record causes an index to have too few entries.

There are many varieties of B-trees, but a description of one of the more common ones, the B+-tree, will illustrate the basic technique. We shall construct a B+-tree to provide access to the records which store the tuples of the CUSTOMER relation in Figure 4.11.

The B+-tree that we shall construct will be of order 1. This means that each index will have a minimum of one test value and a maximum of two. In general a B-tree of order n has a minimum of n and a maximum of $2 \times n$.

A component index, or node, in an order of 1 B+-tree comprises store for three addresses or pointers, and two test values. We depict a component index diagrammatically

$$* \mid \text{test value}_1 \mid * \mid \text{test value}_2 \mid *$$

as shown above, where the asterisks (*) represent pointers to records or to other nodes, and the other boxes contain test values. A test value is an access key value used for searching the index.

CUSTOMER

C_NO	NAME	AREA
C1	Nippers Ltd	W Yorks
C2	Tots-Gear	Middl
C9	Kid-Naps	Middl
C10	Boys Hats	London
C11	Play Time	London
C15	School Kit	London
C19	Smart Kids	Anglia
C23	Bed Socks	London
C25	Slugs	Anglia
C27	Kids Stuff	Middl
C32	Play Ground	Middl
C34	Way In	W Yorks

Figure 4.11   *Example CUSTOMER relation*

Example 4.43

Having created the relation in Figure 4.11, the B+-tree may look as follows.

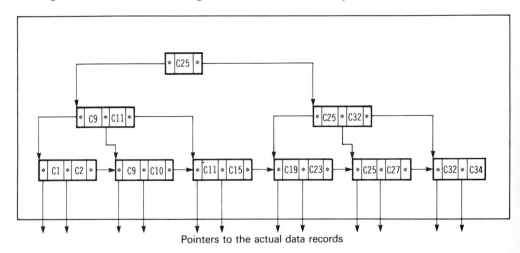

Pointers to the actual data records

Note that each node includes one or two test values, and there is a pointer to another node or to a data record on each side of each test value. A test value indicates the lowest access key value in a particular node. The pointer to the left is the address of the node that indexes the preceding records, and the pointer to the right addresses the node that includes the test value. Note also that the leaf nodes of the B+-tree, i.e. the nodes that point to the data records, are linked so that records can be accessed in access key sequence.

Every record in the example B-tree is accessed by searching two node indexes, as is illustrated by the next example.

Example 4.44

The following SQL,

```
SELECT *
FROM CUSTOMER
WHERE CUSTOMER_NO = 'C15';
```

is executed as described below.

The root node, *C25* is searched. It is scanned from left to right, and the pointer to the left of the first test value greater than the access key of the required record is followed. In this case, since C15 is less than C25, we follow the first pointer and move to node,

```
*C9*C11*
```

The node *C9*C11* is searched. Since C15 is not less than either of the two test values we follow the third pointer to node,

```
*C11*C15*
```

This final node, *C11*C15* is a leaf, and so contains access key values and the addresses of corresponding data records. This node is searched and in it is found the required access key value and hence the address of the required record.

When a new data record is inserted, the index nodes are also updated. Appropriate entries are added and where a node would become larger than is allowed, an extra node is created. This process is illustrated in the following example.

Example 4.45

The SQL,

```
INSERT INTO CUSTOMER
VALUES ('C12', 'Sprog Ware', 'W Yorks');
```

is executed in the following manner. A new data record is created containing the data values of the new tuple. The B+-tree is searched (as in Example 4.44), to locate where in the tree the new record is to be accommodated. The search path followed is the one indicated by the dotted line in the diagram below.

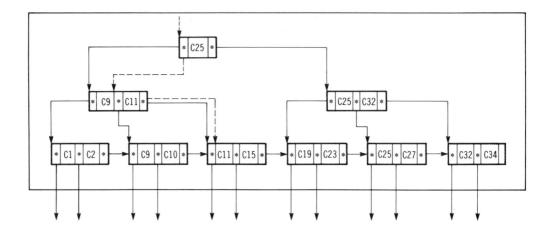

The B+-tree search takes us to node *C11*C15*. It is there that we wish to add test value C12 and the address of the corresponding data record. However, we cannot do this because this node is at its maximum size. What happens now is that the node splits into two so as to make space to accommodate the new value. This operation is called a cellular split. The cellular split takes place in the following way.

a) A new index node is created, and values of the old node and the access key value and address for the new data record are distributed between the old and the new node, giving:

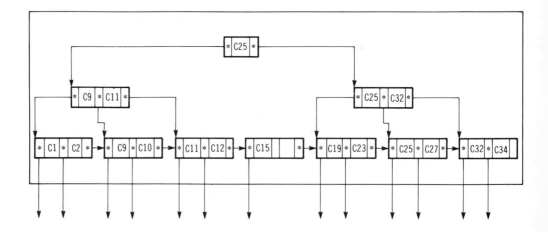

b) The affected parent node, *C9*C11*, is then adjusted to provide access to the new leaf node. To do this we must add C15 and the address of the new node, but the parent node is already full. The parent node must also split in a similar way. The B+-tree therefore becomes as the following diagram.

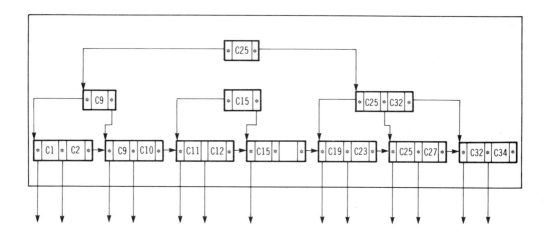

c) The parent node of the nodes adjusted in b), i.e. the root node, is adjusted by adding a test value and address for this new node. This gives the following B+-tree.

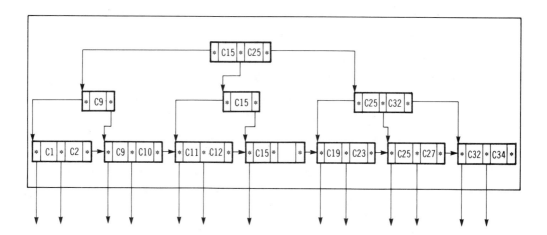

We have now completed the insertion of the new record and corresponding B+-tree update. Note the way in which the effects of the new record 'rippled' up the tree structure so as to accommodate the new record while maintaining the balance of the tree.

Deletion of a record from a B-tree is the insertion process in reverse. Instead of expanding to accommodate the new test values and pointers, the B-tree contracts. When a test value and associated address are removed from a node and that node becomes too small, the node is deleted from the tree, and any test values and addresses that were in the node are redistributed to other nodes. The parent nodes are adjusted in a similar way.

4.20.16 When to use indexes

Indexes are slower but more versatile than hashing. They should be used in the following situations.

a) When pattern matching is used to retrieve tuples. B-tree and ISAM files are based on access key sequence, and so it is possible to retrieve on the basis of the left-most part of the access key. For example it is possible to retrieve EMPLOYEE records with names that start Mac using a NAME index.

b) When tuples are retrieved on the basis of a range of access key values. For example, it is possible to retrieve details of products stored in quantities of 1000 to 2000 from a STOCK relation using an index on Quantity.

c) When using the left-most attributes of a multi-attribute access key. It is possible, for example, to access details of employees at a specific address using an index on (ADDRESS, NAME).

B-trees are preferable to ISAM in the following situations.

a) When the relation is frequently updated. An ISAM file will deteriorate in this situation because its index is fixed and cannot accommodate a changing spread of access key values without resorting to record overflow.

b) When the relation is so large that it is costly to recreate. A B-tree reorganises itself whenever it is updated.

c) When sorting on the access key is required. Updates to an ISAM file will cause the records to lose their access key sequence (see Example 4.43) but the sequence will always be maintained in a B-tree.

ISAM is most appropriate in the following situations.

a) When the file is infrequently updated. An ISAM file which has not been updated will give faster access than a B-tree, because the B-tree has an extra level of indexes, i.e. the leaf nodes which contain the record pointers.

b) When the relation is to be simultaneously manipulated by a number of users. This is because, since the ISAM index does not change, it is not necessary to take any precautions to avoid problems of multiple concurrent updates of the index (see Chapter 5).

c) When all of the data records are to be accessed serially. With a B-tree the sequence is determined via the leaf nodes, but in an ISAM file the data records may be processed without reference to the index.

4.21 Clustering

Clustering is the technique of storing related records physically close together. The advantage of doing this is that it reduces the number of page accesses necessary to process a group of related records.

For example, consider the situation where details of sales orders and order lines are respectively represented in the ORDER and ORDER_LINE relations. An application which produces the invoice for a sales order, one with six order lines say, will have to access the corresponding tuple in the ORDER relation, and also the corresponding six tuples in

ORDER_LINE. If these tuples are all stored in separate pages then the application must access seven different pages. However, if we arrange for records in the file that stores ORDER_LINE to be clustered on ORDER_NO, then the six ORDER_LINE tuples will probably be stored in the same page, and so only two page accesses are necessary. By clustering on ORDER_NO we mean storing records with the same ORDER_NO value physically close together.

Some RDBMSs support cluster indexes (see Section 3.9.4) whereby records with the same access key value are stored physically close together.

When to use clustering
Clustering should be used when an application accesses groups of tuples which have some common attribute value. A relation may have only one clustering index, and so, where there is more than one such application, the designer must decide which is the most important. Where applications have equal importance, then clustering on the tightest attribute is likely to be more effective. This is because a large cluster is likely to spread across a number of pages, thus slowing down the application, and also using up space which should be occupied by other clusters.

4.22 Changes to the logical database design

The logical database design methods described earlier in this chapter attempt to produce a design that reflects the natural structure of the data, rather than the ways in which it is used. However, a consequence may be that data required by any particular application may be dispersed across a number of different relations or stored with other data that the application does not require.

Consider, for example, the following 2NF_CUSTOMER relation.

2NF_CUSTOMER

C_NO	NAME	AREA	SOFF
C1	Nippers Ltd	W Yorks	Leeds
C2	Tots-Gear	Middl	Oxf'd
C9	Kid-Naps	Middl	Oxf'd

Earlier in this chapter it was shown that a theoretically better logical database design is produced by decomposing 2NF_CUSTOMER, giving 3NF_CUSTOMER and 3NF_AREA as shown below (see Section 4.12.3).

3NF_CUSTOMER

C_NO	NAME	AREA
C1	Nippers Ltd	W Yorks
C2	Tots-Gear	Middl
C9	Kid-Naps	Middl

3NF_AREA

AREA	SOFF
W Yorks	Leeds
Middl	Oxf'd

However, a sales analysis application may require details of both customers and the sales office through which each customer places orders. For that application it is more convenient to store the information in the single 2NF_CUSTOMER relation, than to disperse it between 3NF_CUSTOMER and 3NF_AREA, because the application program can then be smaller and execute faster. It will not need to join 3NF_CUSTOMER and 3NF_AREA to access the information it requires.

The designer may sometimes conclude that an application is sufficiently important to justify denormalising the logical design. For instance, if the above sales analysis application is considered sufficiently important, then data will be stored in 2NF_CUSTOMER, rather than 3NF_CUSTOMER and 3NF_ORDER. Of course, a consequence is that some data redundancy is then reintroduced, and applications must be programmed to cope with it (see Section 4.12.3).

Sometimes the logical database design will include relations with many attributes, but where certain applications will need to access just a few. For example, the payroll application will only wish to access attributes in an EMPLOYEE relation which relate to rates of pay. It takes less time to access shorter records, and so the designer may choose to split up a relation so as to place groups of attributes required by different applications in different relations. This is called vertical fragmentation and is discussed in Chapter 6.

4.23 Summary

★ Physical database design is the process of deciding how to store relations. The designer must select the most appropriate of the storage structures supported by the RDBMS for each relation. The choice will be based on the logical database design, the volume and volatility of the data, the ways in which applications will manipulate the data and the costs associated with each representation.

★ A physical database design is usually tested by bench-marking data manipulation of a test database, and will be tuned throughout the life of the database system by monitoring its performance and making adjustments.

★ Four methods of representing relations are the use of heap files, sorted files, hash files, and indexes (e.g. ISAM or B-tree).

★ A heap file is a chain of pages where new records are simply added to the end, and is appropriate when a batch of records is being inserted or when a file is only a few pages long. The disadvantage is that record access is slow because serial searching must be used. Serial searching involves accessing each record, from the first to the last.

★ Other file organisations make it possible to access records speedily, given the value of some access key, i.e. specific attribute or attributes. Attributes used in the search conditions are candidate access keys, and the tightest candidate access keys should be implemented.

★ Record access speed can be improved if the file is sorted. Binary searching may then be used to access records with a specific value of the access key, i.e. the attributes on which the file is sorted. Binary searching is the process of repeatedly halving the part of the file that contains the required record. Sorted files are appropriate when tuples are normally accessed in some specific sequence.

★ Hashing is the process of locating a record by calculating its address from the access key value. Hash files provide the fastest access to records for exact search key matching, but are inappropriate when retrieval is on the basis of pattern or range matching. Also, they do not support sequential access to records.

★ An index is a table of access key values and associated record addresses. Indexes are slower but more versatile than hashing. They should be used when retrieval is based on pattern or range matching.

★ Two types of index structures are ISAM and B-trees. ISAM is an example of a partial index, because the data records are in access key sequence and the index addresses pages rather than records. A B-tree is an example of a full index because every record is addressed by the index. ISAM files have a static index and therefore deteriorate when records are inserted, but provide faster access and give fewer problems than B-trees when simultaneously used by many users. B-trees, on the other hand, maintain themselves by expanding or contracting according to the number of data records, and so are more appropriate when recreating the file structure is expensive, or when the file is frequently updated.

★ Clustering is the technique of storing related records physically close together, and should be used where applications process groups of tuples with some common attribute value.

★ Sometimes the designer may choose to alter the logical database design to favour certain applications. This may be done by combining relations, i.e. denormalising, so as to remove the necessity for an application to perform a join; and by vertical fragmentation, i.e. splitting a relation so as to place the groups of attributes used by different applications in different relations. Vertical fragmentation has the advantage of producing files with shorter records, and these may therefore be accessed faster.

★ Physical database design is a complex and technically demanding task, and the information in this chapter merely gives a brief overview of issues, methods and techniques. In practice the designer should have a good technical knowledge of the operating system and the RDBMS.

Exercises

4.25 What is the purpose of physical database design?

4.26 What information does the designer require as the basis for a physical database design?

4.27 Identify the stages of the physical database design process.

4.28 What are the requirements of a physical representation of a relation?

4.29 What is the relationship between an RDBMS and the operating system file manager?

4.30 How can a relation be represented as a file?

4.31 Draw a diagram to show how the EMPLOYEE_TELEPHONE relation illustrated in Figure 4.12 may be represented:

a) as a heap file,

b) as a sorted file (sorted on EMP_NO),
c) as a hash file (hashed on EMP_NO) using modulo-7 hashing on the numeric part of EMP_NO and progressive overflow,
d) as an ISAM file (indexed on EMP_NO),
e) as an order 1 B+-tree file (indexed on EMP_NO).

Assume pages may each store two records, or three index entries.

EMPLOYEE_TELEPHONE

EMP_NO	OFFICE	EXTENSION
E1	R101	811
E1	R102	813
E2	R10	111
E3	R35	123
E5	R35	123
E6	R35	123
E7	R35	123
E8	R35	123
E9	R35	123
E10	R35	123
E13	R35	123

Figure 4.12   *Example EMPLOYEE__ TELEPHONE relation*

4.32 Under what circumstances would you choose a), b), c), d) or e) in 4.31?

4.33 Use your sorted file diagram (in 4.31) to illustrate a binary search for employee E9's tuple. Contrast this with the equivalent search of the heap file (also in 4.31).

4.34 Demonstrate progressive chained overflow by making any necessary adjustments to your solution to 4.31 c), and then inserting into the hash file the following three tuples ⟨E15, R2, 555⟩, ⟨E20, R2, 555⟩ and ⟨E25, R2, 555⟩.

4.35 Demonstrate the way in which an ISAM deteriorates with update by inserting the three tuples in 4.34 into the ISAM file (in 4.31).

4.36 Demonstrate cellular split by inserting the three tuples in 4.34 into the B+-tree file (in 4.31).

4.37 The manager of the data processing department of a manufacturing organisation has been in that job for the last thirty years, and thinks very much in terms of third generation file-oriented computing. However, he is aware that the newly installed relational database system requires new ways of thinking. He has asked you to write for him a tutorial report that explains and illustrates the way in which the design of the new database system should be approached.

4.38 Much of the literature on 'normalisation' is very difficult for the non-mathematician to understand. You have been asked by the manager (in 4.37) to write a simple explanation of what normalisation is, how to do it, and why it is a good thing.

4.39 Perform a logical database design for a small organisation with which you are familiar. Use either bottom-up or top-down data analysis to produce a conceptual data model, data design to produce a first-cut relational database schema, and normalisation to refine the design.

4.40 Study an RDBMS to which you have access, and write a report, detailing the range of physical representations of relations that it supports, and giving guide-lines for the database designer on when best to use each of them.

5 On keeping a database clean, tidy and safe

5.1 Introduction

There is the potential for many things to go wrong during the lifetime of a database system. The database may become damaged as a result of hardware or software failure or as a consequence of human error, ignorance, or malice. This chapter discusses these problems and describes the ways in which such disasters can be avoided or, if a disaster does occur, how the database system may be recovered.

5.2 Transactions

The concept of a transaction is fundamental to database safeguards against and recovery from failures. We explain this concept by examining the relationship between a database and the real world.

A database may be thought of as a 'snapshot' of the world; it typically represents information about the world as it is at a particular moment. When the world changes, corresponding changes have to be made to the database, and sometimes it may also be necessary to retrieve information from a database in order to decide what changes should be made to the world.

Data retrieval and alterations that correspond to a single change in the world will often require the execution of many instructions of the database language. Such a collection of instructions which must be executed together is called a transaction.

A transaction is a sequence of instructions which alters the database so as to represent a single change in the world, and/or which retrieve information about a single 'snapshot' of the world so as to support some task.

Example 5.1

An example of a transaction is the acceptance and recording of a sales order. This transaction is performed by executing database language instructions to perform the following:
a) accessing information about the customer's credit worthiness on which to base the decision as to whether or not to accept the order,
b) accessing information about the products that the customer wishes to order and details of how many are currently in stock,
c) inserting data that describes an accepted sales order.

A transaction acts as a unit of recovery in a database system. RDBMSs will make sure that either all of the instructions of a transaction are executed, or that the database is as if none of them have been. All instructions of a transaction therefore execute as a single task, and if for any reason it is decided that the task should not be completed, then the effects of any instructions which have already been executed are undone. Also, other users should not be affected by, or be able to affect, the data used by a transaction until that transaction has been completed or has been abandoned.

5.3 Transaction management

There are a number of potential problems associated with transactions, and safeguards are built into RDBMSs so as to avoid them. These problems and the corresponding safeguards are described in the following sections.

5.4 Incomplete or abandoned transactions

An RDBMS will have built-in safeguards which ensure that incorrect data is not left in the database if for some reason a transaction fails (e.g. because of a programming error), or is abandoned (e.g. if it is decided that the change to the world that necessitated the transaction should not proceed).

A relational database language will include instructions for starting a transaction, and for completing it or abandoning it (see Section 3.12). A transaction is *committed* when it has been successfully completed; it is *rolled back* if it is decided that it should not proceed for some reason. COMMIT and ROLLBACK instructions have the following effects.

Execution of a ROLLBACK instruction causes the data values which have been changed by the transaction to be re-assigned the values that they had immediately before the transaction started. It is only after execution of a COMMIT TRANSACTION instruction that the changes made by a transaction are made permanent (until the next update) within the database. Until that time, those changes are unknown to other transactions.

An RDBMS is able to undo the updates made by a failed or abandoned transaction because it automatically records all changes made to the database. This record is stored as a special file, usually on disk, called the transaction log or journal, which contains data values before and after each update. These are respectively called before-images and after-images.

5.5 Interference between transactions

When more than one transaction is executed at the same time, an RDBMS will safeguard against interference between the transactions. This protection is called concurrency control, and in its absence the following problems may occur.

A transaction may retrieve incorrect or inconsistent data from the database because some other transaction which is executing at the same time is altering that data.

Incorrect data values may be introduced into the database because two transactions are altering the same data at the same time.

A database system that supports many simultaneous transactions will manage things such that one transaction does not upset the operations of another. Users will usually be unaware of each other, since concurrency control normally works beneath the surface of a system and so is not visible to users. However, an RDBMS may support a number of alternative concurrency control mechanisms, and so the DBA must be able to monitor the effectiveness of concurrency control and install the most appropriate mechanism.

In the following sections, potential problems caused by concurrent transactions are illustrated, and the most common form of concurrency control, i.e. a locking system, is described.

5.6 Lost operations

When two updates occur at the same time, in the absence of concurrency control it is possible for the effect of one of them to be lost. To illustrate this problem consider the following example.

Example 5.2

Two transactions involving a STOCK relation execute the following SQL.

```
UPDATE STOCK
SET QTY = QTY + w
WHERE WAREHOUSE_NO = x AND BIN_NO = y AND PRODUCT_NO = z;
```

Consider the situation where they execute concurrently, and the variable values are,

```
w = 100 and 50,  respectively
x = 'WH1'
y = 1
z = 'P1'
```

The STOCK relation is as follows.

STOCK

WAREHOUSE_NO	BIN_NO	PRODUCT_NO	QTY
WH1	1	P1	100
WH1	2	P1	150
WH1	3	P4	100

In the absence of concurrency controls the transactions may execute as follows.

Transaction 1	Time	Transaction 2
Read the first tuple ⟨WH1, 1, P1, 100⟩ into a buffer.		
		Read the first tuple ⟨WH1, 1, P1, 100⟩ into a buffer.
		Add 50 to the QTY value, giving ⟨WH1, 1, P1, 150⟩
		Write the tuple back to the relation.
Add 100 to QTY value, giving ⟨WH1, 1, P1, 200⟩		
Write tuple back to the relation.		

On completion of the above sequence, STOCK is as follows.

STOCK

WAREHOUSE_NO	BIN_NO	PRODUCT_NO	QTY	
WH1	1	P1	200	← should be 250
WH1	2	P1	150	
WH1	3	P4	100	

Note that the update performed by the second transaction has been lost. This occurs because both transactions operate upon a copy of the tuple in its original form rather than directly on the attribute values in the relation, and the last copy to be written to the relation, ⟨WH1, 1, P1, 200⟩ over-wrote the previous one, ⟨WH1, 1, P1, 150⟩.

5.7 Retrieval of inconsistent data

Interference between transactions in the absence of concurrency control can cause the retrieval of inconsistent data from the database. This problem is illustrated by the following two examples.

Example 5.3

Consider two transactions operating upon the STOCK relation.

STOCK

WAREHOUSE_NO	BIN_NO	PRODUCT_NO	QTY
WH1	1	P1	100
WH1	2	P1	150
WH1	3	P4	100

Transaction 1 executes the following two instructions in order to retrieve details of stocks of product P1 in warehouse WH1.

```
SELECT BIN_NO, QTY
FROM   STOCK
WHERE  WAREHOUSE_NO = 'WH1'
       AND PRODUCT_NO = 'P1';

SELECT total_quantity = SUM (QTY)
FROM STOCK
WHERE WAREHOUSE_NO = 'WH1' AND PRODUCT_NO = 'P1';
```

Transaction 2 executes the following SQL.

```
UPDATE STOCK
SET QTY = QTY + 100
WHERE WAREHOUSE_NO = 'WH1'
      AND BIN_NO = 2;
```

If both transactions are executed concurrently, without concurrency control, the following sequence of events may occur.

Transaction 1	Time	Transaction 2

`SELECT BIN_NO, QTY`
`FROM   STOCK`
`WHERE  WAREHOUSE_NO = 'WH1';`
`       AND PRODUCT_NO = 'P1';`		

		`UPDATE STOCK`
		`SET QTY = QTY + 100`
		`WHERE WAREHOUSE_NO = 'WH1';`
		`      AND BIN_NO = 2;`

`SELECT total_quantity = SUM(QTY)`
`FROM STOCK`
`WHERE WAREHOUSE_NO = 'WH1'`
`      AND PRODUCT_NO = 'P1';`		

Transaction 1 will retrieve the following:

BIN_NO	QTY
1	100
2	150

total_quantity
350

and the STOCK relation will become,

STOCK

WAREHOUSE_NO	BIN_NO	PRODUCT_NO	QTY
WH1	1	P1	100
WH1	2	P1	250
WH1	3	P4	100

Note that the above sequence has resulted in the first transaction retrieving a total that does not correspond to the retrieved quantities.

Example 5.4 illustrates a further problem which occurs if one transaction accesses or updates data which has been altered by a transaction which is subsequently aborted.

Example 5.4

If the two transactions in Example 5.3 had executed as follows, with the second transaction being aborted, then once again inconsistent results would be retrieved by Transaction 1.

Transaction 1	Time	Transaction 2
| | | ```
UPDATE STOCK
SET QTY = QTY + 100
WHERE WAREHOUSE_NO = 'WH1'
AND BIN_NO = 2;
``` |
| ```
SELECT BIN_NO, QTY
FROM    STOCK
WHERE   WAREHOUSE_NO = 'WH1';
        AND PRODUCT_NO = 'P1';

SELECT total_quantity = SUM(QTY)
FROM STOCK
WHERE WAREHOUSE_NO = 'WH1'
        AND PRODUCT_NO = 'P1';
``` | | |
| | | ROLLBACK |

Transaction 1 will retrieve the following:

BIN_NO	QTY
1	100
2	250

total_quantity
350

and the STOCK relation becomes,

STOCK

WAREHOUSE_NO	BIN_NO	PRODUCT_NO	QTY
WH1	1	P1	100
WH1	2	P1	150
WH1	3	P4	100

Note that the consequence of the above sequence of events is that the first transaction has retrieved self-consistent but incorrect information because it is based on changes made by a transaction which was subsequently aborted.

5.8 Serialisable transactions

One way of preventing the types of interference between transactions described in the previous two sections is not to allow transactions to occur at the same time. If each transaction waits for the previous ones to finish before it starts there can be no interference. However, this is not an acceptable solution, because it causes excessive delays; users have to wait for the database to become 'free'. An acceptable solution should allow transactions to run at the same time, but should ensure that the transactions have the same effect on the database as if they had executed one at a time. This quality is called serialisable execution.

5.9 Locking

Serialisable execution is usually assured by applying locks to the data that is being accessed or updated by transactions. Locks are applied in the following two circumstances.

a) If a transaction needs to access some data, then a lock is applied to that data so as to stop other transactions from changing it. This ensures that the transaction has access to a database that represents a single consistent 'snapshot' of the world.

b) If a transaction is to alter some data, a lock is applied to the data to ensure that other transactions do not access that data until the alterations are complete.

Locking strategies aim to allow as much simultaneous access to a database as possible, while at the same time ensuring that the database contains accurate and consistent data. The ideal is therefore to lock as little of the database as possible for as short a time as possible. Many locking strategies have been devised, but here we describe the simple strategy that forms the basis of these.

In this simple locking strategy, two types of lock are applied.

a) *Shared locks*. These are applied to data that is being read by a transaction. A shared lock stops other transactions from updating the locked data, but other transactions are also allowed to read that data. More than one transaction may apply a shared lock to the same data objects.

b) *Exclusive locks*. These are applied to data that is being updated, and stop other transactions from updating or reading that data. Only one transaction may apply an exclusive lock to a data object at any particular time.

The rules that govern the application of shared and exclusive locks are as follows.

a) If a transaction requests a shared lock on data, then the lock is applied as soon as all exclusive locks have been released from that data. In the meantime the transaction must wait.

b) If a transaction requests an exclusive lock on data, then the lock is applied as soon as all locks (shared or exclusive) on the data are released. In the meantime the transaction must wait.

c) The locks acquired by a transaction are released when that transaction executes either a COMMIT or ROLLBACK.

Locks are used to ensure that data that is being updated is not read, and that data being read is not updated. Locks are applied automatically by RDBMSs, but some also allow users to override the automatic facility and explicitly to apply locks. Also, locks may be applied at a number of levels, e.g. at relation level (i.e. where relations are locked), or at page level (i.e. where pages are locked).

Example 5.3 is re-worked below, but this time exclusive and shared locks are applied such that inconsistent results are avoided.

Example 5.5

Consider the two transactions in Example 5.3. These operate upon the STOCK relation,

STOCK

WAREHOUSE_NO	BIN_NO	PRODUCT_NO	QTY
WH1	1	P1	100
WH1	2	P1	150
WH1	3	P4	100

Transaction 1 executes the following two instructions in order to retrieve details of stocks of product P1 in warehouse WH1.

```
SELECT BIN_NO, QTY
FROM    STOCK
WHERE   WAREHOUSE_NO = 'WH1'
            AND PRODUCT_NO = 'P1';

SELECT total_quantity = SUM(QTY)
FROM STOCK
WHERE WAREHOUSE_NO = 'WH1'
            AND PRODUCT_NO = 'P1';
```

Transaction 2 executes

```
UPDATE STOCK
SET QTY = QTY + 100
WHERE WAREHOUSE_NO = 'WH1'
        AND BIN_NO = 2;
```

If both transactions are executed concurrently, with concurrency control, the following sequence of events may occur.

Transaction 1	Time	Transaction 2

SELECT BIN_NO, QTY
FROM   STOCK
WHERE   WAREHOUSE_NO = 'WH1'
      AND PRODUCT_NO = 'P1';
  (a shared lock is applied
  to the selected data)		

		UPDATE STOCKSET QTY = QTY + 100 WHERE WAREHOUSE_NO = 'WH1' AND BIN_NO = 2; (an exclusive lock on the data to be updated is requested, but transaction 1 already has a shared lock on it. The update must therefore wait until the shared lock is released. Only then will the exclusive lock be granted allowing the update to proceed)
SELECT total_quantity = SUM(QTY) FROM STOCK WHERE WAREHOUSE_NO = 'WH1' AND PRODUCT_NO = 'P1'; COMMIT (shared lock is released)		
		(the locks on the required data have been lifted, so now an exclusive lock is applied and the update proceeds) COMMIT (locks are released)

Transaction 1 will retrieve the following:

BIN_NO	QTY
1	100
2	150

total_quantity
250

The STOCK relation becomes,

STOCK

WAREHOUSE_NO	BIN_NO	PRODUCT_NO	QTY
WH1	1	P1	100
WH1	2	P1	250
WH1	3	P4	100

Note that the above sequence has resulted in the first transaction retrieving a total that does now correspond to the retrieved quantities. The effect of applying the lock was to delay completion of Transaction 2 until after Transaction 1 had finished with the data, i.e. the effect is that of running Transaction 1 and then Transaction 2.

It is left as an exercise for the reader to re-work Examples 5.2 and 5.4 but including locking so as to avoid the problems.

5.10 Deadlock

The use of locking creates problems, as well as solving them. One such problem is that of deadlock or deadly embrace, as illustrated in the following example.

Example 5.6

Consider the situation where two transactions both update data objects X and Y. A deadlock then occurs if the following sequence of events takes place.

Transaction 1	Time	Transaction 2
Apply an exclusive lock to data X.		
		Apply an exclusive lock to data Y.
Request an exclusive lock on data Y.		
		Request an exclusive lock on data X.

The above situation is an impasse. Transaction 1 cannot proceed until Transaction 2 releases its lock on Y, but Transaction 2 will not release its lock on Y until it has obtained access to X, which is currently locked by Transaction 1. Neither transaction can proceed.

When a deadlock occur there are two or more transactions waiting for each other to release locks on data objects, and unless the RDBMS intervenes they will wait for ever!

Deadlocks can be completely prevented by requiring each transaction to lock all the data that it will need when it starts. However, the disadvantages of this strategy are that data is locked for the full duration of a transaction and it is necessary to lock whole relations, since the pages and tuples to be accessed are not identified until the appropriate commands are executed.

This is an example of a pessimistic locking strategy, because it always takes precautions to avoid the deadlock. An optimistic locking strategy allows deadlock to occur, and then breaks the deadlock. Deadlock is detected by periodically searching for a cycle in the 'who is waiting for whom' relationships. In Example 5.6 Transaction 1 has locked X but is waiting for Transaction 2 to release its lock on Y, and Transaction 2 is similarly waiting for Transaction 1 to release its lock on X. These relationships form the cycle shown below.

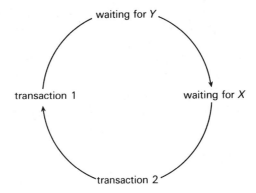

In this example there are only two transactions involved in the deadlock, but in general there may be many. When a deadlock is detected the RDBMS selects a victim transaction and aborts, or rolls it back. Some systems then automatically restart the transaction, while others return an appropriate status message so that the application program may take some appropriate action. Users should be unaware of deadlocks.

The disadvantage of optimistic strategies is that when there are many concurrent transactions, many deadlocks may occur. Some transactions may then be significantly slowed down because they repeatedly deadlock, roll back, and restart.

Some RDBMSs allow the DBA to choose between different locking strategies, both pessimistic and optimistic, and also to set the level at which locks are applied, e.g. to relations or to pages. By monitoring the performance under different strategies, the DBA may then determine the most effective concurrency controls.

Deadlocks can also be avoided by ensuring that where possible each user accesses their own copy of the required data, but this is not always feasible or desirable, since shared access to data is one of the main attractions of database systems.

5.11 Recovery from failure

Recovery from failure of the database system as a whole, rather than of individual transactions, is made possible by keeping copies of past instances of the database, and by recording details of changes that have been made to the database. Types of failure and recovery procedures are described in the following sections.

5.12 Backing up

Back-up copies of the database should be created regularly and should be stored away from the computer on which the database is stored. This is necessary in order to protect the back-up copies from any disaster such as flood or fire that may destroy the database. The frequency with which back-up copies are made depends on the frequency with which the database is changed. The parts of the database which change most frequently may be stored in separate files and may be backed up separately and more frequently than the rest of the database.

An RDBMS will include utility programs or special instructions in the database language for creating back-up copies of all or part of the database and for recreating the database from a back-up copy.

5.13 Transaction logging or audit trails

When a database is destroyed, it may be recreated from the most recent back-up copy, but transactions may have occurred since that copy was made. The effects of these transactions must be recreated in order to install the database as it was just before the system failed. In order to do this it is also necessary to record the changes made to the database by each transaction. The special file on which this information is recorded is called a transaction log or journal. Each time a transaction carries out an update, the altered data is written to the transaction log both before and after that update. These copies of the data are respectively called before-images and after-images.

The transaction log may be used to modify the database recreated from a back-up copy so as to recreate the changes made by transactions that occurred after the back-up was made.

5.14 Checkpointing

One problem remains if a database is recreated from a back-up copy and transaction log. That is, when a database is destroyed or corrupted by some failure there may be transactions which have not yet been completed.

A transaction is deemed not to have been completed when either of the following circumstances hold:

a) the transaction has not yet executed a COMMIT or ROLLBACK instruction,
b) the transaction has executed COMMIT or ROLLBACK, but the data that has been processed by the transaction is still in buffers or temporary files which have yet to be output to the database.

During recovery, these incomplete transactions must be identified and re-executed. This may be done with the aid of checkpoints.

A checkpoint is a special marker record which is periodically written to the transaction log. Before a checkpoint record is written, all data to be written to the database, which is in buffers or temporary files, is written to the database. The checkpoint record contains information about all transactions which have not been completed.

5.15 Recovery using back-up copy and transaction log

The use of back-up copies, transaction logs and checkpointing after database failures is illustrated using the following example sequence of events.

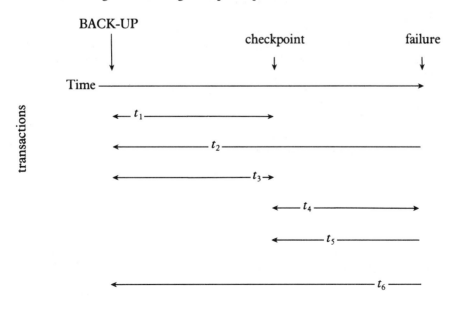

The previous diagram depicts a sequence of transactions, t_1 to t_6, which occur subsequent to a back-up of the database. A checkpoint is made, and then at some time later the system fails. The checkpoint will cause transactions t_1 and t_3 to complete, and the checkpoint record will record details of the two current transactions, t_2 and t_6. The DBA has the problem of reconstructing the database as it was just before the system failed. This must be done using the back-up, which contains a copy of the complete database as it was at the time of backing up, and a transaction log containing:

a) Before-images: a before-image is written before each data object is updated, and contains a copy of the data object to be updated.
b) After-images: an after-image is written after each data object is updated and contains its new values.
c) Checkpoint records: when a checkpoint takes place all input–output operations currently taking place are completed and a checkpoint record identifying all transactions that have not yet completed is written to the transaction log.

There are three types of failure that may have taken place.

a) Storage device failure
There may have been a storage device failure, e.g. a disk crash, which caused the database to be corrupted. In that case a new database must be reconstructed from the most recent back-up copy, and the effects of completed transactions (t_1 and t_3) must be recreated by working forward through the transaction log and applying the after-images.
Incompleted transactions are those in the last checkpoint record (t_2 and t_6) and those which start after it (t_4 and t_5). The effects of those which, according to the transaction log records, have issued a COMMIT (t_4) must be recreated from after-images. The other incomplete transactions which have not executed a ROLLBACK (t_2, t_5 and t_6) fail and have to be re-executed.

b) System failure
If the system fails such that the database is still usable, but cannot be relied on, it is necessary to work backwards from the current database using the transaction log, as follows.
Before-images are applied for incomplete transactions (t_2, t_4, t_5 and t_6). These are all transactions which are in the last checkpoint record, or which started after it. The effects of those incomplete transactions which the transaction log indicates have executed a COMMIT (t_4) are recreated by applying after-images. The other incomplete transactions (t_2, t_5 and t_6) which have not executed a ROLLBACK are deemed to have failed and must be re-executed.

c) Transaction failure
If an individual transaction fails, only those before-images from the transaction log for the failed transaction are applied. A similar recovery takes place if the transaction executes a ROLLBACK.

5.16 Security

Database systems often contain information which the database owner would rather keep private. Examples are databases containing medical information, police or security service records, and financial information. In cases where databases contain financial information, vast sums of money may sometimes be stolen by criminals who can gain access to and alter the data.

The RDBMS should make it possible to restrict access to 'sensitive' data, but this is not an easy facility to provide. For example, in recent years, dedicated 'hackers' have still managed to penetrate many highly sensitive database systems. A problem is that even if the RDBMS is secure from undesirable access through its user interfaces, the intruder may find other ways in, e.g. through the operating system. However, RDBMSs do usually provide security features which make it extremely difficult to access data that the database owner wishes to keep private.

An RDBMS will typically offer a secure means by which some privileged user (the DBA) can specify to the database system authorisation information, i.e.

a) which users are allowed access to the database,
b) times at which users may access the database and the terminal that they may use,
c) the data that may be accessed by each user,
d) the types of access that each user has to data, e.g. for update, for retrieval, for inserting new tuples, for deleting tuples,
e) how a particular user wishing to perform a particular database operation should identify him or herself.

This information, when stored within the database system, should be accessible only to the privileged user, and it should be possible for that user to alter that information instantaneously, e.g. when an intruder is detected.

Database users are assigned user names with which they must identify themselves when they enter the database system. There is often also a password that they must enter. In theory a password should be secret and known only to those who need to use it. In practice unauthorised people do find out passwords, and so the DBA must have the facility to make immediate changes to passwords. Some systems will also support password access to specific data objects, such as relations or attributes.

The external model mechanism can also be used to provide some security, since it can be used to ensure that users see only what it is necessary for them to see. An external model in a relational database system comprises the set of base relations and views to which the user needs to have access. Authorisation information concerning which base relations and views a user may have access to is specified in SQL using the GRANT and REVOKE instructions (see Section 3.9.7). For example, the SQL instruction,

```
GRANT SELECT, UPDATE ON TABLE PRODUCT TO WAREHOUSMAN;
```

will authorise the user identified as WAREHOUSMAN to execute only SELECT and UPDATE commands on the PRODUCT relation.

```
REVOKE UPDATE ON TABLE PRODUCT FROM WAREHOUSMAN;
```

will take away from WAREHOUSMAN authorisation to update the PRODUCT relation, though he may still execute SELECT. GRANT and REVOKE may be used to specify authorisation on both base relations and also views.

An RDBMS will also offer a means by which the users who have tampered with the database and the offending transactions may be tracked down. An audit trail provides this facility. An audit trail is a file into which the database system writes details of users who log on to the database system and of the transactions that they perform. It provides a historic record of the use made of the database over a period of time. This makes it possible, for example, to trace back to the user and transaction that caused a particular data object to be corrupted.

Finally, an RDBMS will offer a means by which sensitive data may be made unintelligible to any person who gains unauthorised access to it. This is done through encryption, which is the technique of applying some transformation to the 1's and 0's that are the data, so as to hide its meaning. This transformation may be reversed so as to recreate the hidden data. Encryption procedures use an encryption key that must be specified when the data is encrypted and when the encryption is reversed. This encryption key acts as a password; it is only people who know the encryption key who can unscramble the 1's and 0's to reveal the hidden data.

5.17 Integrity constraints

Integrity constraints are to prevent applications and users from changing the database in an implausible way. These are rules that must be complied with by all valid instances of the database.

There are two general integrity rules, entity and referential integrity (see Section 2.4) that must be true for all databases. Entity integrity requires all primary key values to be non-null. This ensures that every object in the database has a name. Referential integrity requires all foreign key values to be either null or correspond to a primary key value. This ensures that no cross-references are made to non-existent tuples.

The RDBMS should safeguard against the violation of these two general rules, but in practice this is not always done.

Not all RDBMSs ensure that entity integrity is satisfied; many will allow duplicate tuples within a relation, and will allow null values for primary keys.

Referential integrity is not usually enforced. This is because of the overhead of doing so. To enforce referential integrity involves assessing many tuples in different relations for each update. An exception is the UNIFY RDBMS which does go some way towards supporting referential integrity. UNIFY allows the DBA to specify that an attribute of a relation is a 'reference' to some other attribute. The UNIFY system then ensures that all values of the 'reference' attribute correspond to values of the referenced attribute.

Some RDBMSs also allow the DBA to establish database-specific integrity rules (see Section 3.11.3). For example, INGRES allows a condition to be associated with relations which must be true after any update of that relation.

5.18 Summary

★ A transaction is a set of database language instructions that corresponds to some single real world task, and must be executed as a single task.

★ The effects of a transaction become permanent and known to other database users after the transaction executes a COMMIT, or are removed when it executes a ROLLBACK or ABORT.

★ Locks are used to safeguard against interference between transactions. Shared locks are used to stop transactions updating data that is being read, and exclusive locks stop data being read while it is being updated.

★ When a database system fails, it is recovered from back-up copies, and a transaction log which includes checkpoint records. A transaction log includes before- and after-images of updated data. When a checkpoint takes place all outputs to the database are completed and a checkpoint record describing current transactions is written to the transaction log.

★ A damaged database is recovered from the most recent back-up copy, and then subsequent transactions are applied using the after-images of the transaction log.

★ After a system failure, the database is recovered by using the transaction log to recreate the effects of transactions that were incomplete at the time of the failure.

★ Database security is difficult to ensure, but most systems will allow a privileged user, the DBA, to specify authorisation information and will allow encryption of data. Also, integrity constraints can sometimes be specified to ensure that implausible updates do not take place. An audit trail enables the DBA to trace the culprit after the database has been misused.

Exercises

5.1 What is a transaction?

5.2 What effect does a COMMIT instruction have?

5.3 What effect does a ROLLBACK instruction have?

5.4 Give an example of how an update may be lost when two updates occur simultaneously.

5.5 Give an example of how concurrent transactions can:
a) cause inconsistent data to be retrieved;
b) cause consistent but incorrect data to be retrieved.

5.6 Show how, using exclusive and shared locks, the problems that are illustrated in Examples 5.2 and 5.4 could be avoided.

5.7 Locking strategies can cause deadlock. Explain what deadlock is, and give an example of how it can occur.

5.8 How can deadlock be avoided?

5.9 How can a deadlock be resolved, without the database user knowing anything about it?

5.10 What is a transaction log?

5.11 What is a checkpoint?

5.12 What is a back-up copy?

5.13 How can the DBA recover the database system using back-up copies and a transaction log?
a) after hardware failure
b) after system failure
c) after transaction failure.

5.14 Describe the SQL facilities for ensuring database security.

5.15 Describe the INGRES facilities for ensuring database integrity.

5.16 What is encryption, and what is it used for?

5.17 The director of a financial organisation has been alarmed by horror stories in the newspapers concerning the vulnerability of relational databases. She has asked you to write a report advising her as to the risks to data as a consequence of system failures and the vulnerability of data to unauthorised access. In your report you should identify the potential risks and steps that can be taken to minimise them. (If you have access to an RDBMS, assume that it is the one used by the financial organisation, and make your report specific to its features.)

6 Distributed relational databases

6.1 Introduction

This chapter discusses how relational database systems may be implemented using a number of computers which communicate via a communications network. There are three variations on this theme.

a) *Client/server database systems*. These allow a database stored on one computer to be accessed remotely by programs running on others.

b) *Multi-database systems*. These enable applications to access many databases stored on different computers as if they were a single database.

c) *Distributed database systems*. These allow the parts of a single database to be stored on a number of different computers.

Client/server and multi-database systems are described in Section 6.2, and distributed database systems in Section 6.3. The technologies described are relatively new and some of the issues are complex. This book provides only an introductory overview.

6.2 Client/server and multi-database systems

A client/server DBMS (C/SDBMS) provides facilities by which applications running on a (client) computer may access a database stored on another (server) computer, where the computers are connected by a communications network (as illustrated in Figure 6.1).

Figure 6.1   *Client/server database system*

Examples of this type of system are INGRES's INGRES/NET and ORACLE's SQL*Net.

A remote (client) application must identify the (server) computer and database when the connection between application and database is made. However, all subsequent operations are as if that database and application are on one computer, though data definition and manipulation operations may be slower because of the relatively slow speed of transmitting data over the network.

Client computers typically act as sophisticated workstations on which to run database applications. They will store front-end software, i.e. 4GL tools and applications, which generate statements in SQL or some other database language. Front-end software gains access across the network to a specific database by issuing an appropriate connect instruction to the database networking software. The database networking software subsequently routes all queries issued by the front-end software across the network to the back-end DBMS running on the server computer which manages the specified database, and routes all DBMS responses back to the front-end software.

This type of facility has two advantages. It makes possible wider access to existing databases. For example, a database created and managed by one department on its own departmental computer may be accessed by other departments using a C/SDBMS. It also makes possible computer specialisation. A C/SDBMS enables all database storage and retrieval operations to be devolved to one or a few dedicated computer systems, called database servers or data managers. This means that only the database servers require storage and processing power sufficient to store and manage the database. It is therefore possible to take advantage of any economies of scale which exist. For example, in general the cost and speed of storing or retrieving a character of data is less for large-capacity storage devices.

A computer which does only database processing can be configured and tuned so as to give the best possible performance for that task. In fact an organisation may choose to use a special type of computer designed specifically for database processing, i.e. a database machine. Furthermore, it is easier to manage and maintain data when it is all stored in one place using a single DBMS.

The uncoupling of the back-end and front-end software makes possible an open-systems architecture, i.e. one in which the interface to the back-end conforms to some standard. Given an open-system architecture, software houses and users may establish a range of front-end and back-end products. This is advantageous to users, as it potentially provides them with greater choice and flexibility. They may 'shop around' for the most appropriate software products, rather than having to rely on software which is integrated into a DBMS itself and is supplied only by the DBMS vendor.

A problem with the client/server architecture is the reliance on one or a few (server) computers for all database accesses. If a database server fails then all associated database applications go down with it. A solution is to store the database on more than one database server and execute updates on all the copies, but this strategy of course significantly adds to the cost of the database system.

Some C/SDBMSs, e.g. SYBASE, now support queries and updates to more than one server database. This type of system is called a multi-database system, and has the advantage that:

a) data stored on different databases may be combined; for example, using a multi-database system, it is possible to join relations stored in different databases;

b) users are allowed to administer their own databases without the imposition of some central control (this is not the case if a distributed database system is used to integrate data stored on a number of different computers (see Section 6.3)).

An external model of a database system is a user's view of the database and includes only data that is relevant to that user (see Section 2.7). In a relational system the external model comprises a set of base relations and views (see Section 2.8). A multi-database system extends this notion of external models by supporting them both for individual databases, and also for groups of databases (see Figure 6.2). In this way a user can be presented with a virtual database, i.e. one that does not actually exist, which is formed by integrating data physically stored in one or more actual databases. For example, using a multi-database system a sales analysis application could access a view which is created by joining a relation containing details of sales orders stored in a database on the sales office computer, with a relation containing details of products stored in a database on the computer in the production control office.

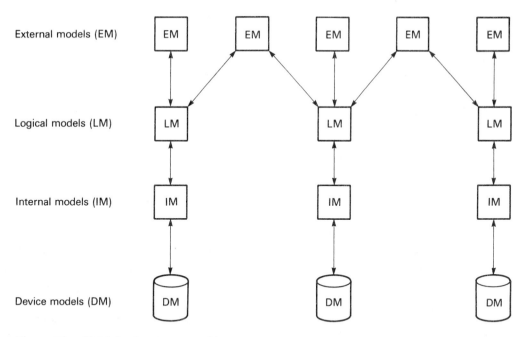

Figure 6.2   *Multi-database system architecture*

6.3 Distributed databases

6.3.1 What is a distributed database and why use one?

In a distributed database system (DDBMS) parts of a single database are stored on a number of computers connected by a communications network (as illustrated in Figure

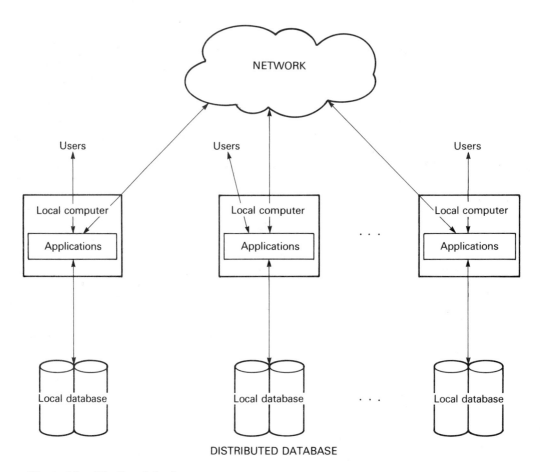

Figure 6.3   *Distributed database system*

6.3). The main advantage is that data may be stored where it is used, while at the same time there are still the benefits of managing data as a single entity (see Section 1.3.2).

For example, using distributed database technology, a large manufacturing organisation may implement its computer systems on a number of separate computers rather than a single mainframe computer. These may be sited in each of the warehouses, in the accounts department, in each sales office, etc. A network which links these computers will then enable them to communicate one with another, and a DDBMS will make it possible for any of the computers to access data stored on another.

Alternatively, a large organisation may already have a number of existing computers sited in different departments, divisions, or areas, and each computer may already maintain its own database. A DDBMS can then be used to integrate the separate databases into a single one, and so make the data more widely available.

Research into distributed database systems started in the 1970s, but true distributed DBMSs did not come on to the market until the mid-1980s. The first DDBMS products were INGRES/STAR from INGRES (previously Relational Technology), SQL*STAR from ORACLE, VAX Data Distribution from DEC, and NonStop SQL from Tandem, though there are now others.

In a distributed database system, the computer at each site possesses the capability of carrying out processing on its own, i.e. each site has some local autonomy, and is also capable of processing data stored on other computers.

Applications that take place in one computer independent of others are called local applications. An example of a local application is where a warehouse clerk updates stock levels which are stored on the computer in the warehouse and nowhere else.

A distributed database system will also support applications which involve accessing data stored on a number of computers. These are called global applications. An example of a global application is where a sales office clerk creates an invoice from information about the customer, stored at the central office computer, and from sales order information stored locally on the sales office computer.

A distributed database system therefore has the following features:

a) a collection of data is distributed over a number of different computers,
b) the computers are linked by a communications network,
c) each computer can perform some local applications,
d) each computer participates in at least one global application.

The general requirements of a database system also apply to a distributed database system, as they do to a single-site one, i.e. that the database should be a natural representation of information as data, sharable by all relevant applications (see Section 1.3.2).

Users of a database system should not be able to discern if it is local or remote, centralised or distributed, since they should access only logical structures of the database as a whole. The fact that a distributed database is split into parts which may be stored on different computers should be hidden. Applications are therefore implemented on a distributed database system in the same way as for a centralised one (see Chapter 3).

There are two consequences of opting for a distributed database system rather than a centralised one. Firstly, there is less central control. Individual computers in the system have some capability for independent processing and therefore some independence. However, the system as a whole must still be managed, and so at least two tiers of management are necessary; there will be both local and global DBAs.

Secondly, there will be greater physical duplication of data. An objective of distributed database design is to store data where it will be used, and so data that is used at two or more sites will often be duplicated. This means that the DDBMS must work harder in order to keep the database consistent and correct. However, this does not cause problems for users, since they will access a single logical database and the usual logical database design techniques such as normalisation (see Chapter 4) will have been applied to ensure that there is no unnecessary duplication of logical data.

Two advantages claimed of a distributed rather than a centralised database are a consequence of the structure and politics of the organisation itself. Distribution may fit naturally into an organisation's structure. For example, relevant parts of the database may be stored within an organisation's divisions, departments, offices, etc. This may be appropriate when sections of an organisation have considerable independence, since the DDBMS then gives each section some control over their own data resources.

The second advantage is that there may be political or legal constraints as to where data is stored. If an organisation is required to store data at some specific location, a DDBMS will then provide wider access to that data.

There are also possible financial advantages. Money is saved in a distributed system by reducing the communications costs. Placing much of the data where it is needed will result in less data transmission across communications lines. Furthermore incremental growth is possible with a distributed system. It may be cheaper and less disruptive to expand a database system by adding an extra (small) computer to the network rather than by upgrading a large mainframe computer. Also, each computer may be tailored to the often diverse requirements of the respective divisions.

Greater reliability is also claimed of a distributed system, in that it is more robust. When a centralised database system crashes, the complete system becomes unusable until it is up again. This problem may be eased by running a 'twin' computer system as a stand-by; all database operations are duplicated on the 'twin' and when a crash occurs, the twin takes over. However, this is expensive as it means running two central computers rather than one. On the other hand, when a computer or communication link of a distributed system fails, it may be possible for much if not all of the system to continue operating. In some cases there may be an alternative route which by-passes the broken communications link, or the data made unavailable by the crash may be duplicated on some other computer. This ability to continue after failure, but with reduced facilities, is called graceful degradation and is a property that human beings also possess. For example, if I break one of my legs, I can still perform many functions, albeit with reduced speed.

Better performance is also claimed of distributed systems because local applications will run faster. A small local computer with data and software for local applications will often run faster than a larger remote computer which stores the complete database and runs all applications.

There are many problems that have not yet been satisfactorily solved for distributed database systems. Organisational problems include the following.

a) *Management of a multi-computer system.* For example, with a single-computer system, time can be scheduled for engineering work, for back-ups, for systems programming work including operating system upgrades, etc. This scheduling becomes more difficult where other computers rely on that computer being available. Computer schedules must then be synchronised so that computers are available when they are needed by others.

b) *Database administration.* The greater complexity of a distributed database system makes administration correspondingly more complex.

c) *Privacy and security of information.* The problems of ensuring privacy and security at site level are much the same as for a centralised system. There is however the additional problem of restricting access across the network.

d) *Recovery from system or transaction failure.* Recovery is harder to ensure as it may involve a number of computers executing a single transaction.

There may also be performance problems which are solved by system tuning. A centralised database is made faster by adjusting the physical representation of the data. Tuning therefore involves consideration of hashing algorithms, indexes, clustering, etc. (see Chapter 4). A distributed database system on the other hand is made faster by reducing the number of records that are transmitted across the network. The access speed within a computer may be negligible compared with the transmission speed across the network.

The newness of distributed database technology is also a cause of problems, owing to lack of experience. There is as yet very little experience of using this technology, and standard methods and approaches to designing and utilising distributed databases are not yet well established.

The above advantages and disadvantages for distributed database systems makes them more desirable for large organisations which are distributed over a wide geographical area, and where the management structure is such that departments and divisions have a large degree of self-management. This may be the case for companies which, having merged, possess a number of existing computer systems and database systems.

6.3.2 The architecture of a distributed database system

The architecture of a computer system is the set of parts from which it is made, and the ways in which they are related. In Chapter 2, a general database systems architecture was introduced (see Figure 2.18). This architecture is extended, as shown in Figure 6.4, to allow for database distribution.

The distributed database system architecture includes the external, logical, internal, and device models of a single-site database system. However, note that there is a separate logical, internal, and device model for each local computer. In addition, there are global, fragmentation, allocation and mapping schemas which collectively allow the local databases to be treated as parts of a single database.

Global schema
A distributed database system will include a logical description of the whole database, as if it were not distributed. This description is called the global schema.

The global schema for a distributed relational database will be the same as the logical schema for an equivalent centralised database, and will include definitions of base relations, and authorisation and integrity constraints (see Section 2.8).

External model
External models may be defined on the global schema to give each application a view of the database that includes only relevant information. As with a centralised database, the external model of a distributed relational database will comprise virtual and base relations relevant to some specific user or application (see Section 2.8).

Fragment schema and allocation schema
Fragments are logical partitions of a distributed database. A fragment is a subset of attribute values of a base relation in the global schema. Values are grouped into a

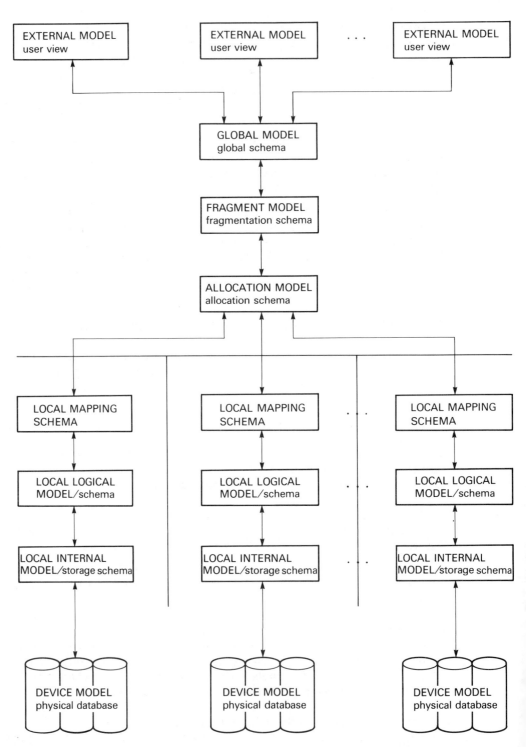

Figure 6.4   *Architecture of a distributed database system*

fragment because they have some common property, e.g. they are accessed by a particular application, or are accessed from specific locations. Fragments are defined in the fragment schema. Each fragment of a distributed database must be stored in one or more of the (local) computers. The location at which each fragment is stored is specified in the allocation schema.

Definition and allocation of fragments is done strategically so as to achieve the following objectives.
a) *Process locality.* Data should be stored where it will be used, when it is economic to do so. A fragment may in fact be used at a number of different sites, in which case it may be desirable to duplicate that fragment and place a copy at each of those sites. This duplication also improves resilience to failure (see the next paragraph), but the cost is paid when the database is updated; when one fragment is updated so must all of its copies.
b) *Resilience to system failures.* Resilience is improved by duplicating fragments so that there is an alternate copy in the event of failure.
c) *Avoidance of bottle-necks and under-utilisation of the resources.* The designer should take into account the availability and cost of storage on each of the computers, for example, by utilising cheap mass storage where appropriate.

The definition and allocation of fragments must therefore be based primarily on how the database is to be used. The designer must analyse major applications in terms of their requirements and statistics. The design should be based on:
a) how frequently and from which locations applications are executed;
b) details of transactions that are initiated when each application is executed, including which relations, attributes and tuples are accessed, and what type of access is required, e.g. for read, insert, delete or update;
c) specific requirements of applications and transactions, such as maximum acceptable execution times;
d) the relative importance of each application compared with others.

The designer must also have knowledge of relative costs associated with accessing data stored in the distributed database.

Using the above information about applications and data access costs, it is possible to estimate relative costs and benefits associated with alternative fragmentation and allocation strategies, and so to seek the most advantageous design. These estimations should take into account the benefit of greater system resilience gained through duplicating fragments, as well as the costs associated with updating duplicated fragments.

The two basic types of fragment are horizontal fragments, which are subsets of tuples, and vertical fragments, which are subsets of attributes. There are two general rules which apply to horizontal and vertical fragments of a relation. These are:

Rule 1: completeness
Every attribute value of the base relations in the global schema must occur within the set of fragments.

Rule 2: reconstructability
It must be possible to reconstruct the base relation from its fragments.

A third rule also applies to horizontal fragments, i.e. tuple subsets.

Rule 3: non-overlapping
Fragments should not overlap. If the tuples of a base relation are divided into a number of fragments, each tuple must occur in one and only one of those fragments.

A horizontal fragment is defined using the restriction operator of relational algebra (see Section 2.3.6). The restriction condition is defined to group together tuples which have some common property, e.g. they are all used by the same application or are all used at the same locations.

As an illustration of horizontal fragmentation, consider a distributed database system which includes a computer in each warehouse and where the global schema includes a WAREHOUSE relation, an example instance of which is given in Figure 6.5. The tuples of WAREHOUSE represent information about the contents of the bins in each warehouse.

WAREHOUSE

WH_NO	BIN_NO	P_NO	QTY
WH1	B1	P1	500
WH1	B2	P1	300
WH1	B3	P4	150
WH1	B4	P2	1000
WH2	B1	P5	5000
WH2	B2	P6	1000
WH2	B3	P6	500

Figure 6.5   *Example WAREHOUSE relation*

An obvious strategy is to split WAREHOUSE into horizontal fragments, each containing tuples for just one warehouse, and to store the fragments on the computers in the appropriate warehouses. The advantage is that warehouse applications, such as recording goods inwards and outwards, and inventory control then become local applications.

These fragments are defined, respectively, by the equivalent in the appropriate database language of the following expressions in relational algebra.

WAREHOUSE_1: RESTRICT WAREHOUSE WHERE WAREHOUSE_NO = 'WH1'
WAREHOUSE_2: RESTRICT WAREHOUSE WHERE WAREHOUSE_NO = 'WH2'

Given the WAREHOUSE relation in Figure 6.5, these fragments are as shown in Figure 6.6. Note that WAREHOUSE_1 and WAREHOUSE_2 satisfy all three of the general rules: (Rule 1) all tuples of WAREHOUSE are included within the fragments; (Rule 2) the WAREHOUSE relation may be recreated from the union of the fragments; and (Rule 3) each tuple is in only one fragment.

WAREHOUSE_1

WH_NO	BIN_NO	P_NO	QTY
WH1	B1	P1	500
WH1	B2	P1	300
WH1	B3	P4	150
WH1	B4	P2	1000

WAREHOUSE_2

WH_NO	BIN_NO	P_NO	QTY
WH2	B1	P5	5000
WH2	B2	P6	1000
WH2	B3	P6	500

Figure 6.6 *Example horizontal fragments of WAREHOUSE*

Vertical fragments are subsets of the attributes of a relation in the global schema, and are defined using the PROJECT operator of relational algebra (see Section 2.4.7). This type of fragment is used to group together attributes that are used by specific applications. The advantage is that vertical fragments may be stored where the relevant applications take place.

Vertical fragmentation is also an important part of the design of non-distributed database systems (see Section 4.22). For instance, if only part of a base relation is used by a frequently occurring application, it may make sense to split that relation into vertical fragments. The frequently occurring application will then execute faster because the tuples in the fragment that it accesses will be shorter than those of the base relation.

As an example of vertical fragmentation, consider a distributed database system which includes computers in the salaries office and in each department. The global schema includes an EMPLOYEE relation, an example of which is given in Figure 6.7.

The salaries office applications require access to EMP_NO, NAME, SALARY and TAX_CODE only; and the departments' work scheduling applications require access to EMP_NO, NAME, MANAGER_NO and DEPARTMENT_NO. An obvious design is therefore to fragment EMPLOYEE vertically so as to place these two subsets of attributes in separate fragments and to store them, as appropriate, in the salaries office and the departments' computers.

EMPLOYEE

EMP_NO	NAME	SALARY	TAX_CODE	MANAGER_NO	DEPT_NO
E1	J Smith	12000.00	T10	E5	D1
E2	B Brown	12000.00	T10	E5	D1
E3	T Red	9123.00	T4	E12	D4
E5	R Bod	22192.00	T12	null	D1
E12	S Pid	20131.00	T12	null	D4

Figure 6.7 *Example EMPLOYEE relation*

The two fragments are respectively defined by the equivalent in some relational database language of the following relational algebra expressions.

EMPLOYEE_1: PROJECT EMPLOYEE ON EMP_NO, NAME, SALARY, TAX_CODE
EMPLOYEE_2: PROJECT EMPLOYEE ON EMP_NO, NAME, MANAGER_NO, DEPT_NO

Given the example EMPLOYEE relation in Figure 6.7, the fragments are as in Figure 6.8. Note that both fragments include the key EMP_NO. This is necessary so that the EMPLOYEE relation may be recreated from its fragments (Rule 2).

EMPLOYEE_1

EMP_NO	NAME	SALARY	TAX_CODE
E1	J Smith	12000.00	T10
E2	B Brown	12000.00	T10
E3	T Red	9123.00	T4
E5	R Bod	22192.00	T12
E12	S Pid	20131.00	T12

EMPLOYEE_2

EMP_NO	NAME	MANAGER_NO	DEPT_NO
E1	J Smith	E5	D1
E2	B Brown	E5	D1
E3	T Red	E12	D4
E5	R Bod	null	D1
E12	S Pid	null	D4

Figure 6.8   *Example vertical fragments of EMPLOYEE*

Vertical and horizontal are the two basic types of fragment, but there are other types, e.g. mixed fragments and derived horizontal fragments. (Derived fragments are based on the SEMI-JOIN operator of relational algebra (see Section 2.44.4) and are used to place joinable fragments at the same location.) However, these are not described here, as a full treatment of the complex issue of distributed database design is beyond the scope of this book.

Local databases
Each computer of a distributed database system will store a set of fragments in its local database, and will run a (local) DBMS. A DDBMS may be categorised as being either heterogeneous or homogeneous, depending on the nature of the (local) computer systems.

A heterogeneous system is one in which the parts are of different types. There are a number of ways in which a distributed database system may be heterogeneous. The local DBMS may be of different types, e.g. network, hierarchical or relational (see Section 2.2.2); or different implementations of the same type of database, e.g. INGRES, ORACLE and DB2 relational DBMSs. Also, the database may be heterogeneous in that it is stored on different hardware, running under different operating systems.

In a homogeneous database system all of the local DBMSs are of the same type.

Current DDBMS products tend to be data-model homogeneous, usually relational, but may allow different RDBMS products at the local computers. For each local computer, the logical structures in the local database must correspond to those in the global database. The mapping between the global structures and the local structures is described in the local mapping schema.

6.3.3 Query processing in a distributed database system

Query processing in a distributed database system is more complicated than in a centralised system. A query must be decomposed into a set of subqueries, one for each local database that is to be searched, and this must be done such that the amount of data transmitted across the network is kept to a minimum. However, the user should be unaware of any of these complexities. A fully distributed database system will look to the user as if it is stored at one site, and so will not require any extensions to the database language, SQL say.

Data manipulation instructions are processed in a distributed database system in the following way. A query submitted by an application is analysed by the DDBMS and translated into a corresponding query expressed in the database language of the DDBMS, i.e. the global language. This global query requires access to data stored on a number of different computers, and so the DDBMS translates it into a set of subqueries, one for each of the local databases to be searched. Subqueries are transmitted across the network to the appropriate local computers, where they are translated into corresponding queries in the database language of the local DBMS. Responses are then routed back across the network, are assembled by the DDBMS software and passed back to the applications. This process is depicted in Figure 6.9.

Concurrency controls are necessary in a distributed database system to safeguard against concurrent transactions interfering with each other. The problems are the same as for a single-site database system (see Chapter 5), with the added complication that many computers may be involved in executing a single transaction.

Distributed database systems will typically provide concurrency control by operating a locking protocol (as described in Chapter 5), but will also operate a two-phase commit protocol to ensure that either all or none of an update operation takes place. This protocol operates in the following way.

Phase 1: prepare for update phase
On receiving an update instruction, the following takes place.
a) The update instruction is split up into subinstructions, one for each participating computer.
b) Subinstructions are transmitted to the appropriate computers.
c) Participating local computers perform the update operations on secure copies of the data, and then return a READY-FOR-UPDATE message.

(Note that the permanent database has not yet been updated; only copies of the data have been changed.)

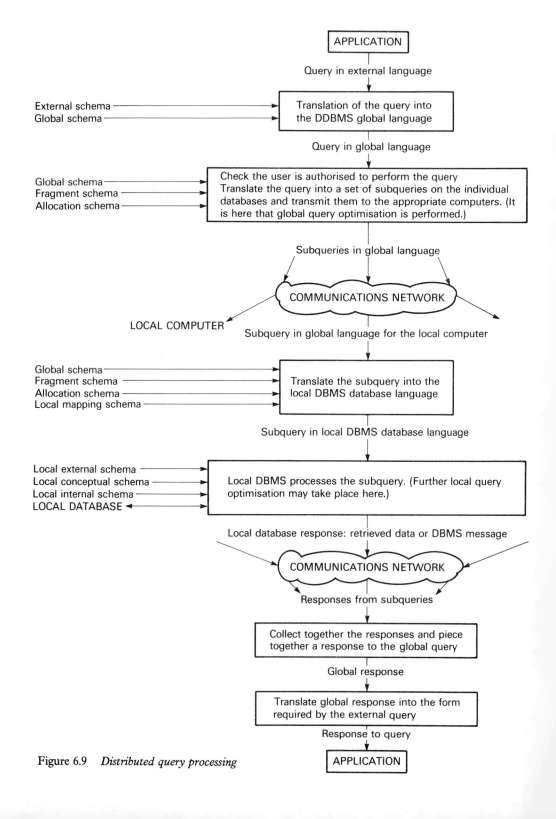

Figure 6.9 *Distributed query processing*

Phase 2: `COMMIT-` **or** `ABORT-UPDATE` **phase**

On receipt of a `READY-FOR-UPDATE` response from all participating computers, the computer from which the subupdates were sent, i.e. the controlling computer, will complete the update as follows. The controlling computer will send to each participating computer a `COMMIT-UPDATE` message. On receipt of `COMMIT-UPDATE`, each participating computer will make the updates permanent.

If the controlling computer does not receive a `READY-FOR-UPDATE` from each participating computer, it will send them each an `ABORT-UPDATE` message, causing them to 'forget' the update.

6.3.4 Objectives of distributed database systems

DDBMS are a fairly recent innovation and the technology is still evolving. To round off this section we summarise the direction in which DDBMS technology is heading by listing C. J. Date's twelve objectives of distributed database systems. (C. J. Date, an eminent database researcher, presented these objectives at the *1987 Conference on Very Large Database Systems* in Brighton, UK.)

The twelve objectives itemise the properties of an ideal DDBMS, and are as follows.

1) *Local autonomy.* Each site should be able to run independently.
2) *No reliance on a central site.* There should be no one site without which the database cannot operate.
3) *Continuous operation.* There should be no planned shut-downs.
4) *Location independence.* The user should be able to access the database from any site. All data should be accessible as if it were stored on a single-site database regardless of where it is physically stored.
5) *Fragmentation independence.* The user should be able to access the data, regardless of how it is fragmented.
6) *Replication independence.* It should not be necessary for the user to be aware that data is duplicated. The user should not need to know that a particular fragment is stored at more than one site.
7) *Distributed query processing.* The system should be capable of processing queries which reference data stored on a number of computers.
8) *Distributed transaction management.* The system should support transactions as the unit of recovery. It should be possible for users to commit or roll back transactions as if they were executing at a single site, and the DDBMS should include necessary safeguards against interference between concurrent transactions (see Chapter 5).
9) *Hardware independence.* The distributed database system may comprise different types of computer.
10) *Operating system independence.* The computers may run different operating systems.
11) *Network independence.* The computers may be linked by any type of network.
12) *DBMS independence.* The computers may run different DBMSs. The local mapping schema will then make the binding between the objects in the local databases and those in the global database.

The above twelve objectives are satisfied by an ideal DDBMS still to be realised. For example, actual DDBMSs have restrictions on the computer hardware, operating systems, and local DBMSs. Also, there are often restrictions on distributed updates. However, Date's objectives do provide a useful indication of what we should expect of DDBMSs of the future.

6.4 Summary

This chapter has described database systems which utilise more than one computer. Three types of system have been described.

★ Client/server database systems, in which applications and database may be on different computers. The advantages are wider access to databases, and benefits of a specialised computer system.

★ Multi-database systems which are client/server database systems, but where a client computer can query or update many database servers. A multi-database system supports external models on individual databases, and also on groups of databases. An advantage is the ability to integrate data stored on separate databases, but without having to impose some central administration on them.

★ Distributed database systems are those in which parts of a single database are stored on a number of computers. Advantages are the ability to place data where it is used, while at the same time managing the data as a single entity. An extended database systems architecture has been described to allow distribution, and query processing with two-phase commit has been described.

Exercises

6.1 How does a client/server DBMS differ from a conventional one?

6.2 What are the two main advantages of a client/server architecture?

6.3 Identify a major weakness of a client/server architecture, and suggest a way of lessening this problem.

6.4 How do views, as supported by a multi-database system, differ from those supported by a conventional RDBMS?

6.5 How do a multi-database system and a distributed database system differ?

6.6 How will distributing a database system affect the user?

6.7 Identify two organisational, two financial, and three performance-based reasons for distributing a database system.

6.8 Identify six reasons for not distributing a database system.

6.9 Sketch the architecture of a distributed database system.

6.10 What are the contents and purposes of each of the following parts of a distributed database system?
a) external model
b) global model
c) fragmentation model
d) allocation model
e) local mapping schema
f) local logical, internal and device models.

6.11 Identify three objectives of database fragmentation and allocation.

6.12 What are the two basic types of fragment?

6.13 Identify and explain the basis of the three fragmentation rules, i.e. the completeness, reconstructability, and non-overlapping rules.

6.14 Describe two-phase commit, and explain why it is necessary in distributed query processing.

6.15 Summarise the likely capabilities and characteristics of a DDBMS of the future.

6.16 You have been asked to advise a small college of further education, which currently uses a relational database system running on a small mainframe for its administration activities, on the advisability of changing to distributed database technology. Write a report for the Principal of the college which identifies and explains the options, i.e. client/server, multi-database, and distributed database systems, and sets out the arguments for and against each of these.

7 And what next?

7.1 Introduction

The relational model has been the main vehicle for research into database systems since the early 1970s, and is the foundation for state-of-the-art database technology. However, it is known to be less than perfect and is inappropriate for a number of applications areas, e.g. office automation, expert systems, and computer-aided design and manufacture (CAD/CAM). In this chapter we take a critical look at the relational model and speculate on the next generation of database technology.

Section 7.2 is a summary of some of the strengths of the relational model. These strengths are not fully exploited in current RDBMSs, since they do not support all of the features of the relational model; there is a gap between theory and practice. This gap is examined in Section 7.3 and criteria are presented for classifying how relational a DBMS is. Codd's twelve rules for RDBMSs are also presented in this section. Though no RDBMSs currently satisfy all twelve rules, the rules do provide an indication of likely capabilities of future RDBMSs.

The relational model itself is inadequate for various important applications but in spite of the known weaknesses there is at present no obvious contender to supersede it. Section 7.4 examines these inadequacies and identifies some promising developments filtering through from database research.

7.2 Strengths of the relational model

The strengths of the relational model are to do with its simplicity, theoretical rigour, practicality and generality. The simplicity of relational technology is a result of the following features.

a) The relational model is not complicated by implementation-type features such as file structures and access methods, but is concerned solely with the logical structure of data.
b) All data can be accessed on the basis of its values and all relationships between data are implicit in the data values; relationships do not have to be built into the database using special structures.
c) The users may view a relational database very simply as a set of tables.
d) The manipulative part of the model, relational algebra (see Section 2.3), provides the basis for simple, powerful, and mainly non-procedural database languages (see Chapter 3). These languages may be thought of as providing comprehensive 'cut and paste' operations for putting together new database 'tables' from the values of existing ones.

The relational model has been developed with theoretical rigour and provides the mathematical tools for modelling databases and their use. This makes it possible to analyse properties of database systems without first having to implement them. The theory has been used successfully to explore problems such as database language design (see Chapter 3) and database design (see Chapter 4).

The relational model provides a practical basis for building actual DBMS products (see Chapter 2). This is in spite of early doubts; for some years the relational model was thought of by many as being impracticable for large databases because of the overheads of implementing the operators of relational algebra. However, the rapid increase of computer power and decrease in hardware costs which has taken place during the 1970s and 1980s has made possible implementations of RDBMs with sufficient performance for handling large databases. RDBMSs are now considered the state-of-the-art for all sizes of database.

The relational model is general in that it has proved appropriate for a wide area of applications, e.g. in business, industry, scientific research and engineering.

7.3 The gap between theory and reality

Current RDBMS products do not implement all features of the relational model. For example, the author knows of no RDBMS which supports domains (see Section 2.2.1). This gap between the theory and reality has given rise to some confusion as to which DBMS products are, and which are not, relational; many DBMSs with very few relational features are marketed as RDBMSs. E. F. Codd, the inventor of the relational model, has helped to clarify the distinction between RDBMSs and other DBMSs by publishing (in the 1981 ACM Turing Award Lecture) the following rule.

Minimum requirements rule. For a DBMS to be considered relational, it must satisfy at least the following requirements.

a) All information should be represented as values in tables without user-visible navigation links between them.
b) The database language should support the three important operators of the relational algebra, RESTRICT, PROJECT and JOIN, as single operators. The user should not have to specify loops, decisions or sequences of instructions in order to execute these, and it should not be necessary first to specify physical access paths to support them. Also, the JOIN operator should be unrestricted, i.e. it should be possible to join on the basis of any pair of attributes which may be matched and which have the same domain or type.

Given the above requirements, DBMSs may be classified as follows.

 i) Tabular DBMSs support a) above, but not b). A tabular DBMS is not relational, though a number of tabular DBMSs have been marketed as being relational.
 ii) Minimally relational DBMSs support both a) and b).
iii) Relationally complete DBMSs support a), b) and also all of the other operators of relational algebra (see Section 2.3). This is the case for systems which support relationally complete database languages such as SQL and QUEL (see Chapter 3).
iv) Fully relational DBMSs support all features of the relational model, including entity and referential integrity (see Section 2.4) and domains (see Section 2.2.1).

Leading RDBMS products, including ORACLE, INGRES, DB2, SQL/DS and SYBASE, are currently relationally complete, but the author knows of none that is fully relational.

The above classifications are based on the relational model as defined by E. F. Codd in the early 1970s (described in Chapter 2), and are concerned only with the data definition and manipulation capabilities. However, there are other requirements of a modern DBMS (these have been described in the preceding chapters of this book) which should also be taken into account. Codd has expanded the relational model so as to embrace these, and has recently (in 1990) published Version 2 of the relational model (RM/V2) (he now calls the original version RM/V1). RM/V2 includes the original three parts, i.e. structural, manipulative and integrity (described in Chapter 2), but also parts concerning other aspects of database management, such as authorisation, the data dictionary or catalogue, views, attribute naming and data types. The flavour of the additional parts in RM/V2 is apparent in the set of Codd's twelve rules (published in *Computerworld*, October 1985) which further clarify the distinction between RDBMSs and other DBMSs. In practice, not one RDBMS yet satisfies all of these rules and so they may be considered as Codd's requirements for an ideal RDBMS. The rules are as follows.

Rule 0
The twelve rules are each based on a single underlying rule (Rule 0) which is that an RDBMS must be able to manage the database entirely through its relational feature.

The above definitions of tabular, minimal, complete and fully relational DBMSs are concerned only with data definition and manipulation. Rule 0 goes further by requiring all aspects of database management to be accomplishable through relational features.

Rule 1: information rule
All information in the relational database must be represented explicitly at the logical level in the form of relations. The entire database must be viewable by the user as a set of tables; there must be no hidden values or relationships.

Rule 2: guaranteed access rule
Each item of data must be logically accessible through a combination of relation name, primary key value and attribute name. This is a consequence of the definition of primary key (see Section 2.3.5) and the entity integrity rule (see Section 2.5.2), which requires primary keys to be unique and not to have null values.

Rule 3: systematic treatment of null values rule
An RDBMS must support the use of null values for representing missing or inapplicable information in a systematic way which is independent of data type.

A null value is not the same as a zero numeric field or a text field filled with spaces; zero and spaces are values but null represents an absence of a value. An RDBMS should therefore treat nulls as being different from other attribute values. Nulls are used where an attribute value is inapplicable or unknown. For example, consider an EMPLOYEE relation which contains a tuple describing an employee called Joan Pearson. One of the attributes, HOME_TELEPHONE_NUMBER, has a null value because Ms Pearson is not on the telephone. Another tuple which describes John Darwin also has a null HOME_TELEPHONE_NUMBER value, but this time it is because Mr Darwin is on the telephone, but has yet to inform us of his telephone number.

Rule 4: database description rule
The database's description, i.e. the data dictionary or catalogue, must be represented at the logical level in the same way as ordinary data, i.e. as relations, and it may be accessed by authorised users using the same relational languages, e.g. using SQL.

Rule 5: comprehensive sublanguage rule
Though there may be many database languages, at least one must be expressible as strings of characters and have a well-defined syntax. It should be usable interactively and also within applications programs, and should support all of the following:
a) data definition; i.e. the creation, deletion and alteration of relations,
b) view definition; the creation and removal of user views,
c) data manipulation; the retrieval and update of data stored in the database,
d) integrity constraints; the specification of the rules that restrict the contents of the database so that it remains sensible and plausible,
e) authorisation; the granting and revoking of permission to use the database,
f) transaction boundaries; i.e. units of recovery (see Section 3.12).

SQL (see Chapter 3) is an example of a database language that satisfies this rule.

Rule 6: view updating rule
An RDBMS must allow all user views that are theoretically updatable to be updatable by the system. The problem with this rule is that further research is necessary in order to pin down exactly which views are theoretically updatable. RDBMSs currently support update on only a subset of relations which are known to be theoretically updatable (see Section 3.11.2).

Rule 7: insert, update and delete rule
Retrieval and update operations should operate on relations (views or base relations). It should be possible to insert, update or delete a set of tuples at a time.

Rule 8: physical data independence rule
Application programs and terminal activities must not be logically affected by changes to the way in which relations are physically represented or access methods used.

Rule 9: logical data independence rule
Applications programs and terminal activities must not be affected by changes to the base relations when those changes do not alter the information used by those programs or activities. It should be possible, for instance, to add an extra attribute to a relation or create a new relation without any repercussions.

Rule 10: integrity independence rule
Integrity constraints must be specifiable in the relational language and should be stored in the data dictionary or catalogue, not in the applications program. Changing those constraints should not affect existing applications.

Rule 11: distribution rule
An RDBMS must have distribution independence. That is to say, applications should not be affected when the database becomes distributed or redistributed over a number of computers networked together (see Chapter 6).

Rule 12: non-subversion rule

When an RDBMS supports a low-level language (one which processes one tuple at a time) then that language must still be constrained by the integrity rule and constraints expressed by a relational language.

At the time of writing, there are no RDBMSs which satisfy all twelve rules. In fact, for any one of the rules it is possible to find RDBMS products which violate it. There are leading RDBMS products which, for example, allow duplicate tuples and null key values (violating Rule 1); or do not support primary keys (violating Rule 2); or do not support null values (violating Rule 3); or use a non-relational storage system to represent and access the database description (violating Rule 4); or support two separate languages, one for use exclusively by the DBA for defining the structures of the database, and the other for database users to manipulate the database (violating Rule 5); or do not support views (violating Rule 6); etc.

Codd's twelve rules are, however, influential and seem to act as a spur to the RDBMS industry. They can be viewed as indicative of the probable characteristics of future RDBMSs.

7.4 Weaknesses of the relational model

Four main weaknesses of the relational model are:

a) a lack of semantic features. Semantic features are those to do with the meaning of the data,
b) inability to represent knowledge, other than simple facts,
c) inability to represent complex structures and operations,
d) inability to remember data.

Each of these has given rise to research which may form a basis for the next generation of database technology. These four weaknesses are discussed and some of the major themes of the resulting research are identified in the following sections.

7.4.1 Semantic features

A valid criticism of the relational model is that it is more a syntactic rather than a semantic model. By this we mean that the relational model provides us with a language (i.e. a syntax) which can be used to model databases and applications, but the model does not include any interpretation of structures, rules and operators, which may be expressed in that language, in terms of the real world things about which they represent information (i.e. there are no real world semantics). A relational database contains no explicit links between data and the real world objects they represent; for example, there is no way of knowing whether a relation, called X say, represents entities or relationships.

There are potential benefits from increasing the amount of meaning (the semantic content) in a database; increased semantics should enable a DBMS to respond more intelligently to users' requests, and to maintain the database as a more complete and correct description of the organisation. For example, a DBMS which understands the real world meaning of databases should be capable of understanding queries expressed in terms of real world objects; presenting retrieved information in a meaningful way; and safeguarding against processing 'silly' questions, and updates which create implausible data.

The relational model is not completely lacking in semantic features: domains (see Section 2.3.2), keys (see Section 2.3.5), and functional, multi-valued and join dependencies (see Chapter 4) are all a consequence of the meaning of the data, rather than the whims of the designer. However, the relational model does not contain any way of representing the types of information that data is about; it does not include concepts of entities, associations, rules, etc.

This weakness has given rise to research into semantic data models, i.e. models which represent more of the meaning of the data. A semantic model includes different types of structure with associated operators and integrity constraints for different types of real world object.

A number of researchers, including E. F. Codd, have attempted to extend the relational model so as to include more of the meaning of data. Codd's semantic extension of the relational model is called RM/T (the T stands for Tasmania, because it was there that Codd first expounded his ideas).

RM/T has special types of relation for representing entities, their properties, and relationships between them. It distinguishes between three types of entity:
a) entities which have independent existence, e.g. customers, employees, products, are called kernel entities,
b) entities which exist to describe some other entity, e.g. home address, spouse, child, which may only be important as properties of an employee, are called characteristic entities,
c) entities which represent relationships between other entities, e.g. 'sales orders' which is an entity relating customer, salesman and products entities, are called association entities.

An RM/T database contains three types of relations, E-relations, P-relations and graph relations. E-relations (the E stands for entity) are unary (i.e. single-attribute) relations which are used to list all the entities represented in an RM/T database. An RM/T database includes one E-relation for each type of entity that can be represented. An E-relation is used to store identifiers of the associated entities. So, for example, a database that represents customers will include a CUSTOMER E-relation in which is stored the identifier of every customer described in the database. Entity identifiers are assigned by the system itself and are called surrogates. When a new entity is stored in the database the system allocates to it a unique surrogate which is then stored in the appropriate E-relations and which acts as its unalterable identifier until that entity is deleted from the database.

A P-relation (the P stands for property) represents properties or facts about entities. Each P-relation includes an attribute in which the surrogates of the associated entities are stored: this acts as the primary key, and also as a foreign key to the corresponding E-relation. A P-relation will also include 'conventional' attributes the values of which represent entity properties. Users may maintain their own keys within P-relations, but the entity surrogates always act as primary key.

Various graph relations represent relationships between the different types of entity. For example, there is a characteristic tree relation called a CG-relation which represents the relationship between entities and associated characteristic entities. A CG-relation has two attributes, SUB and SUP, both defined on the domain of relation names, RN-domain. The SUB value of a tuple is the name of a relation which represents characteristic entities of the entities represented in the relation named by the SUP value.

There are many other such graph relations, each of which describes a different type of relationship between entities, e.g. between entities and their component entities (convoys and ships, etc.), and between entities and other entities which are a subtype of them (employees and salesmen), and so on.

The set of operators in the manipulative part of the relational model, relational algebra, is extended in RM/T to manipulate these different types of relation.

The two integrity rules of the relational model, entity and referential integrity (see Section 2.4), hold for RM/T, but it also has others which take into account the different types of information represented by E-, P- and graph relations. For example, a third rule specifies that E-relations accept insertions and deletions only, but not update. This is to ensure that entities remain uniquely identifiable, regardless of changes to their properties.

Semantically extended relational data models have not had much of an influence on DBMS products (there are no major DBMSs based on RM/T or any other semantic data models). They have, however, had some influence on database design methods; some data analysis methods (see Section 4.6.1) use a semantic data model to capture the meaning and structure of data, and then a data design method (see Section 4.8) implements that semantic model using a data model such as the relational model.

7.4.2 Knowledge

A relational database represents simple facts (see Section 2.3.4), and other knowledge about those facts must be built into applications programs (there is some capability for representing other knowledge within the database as integrity constraints but this facility is very limited). This limitation can be a problem, particularly for rule-intensive applications such as expert systems. A rule-intensive application is one which requires access not only to facts, but also to the logical rules which apply. For example, an expert system for medical diagnosis will require access to both facts about the condition of a patient and also rules by which a consultant may diagnose illnesses.

This weakness has given rise to research into logic databases, in which both facts and rules may be represented. A logical DBMS includes an automatic proving mechanism by which it may solve problems, applying the rules to the facts. This contrasts with a conventional database system where it is necessary to write programs in order to solve problems.

One approach taken in a number of experimental systems has been to combine, or bind, a logic programming language, such as PROLOG, with an RDBMS. The advantage of this strategy is that it exploits two complementary technologies: logic programming languages have the desired capability of representing both facts and rules, and have an automatic proving mechanism, but they lack the capability of handling a large number of shared facts and rules. RDBMSs on the other hand are good at handling many facts but lack the ability to store rules or perform proofs.

7.4.3 Complex structures and operations

The structures and operators of the relational model are too simple to represent directly many real world objects and their behaviour. This is a problem particularly for applications such as computer-aided design and manufacture (CAD/CAM) which involve the manipulation of information about structurally and behaviourally complex objects. For such applications, RDBMSs require that each real world object must be represented by many relations, and single real world operations on the objects must be implemented in an application program, using many statements in the database language.

This weakness has given rise to research into object-oriented database systems (OO-DMBS), non-first normal form (NF^2) RDBMSs, and extendable DBMSs (E-DBMSs).

OO-DBMS support complex data structures which may directly represent complex real world objects but also allow programs which implement complex real world operations (called methods) on those objects to be stored in the database. In this way an object-oriented database represents both perceived real world objects and also their behaviour. In fact the database objects in an object-oriented database may only be used via the associated methods, and so the data structures are hidden or encapsulated. OO-DBMSs also support classes and subclasses of objects; subclasses inherit the structure and behaviour of their superclasses. As an example, consider an object-oriented database which represents clerical and non-clerical employees. This will include three classes of objects, EMPLOYEE, CLERIC and NON-CLERIC, where CLERIC and NON-CLERIC are subclasses of EMPLOYEE. CLERIC and NON-CLERIC will inherit the data structures and methods of an EMPLOYEE, but will also have other properties. OO-DBMSs are based on a non-relational technology and a number of them, e.g. GemStone and ONTOS, have evolved from object-oriented programming languages such as SmallTalk-80 and C++.

There have also been attempts to provide support for complex objects and operations within the framework of the relational model. NF^2 RDBMSs allow relations to have complex structures, e.g. nested relations, sets and arrays, so that tuples may directly represent objects perceived by the user, even when those objects have complex structures. E-DBMSs also allow the user to extend the range of data types and operators that are supported by the DBMS.

7.4.4 Database systems which remember the past

When a relational database is updated, it forgets the past; an update destroys the data that it updates. This causes problems for a number of applications, for example in medicine, geology or archeology, where it is necessary to manipulate historic information. For example, in some medical applications it is necessary to store complete patient histories. In such systems new facts should be added to the database without destroying the facts that they supersede.

This weakness has given rise to research into temporal databases, in which historic data and previous states of the database are stored, and users are allowed to manipulate both present and past data. The three classes of temporal database system that have been researched are: rollback, historic and (fully) temporal.

These classifications are based on a distinction between the time at which data is valid, and the time at which a database is updated. A relational database provides a 'snapshot' of its organisation. Over a period of time the database will change in response to changes in the organisation thus creating new snapshots. The times at which a database is updated are called transaction times. The times for which facts recorded in the database are valid are called valid times.

Tuples in a rollback database include special attributes which store the transaction times. Whenever new data is added to the database the time at which it is added, i.e. its transaction time, is automatically recorded; this process is called time-stamping. Also, when new data is added, the data that it supersedes is retained. In this way, a rollback database retains all instances of the database. The database language allows a user to access not only the present instance of the database, but also previous ones.

Tuples in a historic database include special attributes for storing valid time, i.e. the time at which the facts represented by the data apply to the organisation. When new data is added the superseded data is retained, and thus the database stores a history of the entities. The database language makes it possible to ask questions about the present, but also about the past histories of entities.

A (fully) temporal database supports both transaction and valid time. It combines the features of historic and rollback systems.

7.4.5 The next generation of database technology

At the time of writing it seems probable that the relational model and SQL are here to stay for some time. However, the inadequacies of the relational model do leave room for other complementary database technologies and the main contenders seem to be the object-oriented and logic database technologies.

There are as yet relatively few OO-DBMSs on the market but the indications are that the future will bring many more. Object-oriented systems are based on a technology that is fundamentally different from that of RDBMSs and so RDBMSs are unlikely to evolve into next generation systems through the addition of object-orientation front-end software. There are however a number of extended relational systems which implement some of the features of object-oriented databases. For example, the POSTGRES system sits on top of the INGRES RDBMS and extends the relational model to include features such as complex structures, abstract data types and inheritance.

Temporal databases are expensive; all data must be retained and so they require massive storage capacity and very fast data access methods. However, certain application areas may warrant this investment and the cost will reduce as the cost of high-speed storage devices continue to fall. Temporal features are likely to be incorporated into relational and object-oriented technologies; POSTGRES, for example, already includes some temporal database facilities.

Logic database systems are a natural extension of current logic programming systems, and it seems probable that the number of commercially available logic DBMSs will increase significantly in the near future.

7.5 Summary and conclusions

Relational technology is currently the state-of-the-art and has the advantage of being based on clear ideas and thinking, underpinned by a formal data model. However, relational technology has a number of weaknesses, and researchers are looking for something better.

In this book we have tried to give details of the thinking and ideas that lie behind the database approach and relational databases in particular. For relational databases these ideas are formalised as the relational model, which is described in Chapter 2. We have summarised features and facilities of actual RDBMSs, and in particular this book has tried to answer the question, 'how does one design, use, and maintain a relational database?'. We have considered the case where the database system is implemented on a single computer, but also where many computers are used (Chapter 6). Finally we have pointed out some of the weaknesses of relational technology and have identified research towards the next generation of database technology, i.e. semantic, logic, object-oriented, non-first normal form, extended relational and temporal database systems research.

Exercises

7.1 Identify and discuss five strengths of the relational model.

7.2 What is meant by the following classifications?
a) tabular DBMS,
b) minimally relational DBMS,
c) relationally complete DBMS,
d) fully relational DBMS.

7.3 Explain the ways in which standard SQL satisfies the fifth of Codd's twelve rules.

7.4 What is the justification for the criticism that the relational model is syntactic, rather than semantic?

7.5 What is a semantic model?

7.6 In what ways does RM/T extend the relational model so as to represent more of the meaning of data?

7.7 In what ways is the relational model inadequate for rule-intensive applications?

7.8 What is a logic database?

7.9 In what ways is the relational model inadequate for modelling the complexities of many real world objects and activities?

7.10 Explain the main features of:
a) object-oriented database systems,
b) non-first normal form database systems,
c) extensible database systems.

7.11 In what way can an RDBMS be said to be forgetful?

7.12 What are the main features of?
a) rollback DBMSs,
b) historic DBMSs,
c) temporal DBMSs.

7.13 Analyse a 'relational DBMS' with which you are familiar, and write a report which discusses the extent to which it satisfies Codd's twelve rules (see Section 7.3).

CHAPTER 1

1.1 ... organisation ... information ... activities.
1.2 See Section 1.2.1.
1.3 See Section 1.2.4.
1.4 See Section 1.2.5.
1.5 ... natural ... shared ... duplication.
1.6 See Section 1.3.2.
1.7 See Section 1.3.3.
1.8 See Section 1.3.2 first paragraph.
1.9 See Section 1.3.3.
1.10 See Section 1.3.4.
1.11 ... tables.
1.12 See Section 1.4.

CHAPTER 2

2.1 See Section 2.2.1.
2.2 See Section 2.2.1.
2.3 See Section 2.2.2.
2.4　a) Relations are EMPLOYEE, DEPARTMENT and EMPLOYEE_EXTENSION.

b) Attribute names are EMP_NO, NI_NO, NAME, DEPT_NO, NAME, MANAGER, OFFICE and EXTENSION. Attribute values are E1, E2, E3, E5, 123, 159, 5432, 7654, etc.

c) Tuples are ⟨E1, 123, J Smith, D1⟩, ⟨D1, Accounts, E1⟩, ⟨E1, R101, 811⟩, etc.

d) Domains are employee numbers (EMP_NO), national insurance numbers (NI_NO), employee names (EMPLOYEE_NAME), department numbers (DEPT_NO), department names (DEPARTMENT_NAME), office numbers (OFFICE), and extension numbers (EXTENSION).

e) For relation EMPLOYEE, candidate keys are EMP_NO and NI_NO. EMP_NO is an appropriate choice of primary key, in which case NI_NO is an alternate key. DEPT_NO is a foreign key.

For relation DEPARTMENT, DEPT_NO, NAME and MANAGER are all candidate keys. DEPT_NO is an appropriate choice of primary key, in which case NAME and MANAGER are alternate keys. MANAGER is a foreign key.

For relation EMPLOYEE_EXTENSION there are two candidate keys (EMP_NO,OFFICE) and (EMP_NO,EXTENSION). (EMP_NO,OFFICE) is a suitable primary key, in which case (EMP_NO,EXTENSION) is an alternate key. EMP_NO is a foreign key.

2.5　a)

DEPT_NO	DNAME	MANAGER
D1	Accounts	E1

b)

EMP_NO	NI_NO	ENAME	DEPT_NO
E1	123	J Smith	D1
E2	159	J Smith	D1
E3	5432	R Brown	D2
E5	7654	M Green	D3

Note that all tuples of EMPLOYEE are included in the result. This is because there are no J. Smiths in department D2, and so NOT (ENAME = 'J Smith' AND DEPT_NO = D2) is always true.

c)

ENAME
J Smith
R Brown
M Green

d)

OFFICE	EXTENSION
R101	811
R102	813
R10	111
R35	123

e)

ENAME
J Smith

f)

EMP_NO	NI_NO	ENAME	DEPT_NO
E1	123	J Smith	D1
E2	159	J Smith	D1
E3	5432	R Brown	D2
E5	7654	M Green	D3
E4	2222	R Grey	D3

g)

E1
E2
E5
E3

h)

EMP_NO
E3

i)

EMP_NO	NI_NO	ENAME	EMPLOYEE. DEPT_NO	DEPARTMENT. DEPT_NO	DNAME	MANAGER
E1	123	J Smith	D1	D1	Accounts	E1
E2	159	J Smith	D1	D1	Accounts	E1
E3	5432	R Brown	D2	D1	Accounts	E1
E5	7654	M Green	D3	D1	Accounts	E1
E1	123	J Smith	D1	D2	Stores	E2
E2	159	J Smith	D1	D2	Stores	E2
E3	5432	R Brown	D2	D2	Stores	E2
E5	7654	M Green	D3	D2	Stores	E2
E1	123	J Smith	D1	D3	Sales	E5
E2	159	J Smith	D1	D3	Sales	E5
E3	5432	R Brown	D2	D3	Sales	E5
E5	7654	M Green	D3	D3	Sales	E5

j)

EMP_NO
E1
E2
E3
E5

k)

EMP_NO	EXTENSION

l)

EMP_NO
E1

m)

EMP_NO	NI_NO	ENAME	DEPT_NO	DNAME	MANAGER
E1	123	J Smith	D1	Accounts	E1
E2	159	J Smith	D1	Accounts	E1
E3	5432	R Brown	D2	Stores	E2
E5	7654	M Green	D3	Sales	E5

n)

EMP_NO	NI_NO	ENAME	EMPLOYEE. DEPT_NO	DEPARTMENT. DEPT_NO	DNAME	MANAGER
E1	123	J Smith	D1	D1	Accounts	E1
E2	159	J Smith	D1	D2	Stores	E2
E5	7654	M Green	D3	D3	Sales	E5

o)

EMP_NO	NI_NO	ENAME	EMPLOYEE. DEPT_NO	DEPARTMENT. DEPT_NO	DNAME	MANAGER
E1	123	J Smith	D1	D1	Accounts	E1
E2	159	J Smith	D1	D2	Stores	E2
E5	7654	M Green	D3	D3	Sales	E5
E3	5432	R Brown	D2	null	null	null

p)

EMP_NO	NI_NO	ENAME	DEPT_NO
E1	123	J Smith	D1
E2	159	J Smith	D1
E3	5432	R Brown	D2
E5	7654	M Green	D3

q)

EMP_NO	NI_NO	ENAME	DEPT_NO
E1	123	J Smith	D1
E2	159	J Smith	D1
E5	7654	M Green	D3

r)

DNAME
Sales
Stores

2.6   See Section 2.5.2 and Section 2.5.3.
2.7   See Section 2.5.2 and Section 2.5.3.
2.8   a) O.K.
　　　　b) O.K.
　　　　c) Violates the referential integrity rule. (C52 does not exist.)
　　　　d) O.K.
　　　　e) Violates the entity integrity rule (ORDER_NO is the primary key and so may not be null).
2.9   See Section 2.6.
2.10 See Section 2.7 Levels.
2.11 See Section 2.7 Models.
2.12 See Section 2.7 Models.
2.13 See Section 2.7 Programs.
2.14 See Section 2.8.
2.15 See Section 2.8 Global level.
2.16 See Section 2.8 User/application level.
2.17 See Section 2.7 Data dictionary and Section 2.8 Data dictionary.
2.18 See Section 2.8 User/application level.
2.19 See Section 2.8 User/application level.

CHAPTER 3

3.1   See Section 3.2.
3.2   See Section 3.2.
3.3   See Section 3.3.
3.4   See Section 3.3 Database languages + third generation languages.
3.5   See Section 3.3 Fourth generation language environment.
3.6   See Section 3.3 Fourth generation language environment.
3.7   A relationally complete relational database language has the expressive power of the manipulative part of the relational model, i.e. relational algebra (see Chapter 2).
3.8   See Section 3.6.
3.9   See Section 3.7.
3.10 See Section 3.8.
3.11 a) CREATE TABLE EMPLOYEE
```
      (EMP_NO    CHARACTER (5) NOT NULL,
       NI_NO     INTEGER,
       NAME      CHARACTER (10),
       AGE       INTEGER,
       DEPT_NO   CHARACTER (3) UNIQUE EMP_NO);

      CREATE TABLE DEPARTMENT
      (DEPT_NO   CHARACTER (3) NOT NULL,
       NAME      CHARACTER (10),
       MANAGER   CHARACTER (5) UNIQUE DEPT_NO);
```

```
      CREATE TABLE EMPLOYEE_EXTENSION
      (EMP_NO     CHARACTER (5) NOT NULL,
       OFFICE     CHARACTER (5) NOT NULL,
       EXTENSION  INTEGER UNIQUE (EMP_NO,OFFICE));
```
　　　b) INSERT INTO EMPLOYEE
```
      VALUES ('E1', 123, 'J Smith', 21, 'D1');
      INSERT INTO DEPARTMENT
      VALUES ('D1', 'Accounts', 'E1');
      INSERT INTO EMPLOYEE_TELEPHONE
      VALUES ('E1', 'R101', 811);
      etc.
```

3.12 CREATE INDEX EMPIND ON EMPLOYEE (EMP_NO);
CREATE INDEX DEPIND ON DEPARTMENT (DEPT_NO);
CREATE INDEX ET ON EMPLOYEE_EXTENSION (EMP_NO, OFFICE);

3.13.1 SELECT *
FROM EMPLOYEE;

EMP_NO	NI_NO	NAME	AGE	DEPT_NO
E1	123	J Smith	21	D1
E2	159	J Smith	31	D1
E3	5432	R Brown	65	D2
E5	7654	M Green	52	D2

3.13.2 SELECT NAME
FROM EMPLOYEE;

NAME
J Smith
J Smith
R Brown
M Green

3.13.3 SELECT NAME, NI_NO
FROM EMPLOYEE;

NAME	NI_NO
J Smith	123
J Smith	159
R Brown	5432
M Green	7654

3.13.4 SELECT DISTINCT NAME
FROM EMPLOYEE;

NAME
J Smith
M Green
R Brown

3.13.5 SELECT NI_NO
FROM EMPLOYEE
WHERE NAME = 'J Smith';

NI_NO
123
159

3.13.6 SELECT NI_NO
FROM EMPLOYEE
WHERE (NAME = 'J Smith' AND DEPT_NO ! = 'D2')
OR (NAME ! = 'J Smith' AND DEPT_NO = 'D2');

NI_NO
123
159
5432
7654

3.13.7 SELECT *
FROM EMPLOYEE
WHERE AGE > 50;

EMP_NO	NI_NO	NAME	AGE	DEPT_NO
E3	5432	R Brown	65	D2
E5	7654	M Green	52	D2

3.13.8 SELECT *
FROM EMPLOYEE
WHERE AGE BETWEEN 20 AND 40;

EMP_NO	NI_NO	NAME	AGE	DEPT_NO
E1	123	J Smith	21	D1
E2	159	J Smith	31	D1

3.13.9 SELECT *
FROM EMPLOYEE
WHERE AGE > 21 AND NAME LIKE 'Sm%';

EMP_NO	NI_NO	NAME	AGE	DEPT_NO

3.13.10 SELECT *
FROM DEPARTMENT
WHERE NAME LIKE 'S_r%';

DEPT_NO	NAME	MANAGER
D2	Stores	E2

3.13.11   SELECT *
FROM DEPARTMENT
WHERE NAME NOT LIKE '%/*\%%'
    ESCAPE '\';

DEPT_NO	NAME	MANAGER
D1	Accounts	E1
D2	Stores	E2
D3	Sales	null

3.13.12   SELECT *
FROM DEPARTMENT
WHERE MANAGER IS NULL;

DEPT_NO	NAME	MANAGER
D3	Sales	

3.13.13   SELECT *
FROM DEPARTMENT
WHERE MANAGER IS NOT NULL;

DEPT_NO	NAME	MANAGER
D1	Accounts	E1
D2	Stores	E2

3.13.14   SELECT NAME, over_21 = age - 21
FROM EMPLOYEE;

NAME	over_21
J Smith	0
J Smith	10
R Brown	44
M Green	31

3.13.15   SELECT average = AVG (AGE), young = MIN
(AGE), old = MAX (AGE) FROM EMPLOYEE;

average	young	old
42.250	21	65

3.13.16   SELECT DEPT_NO, average = AVG (AGE), old =
MAX (AGE), young = MIN (AGE) FROM EMPLOYEE
GROUP BY DEPT_NO;

DEPT_NO	average	old	young
D1	26.000	31	21
D2	58.500	65	52

3.13.17   SELECT DEPT_NO, average = AVG (AGE), old =
MAX (AGE), young = MIN (AGE) FROM EMPLOYEE
GROUP BY DEPT_NO
ORDER BY AVERAGE;

DEPT_NO	average	old	young
D1	26.000	31	21
D2	58.500	65	52

3.13.18   SELECT *
FROM EMPLOYEE
ORDER BY DEPT_NO, AGE DESC;

EMP_NO	NI_NO	NAME	AGE	DEPT_NO
E2	159	J Smith	31	D1
E1	123	J Smith	21	D1
E3	5432	R Brown	65	D2
E5	7654	M Green	52	D2

3.13.19   SELECT EMPLOYEE.NAME, DEPARTMENT.NAME
FROM EMPLOYEE, DEPARTMENT
WHERE EMPLOYEE.DEPT_NO = DEPARTMENT.DEPT_NO;

NAME	NAME
J Smith	Accounts
J Smith	Accounts
M Green	Stores
R Brown	Stores

3.13.20
```
SELECT EMPLOYEE.*, DEPARTMENT.DEPT_NO, DEPARTMENT.NAME, MANAGER
FROM EMPLOYEE, DEPARTMENT
WHERE EMPLOYEE.DEPT_NO = DEPARTMENT.DEPT_NO AND
      EMPLOYEE.NAME = DEPARTMENT.NAME;
```

EMP_NO	NI_NO	NAME	AGE	DEPT_NO	DEPT_NO	NAME	MANAGE

Note that the above query will always retrieve an empty relation because department name and employee name will not match.

3.13.21
```
SELECT E.*
FROM EMPLOYEE E, EMPLOYEE_TELEPHONE ET
WHERE E.EMP_NO = ET.EMP_NO AND
      EXTENSION = 123;
```

EMP_NO	NI_NO	NAME	AGE	DEPT_NO
E3	5432	R Brown	65	D2
E5	7654	M Green	52	D2

3.13.22
```
SELECT E1.*
FROM EMPLOYEE E1, EMPLOYEE E2
WHERE E1.AGE = E2.AGE AND
      E2.EMP_NO = 'E1'  AND
      E1.EMP_NO ! = E2.EMP_NO;
```

EMP_NO	NI_NO	NAME	AGE	DEPT_NO

3.13.23
```
SELECT DISTINCT E.*
FROM EMPLOYEE E, EMPLOYEE E1, EMPLOYEE E5
WHERE E.AGE > E1.AGE AND
      E.AGE < E5.AGE AND
      E1.EMP_NO = 'E1' AND
      E5.EMP_NO = 'E5';
```

EMP_NO	NI_NO	NAME	AGE	DEPT_NO
E2	159	J Smith	31	D1

3.13.24
```
SELECT E.*,D.*
FROM EMPLOYEE E, DEPARTMENT D
WHERE E.DEPT_NO = D.DEPT_NO (+);
```
(same result as for 3.13.25)

3.13.25
```
SELECT E.EMP_NO, NI_NO, E.NAME, AGE,
       E.DEPT_NO, D.DEPT_NO, D.NAME,
       MANAGER
FROM EMPLOYEE E, DEPARTMENT D
WHERE E.DEPT_NO = D.DEPT_NO
UNION
SELECT E.EMP_NO, NI_NO, E.NAME, AGE,
 E.DEPT_NO, NULL, NULL, NULL
FROM EMPLOYEE E
WHERE NOT EXISTS
 (SELECT *
 FROM DEPARTMENT D
```

```
WHERE D.DEPT_NO = E.DEPT_NO)
UNION
SELECT NULL, NULL, NULL, NULL, NULL,
  D.DEPT_NO, D.NAME, MANAGER
FROM DEPARTMENT D
WHERE NOT EXISTS
  (SELECT *
   FROM EMPLOYEE E
   WHERE E.DEPT_NO = D.DEPT_NO);
```

EMP_NO	NI_NO	NAME	AGE	DEPT_NO	DEPT_NO	NAME	MANAGER
E1	123	J Smith	21	D1	D1	Accounts	E1
E2	159	J Smith	31	D1	D1	Accounts	E1
E3	5432	R Brown	65	D2	D2	Stores	E2
E5	7654	M Green	52	D2	D2	Stores	E2
null	null	null	null	null	D3	Sales	

3.13.26
```
SELECT NAME = E.NAME, ROOM = ET.OFFICE,
DEPT = E.DEPT_NO, ET.EXTENSION
FROM EMPLOYEE E, EMPLOYEE_TELEPHONE ET
WHERE E.EMP_NO = ET.EMP_NO
ORDER BY E.DEPT_NO, E.NAME;
```

NAME	ROOM	DEPT	EXTENSION
J Smith	R10	D1	111
J Smith	R101	D1	811
J Smith	R102	D1	813
M Green	R35	D2	123
R Brown	R35	D2	123

3.13.27
a)
```
SELECT EMP_NO
FROM EMPLOYEE_TELEPHONE
WHERE EXTENSION = 123;
```

EMP_NO
E3
E5

b)
```
SELECT DEPT_NO
FROM EMPLOYEE
WHERE EMP_NO NI
    (SELECT EMP_NO
     FROM EMPLOYEE_TELEPHONE
     WHERE EXTENSION = 123);
```

DEPT_NO
D2
D2

c)
```
SELECT DISTINCT NAME
FROM DEPARTMENT
WHERE DEPT_NO IN
    (SELECT DEPT_NO
     FROM EMPLOYEE
     WHERE EMP_NO NI
        (SELECT EMP_NO
         FROM EMPLOYEE_TELEPHONE
         WHERE EXTENSION = 123));
```

NAME
Stores

3.13.28
```
SELECT NAME
FROM EMPLOYEE
WHERE AGE >
    (SELECT MAX(AGE)
     FROM EMPLOYEE
     WHERE DEPT_NO = 'D1');
```

NAME
M Green
R Brown

3.13.29
```
SELECT NAME
FROM EMPLOYEE
WHERE AGE > ANY
    (SELECT AGE
     FROM EMPLOYEE
     WHERE DEPT_NO = 'D1');
```

NAME
J Smith
M Green
R Brown

3.13.30
```
SELECT E.NAME
FROM EMPLOYEE E
WHERE EMP_NO ! = 'E1' AND
  AGE =
    (SELECT AGE
     FROM EMPLOYEE
     WHERE EMP_NO = 'E1');
```

NAME

3.13.31 a)
```
SELECT NAME
FROM EMPLOYEE E
WHERE EXISTS
  (SELECT *
   FROM DEPARTMENT D
   WHERE D.MANAGER = E.EMP_NO);
```

NAME
J Smith
J Smith

b)
```
SELECT NAME
FROM    EMPLOYEE E
WHERE      EXISTS
  (SELECT *
   FROM EMPLOYEE_TELEPHONE ET1
   WHERE E.EMP_NO = ET1.EMP_NO AND
     NOT EXISTS
     (SELECT *
      FROM EMPLOYEE_TELEPHONE ET2
```

```
      WHERE ET1.EMP_NO ! = ET2.EMP_NO
        AND ET1.EXTENSION =
        ET2.EXTENSION));
```

NAME
J Smith
J Smith

c)
```
SELECT NAME
FROM EMPLOYEE E
WHERE EXISTS
  (SELECT *
   FROM DEPARTMENT D
   WHERE D.MANAGER = E.EMP_NO)
UNION
SELECT NAME
FROM    EMPLOYEE E
WHERE      EXISTS
  (SELECT *
   FROM EMPLOYEE_TELEPHONE ET1
   WHERE E.EMP_NO = ET1.EMP_NO AND
     NOT EXISTS
     (SELECT *
      FROM EMPLOYEE_TELEPHONE ET2
      WHERE ET1.EMP_NO ! = ET2.EMP_NO
        AND ET1.EXTENSION =
        ET2.EXTENSION));
```

NAME
J Smith

3.13.32
```
UPDATE EMPLOYEE
SET AGE = AGE + 1;
```

EMP_NO	NI_NO	NAME	AGE	DEPT_NO
E1	123	J Smith	22	D1
E2	159	J Smith	31	D1
E3	5432	R Brown	66	D2
E5	7654	M Green	53	D2

3.13.33
```
UPDATE EMPLOYEE
SET NAME = 'J Smyth'
WHERE EMP_NO = 'E1';
```

EMP_NO	NI_NO	NAME	AGE	DEPT_NO
E1	123	J Smyth	23	D1
E2	159	J Smith	33	D1
E3	5432	R Brown	67	D2
E5	7654	M Green	54	D2

3.13.34 UPDATE EMPLOYEE
  SET DEPT_NO = 'D2'
  WHERE DEPT_NO = 'D1'

EMP_NO	NI_NO	NAME	AGE	DEPT_NO
E1	123	J Smyth	23	D2
E2	159	J Smith	33	D2
E3	5432	R Brown	67	D2
E5	7654	M Green	54	D2

3.13.35 INSERT INTO EMPLOYEE (EMP_NO, NAME,AGE)
  VALUES ('E9', 'B Eagles',41);

EMP_NO	NI_NO	NAME	AGE	DEPT_NO
E1	123	J Smyth	23	D2
E2	159	J Smith	33	D2
E3	5432	R Brown	67	D2
E5	7654	M Green	54	D2
E9		B Eagles	41	

3.13.36 CREATE TABLE OLD_EMPLOYEE
  (EMP_NO   CHARACTER(3),
   NAME   CHARACTER(10));

INSERT INTO OLD_EMPLOYEE
SELECT EMP_NO, NAME
FROM EMPLOYEE
WHERE AGE > 60;

OLD_EMPLOYEE

EMP_NO	NAME
E3	R Brown

3.13.37 DELETE FROM EMPLOYEE
  WHERE AGE > 60;

3.13.38 DELETE FROM EMPLOYEE
  WHERE EMP_NO IN
  (SELECT MANAGER
   FROM DEPARTMENT
   WHERE DEPT_NO = 'D1');

3.13.39 CREATE VIEW Q31339 (EMP_NO, ENAME, DNAME)
  AS SELECT E.EMP_NO, E.NAME, D.NAME
     FROM EMPLOYEE E, DEPARTMENT D
     WHERE E.DEPT_NO = D.DEPT_NO;

Q31339

EMP_NO	ENAME	DNAME
E1	J Smith	Accounts
E2	J Smith	Accounts
E3	R Brown	Stores
E5	M Green	Stores

The view is not updatable (see Section 3.11.2).

3.13.40 SELECT V1.ENAME
  FROM Q31339 V1, Q31339 V2
  WHERE V2.EMP_NO = 'E1' AND
     V1.DEPT_NO = V2.DEPT_NO AND
     V1.EMP_NO != V2.EMP_NO;

ENAME
J Smith

3.13.41 CREATE VIEW Q31341 (ENAME,DEPT_NO)
  AS SELECT DISTINCT NAME, DEPT_NO
     FROM EMPLOYEE;

Q31341

ENAME	DEPT_NO
J Smith	D1
R Brown	D1
M Green	D2

The view is not updatable.

3.13.42 CREATE VIEW Q31342 (EMP_NO, DEPT_NO)
  AS SELECT E.EMP_NO, E.DEPT_NO
     FROM EMPLOYEE E, DEPARTMENT D
     WHERE E.EMP_NO = D.MANAGER;

Q31342

EMP_NO	DEPT_NO
E1	D1
E2	D1
E3	D2
E5	D2

Q31342 is updatable.

3.13.43
```
CREATE VIEW Q31343 (EMP_NO, NAME)
AS SELECT EMP_NO, NAME
   FROM EMPLOYEE
   WHERE DEPT_NO = 'D1';
```

EMP_NO	NAME
E1	J Smith
E2	J Smith

Q31343 is updatable.

3.13.44
```
CREATE INTEGRITY ON EMPLOYEE
   IS AGE >20 AND AGE <66;
```

3.13.45
```
DROP INTEGRITY ON EMPLOYEE 1;
```

3.13.46 and 3.13.47 See Section 3.12.

3.14 See Section 3.15.

3.15 See Section 3.15.

3.16.1
```
EMPLOYEE
RETRIEVE (EMPLOYEE.ALL);
```

3.16.2
```
EMPLOYEE.NAME
RETRIEVE (EMPLOYEE.NAME);
```

3.16.3
```
EMPLOYEE.NAME, EMPLOYEE.NI_NO
RETRIEVE (EMPLOYEE.NAME, EMPLOYEE.NI_NO);
```

3.16.4
```
EMPLOYEE.NAME
RETRIEVE UNIQUE (EMPOYEE.NAME);
```

3.16.5
```
EMPLOYEE.NI_NO: EMPLOYEE.NAME = 'J Smith'
RETRIEVE (EMPLOYEE.NI_NO) WHERE EMPLOYEE.NAME
= 'J Smith';
```

3.16.6
```
EMPLOYEE.NI_NO: (EMPLOYEE.NAME = 'J Smith'
AND NOT(EMPLOYEE.DEPT_NO = 'D1'))
OR NOT(EMPLOYEE.NAME = 'J.Smith' AND
EMPLOYEE.DEPT_NO = 'D1'))

RETRIEVE EMPLOYEE.NI_NO WHERE (EMPLOYEE.NAME
= 'J Smith' AND NOT(EMPLOYEE.DEPT_NO = 'D1'))
OR NOT(EMPLOYEE.NAME = 'J.Smith' AND
EMPLOYEE.DEPT_NO = 'D1'));
```

3.16.7
```
EMPLOYEE: EMPLOYEE.AGE >50
RETRIEVE (EMPLOYEE.ALL) WHERE AGE >50;
```

3.16.8
```
EMPLOYEE.NAME, DEPARTMENT.NAME: ∀ EMPLOYEE
   ∃ DEPARTMENT (EMPLOYEE.DEPT_NO
      = DEPARTMENT.DEPT_NO)

RETRIEVE (EMPLOYEE.NAME, DEPARTMENT.NAME)
WHERE DEPARTMENT.DEPT_NO = EMPLOYEE.DEPT_NO;
```

3.16.9
```
EMPLOYEE: ∃ EMPLOYEE_TELEPHONE
   (EMPLOYEE.EMP_NO = EMPLOYEE_TELEPHONE.EMP_NO
AND EMPLOYEE_TELEPHONE.EXTENSION = 123)
```

```
RETRIEVE (EMPLOYEE.ALL) WHERE EMPLOYEE.EMP_NO
   = EMPLOYEE_TELEPHONE.EMP_NO AND
   EMPLOYEE_TELEPHONE.EXTENSION = 123;
```

3.17 See Sections 3.3 and 3.21.
3.18 See Section 3.3.
3.19 See Section 3.22.
3.20 See Section 3.24.
3.21 See Section 3.25.
3.22 See Section 3.27.
3.23 See Sections 3.3 and 3.35.
3.24 See Section 3.35.
3.25 See Section 3.30.
3.26 See Section 3.28.

CHAPTER 4
4.1 See Section 4.1.
4.2 Entity types: Customer, Order, Product,
Salesperson, Sales Office.
Attribute types: Customer number, Customer
name, Order number, Order quantity,
Product name, Product colour, Product
number, Product price, Salesperson name,
Salesperson number, Sales Office name, Order
date.
Relational Types: Customer—placed—Order,
Order—ordered—Product,
Order—sold__by—Salesperson,
SalesPerson—works__through—SalesOffice.
4.3 See Section 4.5.
4.4 See Section 4.6.1.
4.5 See Sections 4.6.3 and 4.6.4.
4.6 *Top-down analysis:*
a) Identify entities

b) Identify relationships between entities

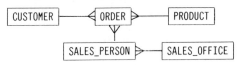

c) Identify entity attributes
Customer : Customer number, Customer
name
Order : Order number, Product ordered,
Quantity, Price, Date
Product : Product number, Product name,
Colour
Sales person: Employee number, Name
Sales office : Address

Bottom-up analysis:

a) Identify data items:
Customer number, Customer name,
Order number, Ordered quantity, Product
number, Product colour, Product price,
Sales person name, Sales person number,
Sales office address, Order date.

b) Identify relationships between data items:
   i) Customer Number ⟩————— Customer Name
   ii) Customer Number ————⟨ Order number
   iii) Order number ⟩————— Ordered quantity
   iv) Order number ⟩————— Product Number
   v) Order number ⟩————— Order date
   vi) Order number ⟩————— Salesperson number
   vii) Salesperson number ⟩——— Salesperson name
   viii) Salesperson number ⟩——*** Sales office address
   ix) Product number ⟩————— Product name
   x) Product number ⟩————— Colour

c) Identify entities
The following conceptual data model is
implied by the above relationships. Note
the components of the diagram are
labelled with references to the
relationships from which they were
implied.

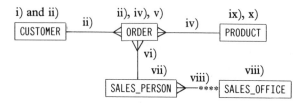

Entity/attributes
Customer   : Customer number, Customer
             name
Order   : Order number, Product ordered,
             Quantity, Price, Date
Product   : Product number, Product name,
             Colour
Sales person: Employee number, Name
Sales office : Sales office address

4.7 The following relation schemas are an
implementation of the conceptual data model in
the solution to 4.6. Note that each entity is
implemented as a relation; each many-to-one
relationship is represented by a foreign key
attribute in the 'many' relation. Note also that
the zero-or-one-to-many relationship is

represented by a separate relation with foreign key attributes for the two relations involved in the relationship.

CUSTOMER

CUST_NO	CNAME

ORDER

CUST_NO	DATE	PROD_NO	QTY	PRICE

PRODUCT

PROD_NO	PNAME	COLOUR

SALES_PERSON

SP_NO	SP_NAME

SALES_PERSON_OFFICE

SP_NO	SO_ADDR

SALES_OFFICE

SO_ADDR

4.8 See Section 4.10.

4.9 See Section 4.11.

1NF_PARENT_CHILD

PARENT_ID	PARENT_NAME	CHILD_NAME	CHILD_AGE
P1	Barry	David	12
P1	Barry	Michael	11
P2	John	Nicky	14
P2	John	Kim	11

4.10 See Section 4.12.2.

4.11 See Section 4.12.2.

4.12 BRAND_NAME → MANUFACTURER
BRAND_NAME,SIZE → PRICE
BRAND_NAME,PRICE → SIZE
(assuming different sizes of a brand have different prices)

4.13 See 4.12.3.

2NF_BRAND

BRAND_NAME	MANUFACTURER
Bonzo	Fat_Dog
Woffles	Fat_Dog
Dog Drops	Pet Treats

2NF_BRAND_SIZE

BRAND_NAME	SIZE	PRICE
Bonzo	Large	£2.99
Bonzo	Economy	£1.99
Woffles	Large	£3.00
Woffles	Small	£1.00
Dog Drops	Standard	£3.50
Dog Drops	Large	£5.50

4.14 EMP_NO → NAME, ADDRESS, DEPARTMENT, DEPARTMENT_MANAGER
DEPARTMENT → DEPARTMENT_MANAGER

4.15 See Section 4.12.4.

3NF_EMPLOYEE

EMP_NO	NAME	ADDRESS	DEPARTMENT
E1	Smith	Chez Nous	D1
E2	Brown	Mon Repose	D1
E3	Smith	Mon Repose	D1
E4	Jones	Sea View	D2
E9	Bloggs	The Nook	D2

3NF_DEPARTMENT

DEPARTMENT	MANAGER
D1	E1
D2	E9

4.16 P_NO → WAREHOUSE

4.17 See Section 4.12.6.

BCNF_MAKE

P_NO	FACTORY
P1	F1
P1	F2
P2	F2
P3	F2
P4	F2

BCNF_STORE

P_NO	WAREHOUSE
P1	Wh1
P2	WH1
P3	WH2
P4	WH2

4.18 See Section 4.13.1.

4.19 P_NO →→ COLOUR|SIZE

4.20 See 4.13.2.

4NF_PC

P_NO	COLOUR
P1	Red
P2	Green
P2	Black

4NF_PS

P_NO	SIZE
P1	Large
P1	Medium
P1	Small
P2	Large
P2	Small

4.21 No MVDs hold, because COLOUR and SIZE are no longer independent. PCS now satisfies 4NF.

4.22 See Section 4.13.3.

4.23 JD ((PARENT,CHILD), (PARENT,HOBBY), (CHILD,HOBBY))

4.24 See Section 4.13.3.

5NF_PC

PARENT	CHILD
Barry	David
Barry	Michael
John	Nicky
John	Kim

5NF_PH

PARENT	HOBBY
Barry	Horn Playing
Barry	ConcertGoing
Barry	Sailing
John	Sailing
John	Golf

5NF_CH

CHILD	HOBBY
David	Horn Playing
David	ConcertGoing
Michael	Sailing
Nicky	Sailing
Kim	Sailing
Kim	Golf

4.25 See Section 4.16 and 4.17.
4.26 See Section 4.18.
4.27 See Section 4.18.
4.28 See Section 4.19.
4.29 See Figure 4.9.
4.30 See Example 4.35.

4.31 a) and b) The only difference is that records may be out of sequence in a heap file.

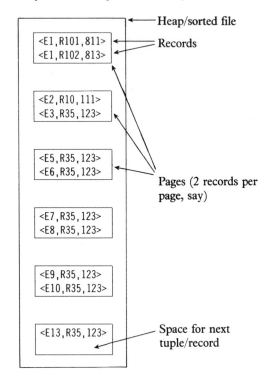

c) Assume: 7 pages of file space; 2 records per page; modulo-7 hashing on the numeric part of EMP_NO; progressive overflow; records are inserted in the order in which they appear in Figure 4.12.

$$\langle \text{Record Key} \rangle \longrightarrow [\text{Hashing Function}] \longrightarrow \langle \text{Home Address} \rangle$$

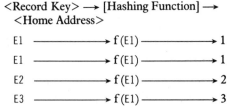

E1	$f(E1)$	1
E1	$f(E1)$	1
E2	$f(E1)$	2
E3	$f(E1)$	3
E5	$f(E1)$	5
E6	$f(E1)$	6
E7	$f(E1)$	0
E8	$f(E1)$	1
E9	$f(E1)$	2
E10	$f(E1)$	3
E13	$f(E1)$	6

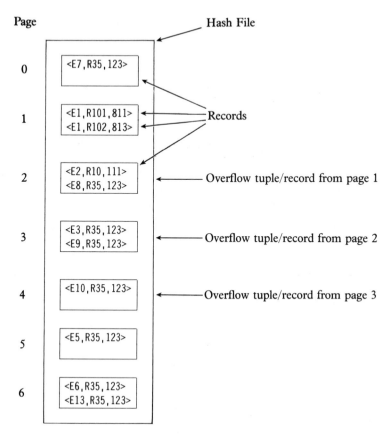

d) ISAM

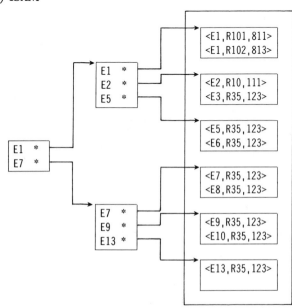

e) B+ – tree   Pointers to the actual data records

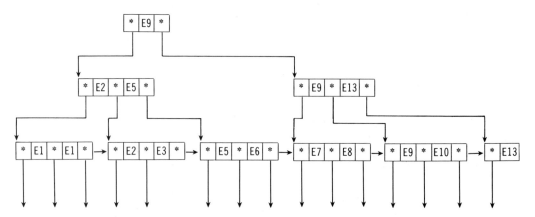

4.32   See Sections 4.20.2 for a), 4.20.5 for b), 4.20.10 for
c) and 4.20.16 for d) and e).

4.33   Binary Search   Serial search

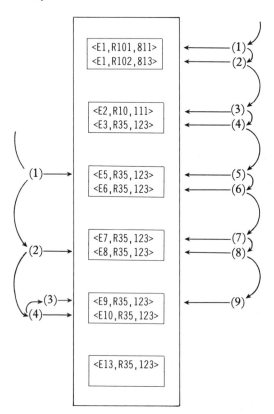

4.34

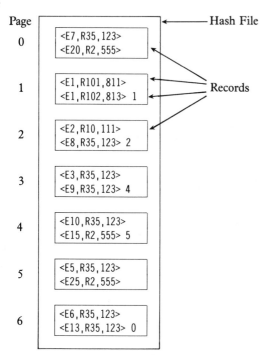

Page
Hash File

0
<E7,R35,123>
<E20,R2,555>

1
<E1,R101,811>
<E1,R102,813> 1

Records

2
<E2,R10,111>
<E8,R35,123> 2

3
<E3,R35,123>
<E9,R35,123> 4

4
<E10,R35,123>
<E15,R2,555> 5

5
<E5,R35,123>
<E25,R2,555>

6
<E6,R35,123>
<E13,R35,123> 0

4.35

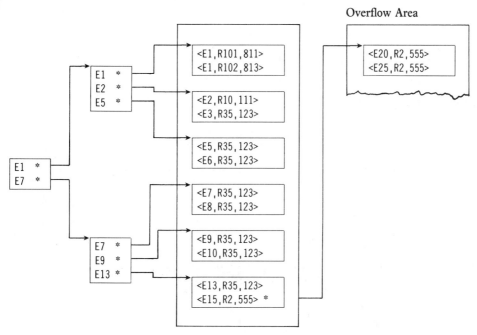

Overflow Area

E1 *
E2 *
E5 *

E1 *
E7 *

E7 *
E9 *
E13 *

<E1,R101,811>
<E1,R102,813>

<E2,R10,111>
<E3,R35,123>

<E5,R35,123>
<E6,R35,123>

<E7,R35,123>
<E8,R35,123>

<E9,R35,123>
<E10,R35,123>

<E13,R35,123>
<E15,R2,555> *

<E20,R2,555>
<E25,R2,555>

4.36   After inserting E15

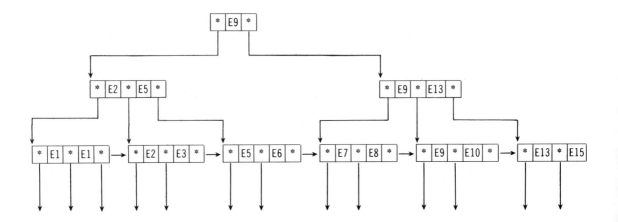

After inserting E20, the E20 must be added to the | * | E9 | * | E13 | * | cell, but this then becomes too large, and must therefore be split as shown. The root cell, | * | E9 | * | is then altered to address the new index.

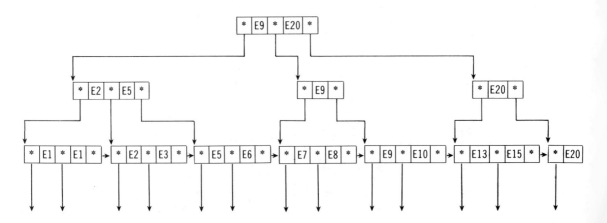

E25 may be inserted without having to change the indexes, because there is room for its address in the | * | E20 | cell.

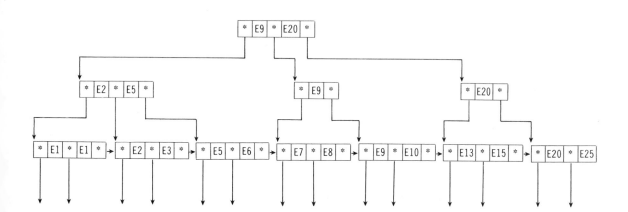

CHAPTER 5

5.1 See Section 5.2.
5.2 See Section 5.4.
5.3 See Section 5.4.
5.4 See Example 5.2.
5.5 a) See Example 5.3.
  b) See Example 5.4.
5.6 Example 5.2 with locking

Transaction 1	Time	Transaction 2
(Apply an exclusive lock on <WH1,1,P1,100>) Read the first tuple <WH1,1,P1,100> into a buffer		
		(Request an exclusive lock on <WH1,P1,100>, but the data is already locked, so Transaction 2 must wait)
Add 100 to QTY value giving <WH1,1,P1,200>		
Write tuple back to the relation (release exclusive lock)		
		(Exclusive lock is applied) Read <WH1,1,P1,200> Add 50 to QTY giving <WH1,1,P1,250> Write tuple back to the relation. (Release exclusive lock)

Example 5.4 with locking

| | Transaction 1 | Time | Transaction 2 |

Transaction 2:
```
UPDATE STOCK
SET QTY = QTY + 100
WHERE WAREHOUSE_NO = 'WH1'
AND BIN_NO = 2;
```
(Exclusive lock is applied to <WH1,2,P1,150>)

Transaction 1:
```
SELECT BIN_NO
FROM STOCK
WHERE WAREHOUSE_NO = 'WH1'
  AND PRODUCT_NO = 'P1';
```
(Request shared lock on <WH1,1,P1,100> and <WH1,2,P1,150>, but the second of the tuples is already locked, so Transaction 1 must wait until the lock is released.)

Transaction 2:
```
ROLLBACK
```
(Release locks)

Locks are applied and SQL is executed

```
SELECT total_quantity = SUM(QTY)
FROM STOCK
WHERE WAREHOUSE_NO = 'WH1';
```

(Release locks)

Transaction 1 will retrieve the following:

BIN_NO	QTY
1	100
2	150

total_quantity
250

5.7   See Section 5.10.
5.8   See Section 5.10.
5.9   See Section 5.10.
5.10   See Section 5.13.
5.11   See Section 5.14.
5.12   See Section 5.12.
5.13   See Section 5.15.
5.14   See Sections 5.16 and 3.9.7.
5.15   See Sections 5.17 and 3.11.3. (Readers who have access to INGRES with Knowledge Management Extensions should also look at Database Procedures and Rules.)
5.16   See Section 5.16.

CHAPTER 6

6.1   See Section 6.2.
6.2   See Section 6.2.
6.3   See Section 6.2.
6.4   See Section 6.2.
6.5   See Sections 6.2 and 6.3.1.
6.7   See Section 6.3.1.
6.8   See Section 6.3.1.
6.9   See Figure 6.4.
6.10   See Section 6.3.2.
6.11   See Section 6.3.2.
6.12   See Section 6.3.2.
6.13   See Section 6.3.2.
6.14   See Section 6.3.3.
6.15   See Section 6.3.4.

CHAPTER 7

7.1   See Section 7.2.
7.2   See Section 7.3.
7.3   See Sections 3.9, 3.10, 3.11, 3.12 and 7.3.
7.4   See Section 7.4.1.

7.5 See Section 7.4.1.

7.6 See Section 7.4.1.

7.7 See Section 7.4.2.

7.8 See Section 7.4.2.

7.9 See Section 7.4.3.

7.10 See Section 7.4.3.

7.11 See Section 7.4.3.

7.12 See Section 7.4.3.

Index